W9-ACA-621

Zondervan 2017

Church and Nonprofit

Tax *&* Financial Guide

For 2016 Tax Returns

2017

EDITION

Dan Busby

Michael Martin

John Van Drunen

ZONDERVAN

Zondervan 2017 Church and Nonprofit Tax and Financial Guide
Copyright © 2017 by ECFA (Evangelical Council for Financial Accountability)

Requests for information should be addressed to:
Zondervan, *3900 Sparks Dr. SE, Grand Rapids, Michigan 49546*

ISBN 978-0-310-52086-3

Publisher's note: This guide is published in recognition of the need for clarification of tax and other laws for churches and nonprofit organizations. Every effort has been made to publish a timely, accurate, and authoritative guide. The publisher, author, and reviewers do not assume any legal responsibility for the accuracy of the text or any other contents.

Readers are cautioned that this book is sold with the understanding that the publisher is not rendering legal, accounting, or other professional service. Organizations with specific tax problems should seek the professional advice of a tax accountant or lawyer.

References to IRS forms and tax rates are derived from preliminary proofs of 2016 forms or 2015 forms. Some adaptation for changes may be necessary. These materials should be used solely as a guide in filling out 2016 tax and information returns. To obtain the final forms, schedules, and tables for filing returns and forms, contact the IRS or a public library.

The term "nonprofit organization" covers a broad range of entities such as churches, colleges, universities, health care providers, business leagues, veterans groups, political parties, country clubs, and united-giving campaigns. The most common type of nonprofit is the charitable organization.

The "nonprofit organization" concept is basically a state law creation, but tax-exempt organizations are based primarily on federal law. The Internal Revenue Code does not use the word "nonprofit." The Code refers to nonprofits as "exempt organizations." Certain state statutes use the term "not-for-profit." A not-for-profit organization under state law may or may not be tax-exempt under federal law. In this book, the term "nonprofit" refers to nonprofit organizations that are exempt from federal income tax.

Any Internet addresses (websites, blogs, etc.) and telephone numbers in this book are offered as a resource. They are not intended in any way to be or imply an endorsement by Zondervan, nor does Zondervan vouch for the content of these sites and numbers for the life of this book.

All rights reserved. With the exception of the sample board resolutions, checklists, charts, and procedures, no part of this publication may be reproduced, stored in a retrieval system, or transmitted in any form or by any means—electronic, mechanical, photocopy, recording, or any other—except for brief quotations in printed reviews, without the prior permission of the publisher.

Printed in the United States of America

16 17 18 19 20 21 22 23 24 25 / DHV / 20 19 18 17 16 15 14 13 12 11 10 9 8 7 6 5 4 3 2 1

Contents . . .

SPECIAL INDEX
FOR CHURCH TREASURERS
A guide within a guide

Sample Board Resolutions, Checklists, Charts, and Procedures

Caution: You may need to consult with a tax or legal professional before adapting these materials to the specific needs of your organization.

Sample Charitable Contribution Letters and Forms

INTRODUCTION

The 26th annual edition of this guide is designed to help church and nonprofit leaders understand what is required by federal and state laws and how to comply. But it is much more!

Last year brought a fresh round of tax changes that are integrated throughout the text. The voluminous laws and regulations that apply to churches and other nonprofits are mind-boggling. Our goal is to provide easy-to-understand information on complex topics.

This guide challenges those who lead these organizations not just to meet the minimum requirements of the law or to meet fundamental ethical levels but to strive for levels of integrity far beyond the basics.

This book includes the basic rules for reporting to the IRS, handling charitable contributions, compensation to nonprofit employees, and much more. It also highlights issues raised in workshops where we have been the presenters and in the hundreds of emails and telephone calls we receive from church and other nonprofit leaders each year! It is a veritable one-stop resource for answers to the tax and finance issues most frequently asked by churches and other nonprofits.

Proper understanding and treatment of the issues addressed in this guide are essential if Christ-centered organizations are to earn the public's trust by practicing accountability and God-honoring ethical practices while fulfilling the Great Commission.

Dan Busby

Michael Martin

John Van Drunen

Recent Developments

Churches and nonprofit organizations continue to be faced with a plethora of tax and finance developments. A summary of some of the more significant developments follow (see the "In the News" page at ECFA.org for current updates on these issues and much more):

Freedom of speech legislation. Introduced in 1954 by then-Senator Lyndon B. Johnson, the "Johnson amendment" restricts the ability of churches and other nonprofits to speak out on political campaigns, and in some instances, even on the issues. Violating the law can result in fines and/or a loss of tax-exempt status. Simply put, the Johnson amendment restricts freedom of religion and freedom of speech.

On September 28, 2016, the Free Speech Fairness Act (H.R. 6195) was introduced in the House. The bill amends current law to clarify that churches and other nonprofits (including their pastors, leaders, etc.) can make political statements, so long as 1) made in the ordinary course of the organization's regular and customary activities in carrying out its exempt purpose, and (2) any expenditure related to such statements are *de minimus*.

For example, the bill would allow a minister, as part of a sermon, to make positive or negative comments about a political candidate. If a nonprofit normally sends out a monthly newsletter related to its core purpose, the bill allows them to occasionally include comments on political issues or candidates. They would not, however, be allowed to create an entirely new direct mail or ad campaign solely to intervene in political campaigns.

Changing the law in this way would restore the religious liberty and free speech rights of churches and other religious institutions, and nonreligious educational and charitable entities, but still avoids the problematic consequence of turning such organizations into political advocacy or action committees by repealing the Johnson Amendment altogether.

Our country has a rich tradition of free speech. Churches, in particular, play an important role in speaking to our national conscience on fundamental issues of the day. The threat, however, of an IRS investigation, fines, and loss of tax exemption has had a chilling effect on pastors from speaking out from the pulpit. To protest and challenge the Johnson amendment, every year a handful of ministers defy the IRS and speak on political matters during "Pulpit Freedom Sunday." Before being elected to Congress, Representative Hice served as a pastor for almost 30 years and in 2008 was one of the original 33 pastors to participate in Pulpit Freedom Sunday.

While no Congressional action is expected on this bill in 2016, it could be the template for consideration in 2017.

Health care reform. The Patient Protection and Affordable Care Act (ACA), passed by Congress in 2010, overhauled the nation's health care industry and has brought with it numerous changes to the tax code. The following is a summary of major ACA changes impacting churches and nonprofits (see also Chapter 4):

- **Employer shared responsibility provision ("employer mandate").** The ACA's employer shared responsibility provision ("employer mandate") applies to churches and nonprofits with 50 or more full-time equivalent employees (FTEs), effective with 2015. Employers with 50 to 99 FTEs had to fulfill their reporting obligations beginning in 2015 (see page 78); however, they have until 2016 to comply with the coverage requirements or pay tax penalties. For employers with 100 or more FTEs, the mandate became effective in 2015, but employers that qualified for transition relief rules were only required to provide coverage to 70% (instead of 95%) of their FTEs in 2015. The definition of "full-time" also remains at an average of 30 hours per week or more under the final regulations.

- **Health FSAs limits.** Health FSAs have traditionally been subject to a "use-or-lose" rule, under which employees must forfeit any remaining FSA amounts that are not used up during the plan year. Additionally, health FSAs are subject to a $2,500 annual limit indexed for inflation due to health care reform ($2,550 limit for 2016). Employers sponsoring health FSAs have the option of amending their written plans to allow employees to carry over up to $500 of unused amounts remaining at the end of a plan year to the immediately following plan year, subject to certain limitations. The carryover does not otherwise affect the annual limit on FSAs.

- **Contraception mandate.** After several years and a growing number of court challenges, concerns continue over the health care law's so-called "contraception mandate." The issue began in August 2011 when the Department of Health and Human Services (HHS) specified that coverage for no-cost preventative health services must include all FDA-approved contraceptives, including some considered to be abortifacients.

  Churches, church-related organizations, and religious orders that provide health insurance policies for their employees have been granted a complete exemption from this mandate, while religious nonprofit employers have only been afforded a lesser accommodation. Meanwhile, for-profit employers with religious or moral objections to the required contraceptive coverage had not been given any relief from the mandate by the federal government.

  In June 2014, the U.S. Supreme Court issued its highly anticipated decision in *Burwell v. Hobby Lobby Stores, Inc.*, ruling that the contraception mandate violates the Religious Freedom Restoration Act (RFRA) as applied to two closely-held businesses owned by Christian families with religious objections to providing the mandated abortifacient drugs. In response to the Hobby Lobby decision and other developments, the government crafted additional relief for closely-held corporations and alternative procedures for nonprofits requesting an accommodation.

Payments or reimbursements of employee healthcare-related expenses. By now, most smaller churches and ministries across America are probably aware they are exempt from the ACA employer mandate because they have fewer than 50 full-time equivalent employees (FTEs).[1] That's the good news.

The bad news: Without even knowing it, many of these same organizations may be subjecting themselves to penalties of up to $100 per employee, per day, per violation for making voluntary healthcare payments on behalf of employees (i.e., for individual policy premiums or for other out-of-pocket medical costs) that do not comply with ACA market reforms. These onerous penalties became effective for health plan years beginning on or after January 1, 2014, so care must be taken now to understand and follow the existing guidance.

- **Background.** For decades, it has been the common practice of many smaller churches and ministries that are unable to offer group health insurance coverage to assist employees with the cost of their individual health insurance coverage and/or other out-of-pocket medical expenses. Employers would pay these costs directly on behalf of employees or provide employees with reimbursements after incurring the expenses. If certain formalities were followed, generally these arrangements were blessed by the IRS and even allowed on a tax-free basis for employees.

  That all changed recently as the result of the issuance of certain guidance relating to the ACA market reforms. When the ACA guidance was initially issued related to reimbursements,[2] it was clear that the tax-free reimbursement of individual healthcare insurance premiums would trigger an excise tax of $100 per employee, per day, per violation. However, many people interpreted the initial guidance as permitting the employer to avoid ACA excise tax problems if they reimbursed the individual healthcare insurance premiums on a post-tax basis.

  A year later, the government issued additional guidance[3] clarifying (changing its position) that an employer is not permitted to reimburse individual healthcare insurance premiums on either a pre- or post-tax basis. That means employers who adjusted their practices to align with the initial guidance by paying after-tax reimbursements should discontinue these payments or reimbursements on either a pre- or post-tax basis to avoid excise tax liability.

- **Excise tax liability.** Smaller churches and ministries are most likely to be impacted by these penalties. This is because employers with 100 or more full-time equivalent employees (FTEs) are subject to the ACA mandate to provide qualified group

---

[1] Or fewer than 100 FTEs through 2015.

[2] IRS Notice 2013-54 published on September 13, 2013.

[3] "FAQs about Affordable Care Act Implementation (Part XXII)" prepared jointly by the Departments of Labor (DOL), Health and Human Services (HHS), and the Treasury published on November 6, 2014.

coverage to employees beginning with their 2015 health plan year. Similarly, employers with 50 or more FTEs who qualify for the employer mandate transition relief for 2015 must provide group health coverage beginning in 2016.

For more information, see the *5 Roads for Healthcare Reimbursement by Churches and Ministries* on the ECFA website.

Housing benefits for ministers are back under attack. Freedom From Religion Foundation (FFRF) has filed a new lawsuit in federal court challenging the constitutionality of the ministers' housing exclusion.

Under current law (Internal Revenue Code, § 107), qualified ministers may exclude from income tax, within certain limits, the rental value of church-provided housing or housing allowances for ministers owning or renting their homes. FFRF charges the law unconstitutionally provides "preferential and discriminatory tax benefits" and violates equal protection principles.

This attack on the housing exclusion is just the latest attempt by FFRF, a group which describes itself as a promoter of nontheism and separation between religion and government. In 2014, a U.S. Appeals Court denied a similar challenge by FFRF on the procedural ground of standing.

The court concluded FFRF could not proceed with its case at the time because its leadership had not suffered any "concrete and particularized" injury. In other words, FFRF could not sue because its leaders were never actually denied the benefit of a housing allowance from the IRS. The court went on to suggest, though, FFRF may have standing if its leaders were to pay income taxes on a designated housing allowance, claim a refund from the IRS, and then sue if the IRS rejected or failed to act upon their claims.

According to the latest court filings, FFRF appears to have followed the appeals court's roadmap in bringing this suit. It claims standing is now met because its leaders have paid taxes on designated housing allowances and been denied refunds after requesting them from the IRS.

Interestingly, the federal government who has the responsibility for defending this provision of the tax code conceded in its first filing in the case that based on its understanding of the facts FFRF has the legal standing required to challenge the housing allowance exclusion (while maintaining there is no standing to challenge the exclusion for parsonages). While this is simply a procedural update—there has been no decision by the court on the merits—it is an important one. FFRF's previous attack on the housing allowance was ultimately rejected by the appeals court based on standing.

With standing now conceded by the federal government in this case, this removes an important barrier to allowing FFRF to proceed for the time being with its latest challenge to the housing allowance at the federal district court level.

What is the immediate impact for ministers and churches? This lawsuit is still in the early stages. The mere filing of the case and initial briefs by the parties do not have any effect on ministers who are eligible for the housing exclusion under current law.

IRS audits of churches. A court settlement between the IRS and the Freedom From Religion Foundation (FFRF) in a case regarding church political activity has shifted focus back to the issue of IRS audits of churches. The IRS began the process over five years ago of adopting updated procedures for auditing churches, but has failed to publicly announce the results. This left many, including FFRF, to wonder if the IRS was actively auditing churches for federal income tax compliance.

FFRF agreed to drop its case after the IRS disclosed procedures it had developed behind closed doors for auditing houses of worship, along with an indication that nearly 100 churches are possible targets for future IRS examinations based on concerns surrounding their political activity. At the same time, ECFA has also observed an uptick in the number of IRS payroll tax audits of churches and other ministries prompted by health care reform.

This settlement between the IRS and FFRF does not mark the end to disputes over church political activity. The recommendations of the Commission on Accountability and Policy for Religious Organizations (report issued in 2013) remains a balanced approach to this issue of constitutional significance to thousands of churches across the U.S.

Department of Labor issues modifications to overtime rules. The U.S. Department of Labor (DOL) has issued modifications to the overtime rules of the Fair Labor Standards Act (FLSA). Some have projected that as many as 15 million workers may be newly eligible for overtime when the new rules were implemented on December 1, 2016.

Perhaps the most significant aspect of the proposed rules is the increase of the salary threshold for exempt workers from $23,660 to $47,476 ($913 per week) per year (which equals the 40th percentile of wages for full-time salaried workers). This means that exemption from overtime rules requires salaried workers to earn at least $47,476 even if they are classified as executives, administrators, or professionals (the so-called "EAP" exemption). The last time the overtime threshold was significantly raised was in 1975.

The salary threshold will be adjusted annually, based on either a fixed percentile of wages or the consumer price index (the DOL has invited comment on which adjustment method would be the most appropriate). The salary threshold for exemption of highly compensated employees also increased from $100,000 to $134,004 on December 1, 2016.

CHARITY Act introduced in U.S. Senate with bipartisan support. Senators John Thune (R-SD) and Ron Wyden (D-OR) have introduced the Charities Helping Americans Regularly Throughout the Year Act (CHARITY Act).

The bill begins by expressing support for nonprofits and charitable giving and states the charitable contribution deduction should be protected as Congress contemplates future tax reform efforts.

If enacted, other provisions of the legislation include making donor advised funds eligible for the IRA charitable rollover, requiring all Form 990 filers to do so electronically regardless of size, and allowing the charitable mileage rate fixed by Congress at 14 cents per mile since 1997 to be indexed annually for inflation by the Treasury Department similar to the business and medical/moving rates.

House bill would expand IRA charitable rollover to include donor advised funds. The "Grow Philanthropy Act" (H.R. 4907) would amend current law to allow distributions to donor advised funds to qualify for the tax-favored IRA charitable rollover.

The bipartisan bill was introduced in the U.S. House of Representatives back in April and was recently discussed at a hearing of the Ways and Means Committee.

Lawmakers push back against donor disclosure with proposed legislation. Legislation has been introduced in the U.S. House of Representatives that, if passed and signed into law, would eliminate the schedule of contributors (Schedule B) currently required on IRS Form 990. Through this schedule on their annual information return to the IRS, nonprofits must report information including the names of major donors and their contribution amounts.

Although Schedule B is not available for public inspection, proponents of "Preventing IRS Abuse and Protecting Free Speech Act" (H.R. 5053) argue the information on the form can be abused by the IRS to target taxpayers and that some state attorneys general are improperly demanding the schedule be included in their charitable solicitation registration process.

IRS withdraws controversial proposed gift substantiation alternative. Opposition was overwhelming to a recent IRS proposal related to charitable gift substantiation rules under the tax law.

The proposal would have allowed—but not required—nonprofits to annually file a new form with the IRS as an alternative to providing donors with written charitable gift acknowledgements to substantiate their single contributions of $250 or more for tax deductibility purposes.

The IRS withdrew its proposed gift substantiation alternative after receiving nearly 38,000 public comments.

The primary concerns with the proposal were related to donor privacy and identity theft because the new reporting form would have required nonprofits to keep donor taxpayer identification numbers (social security numbers) on file to report to the federal government.

Changes coming soon to presentation standards for Not-for-Profit Financial Statements. The Financial Accounting Standards Board (FASB) has announced the first major changes in over 20 years to its standards governing financial statement presentation by not-for-profits, including churches and ministries.

Among other requirements, organizations will have to provide greater disclosure about how they allocate expenses and change the way they report net assets.

Nonprofits will also need to:

- Report more and clearer information concerning resources available to make general expenditures.

- Provide additional information about endowments whose values fall below the original gift amount.

- Classify net assets in two categories: those with donor restrictions and those without donor restrictions.

The changes become effective for GAAP-prepared financial statements for fiscal years beginning after December 15, 2017, and for interim periods within fiscal years beginning after December 15, 2018.

New Form I-9 released. A new version of Form I-9 has been released. Ministries may continue using the current version of Form I-9 with a revision date of March 8, 2013 until January 21, 2017. After that date, all previous versions of the Form I-9 will be invalid.

The new form will have some "smart" error checking features. It will have an expiration date of August 31, 2019.

It is important to note that the new I-9 form is not an electronic I-9. Employers filling out the new form I-9 using Adobe Reader will still need to print the form, obtain handwritten signatures, store in a safe place, monitor reverifications and updates with a calendaring system, and retype information into E-Verify as required.

Legislation would provide for stand-alone health reimbursement arrangements (HRAs). The Small Business Healthcare Relief Act (SBHRA) was approved by the House leaving the bipartisan bill in the hands of the Senate.

In 2013, the Department of Labor decided that stand-alone HRAs would be subject to annual limit regulations. This effectively limited an employer's ability to offer HRAs to their employees.

Under the bill passed by the House (H.R. 5447, S. 3060), stand-alone HRAs would open back up. The SBHRA defines "qualified small employer" based on two major criteria and specifies that employees receiving HRAs must be signed up for minimum essential coverage as defined by the ACA. Those two criteria are:

- The employer is not a large employer—employing an average of at least 50 full-time employees on business days during the preceding calendar year.

- The employer "does not offer a group health plan to any of its employees."

Nationwide church survey identifies governance trends. U.S. church leaders now have the opportunity to gain insight into trends in church governance. ECFA polled more than 500 churches with questions about board member selection processes and criteria, the division of power between pastors and board members, church spending patterns, and measurement of institutional effectiveness.

Key findings include the following:

- Financial experience (18.1 percent) and legal experience (5.5 percent) are among the least desired qualifications for board membership while the most desirable characteristic for board members is faithfulness (89.8 percent), followed by consistent giving (51.9 percent).

- In 93.7 percent of churches surveyed, the lead pastor is on the board in some capacity. The lead pastor is a voting member of the board at 42.7 percent of churches, and at 29.8 percent of these churches the lead pastor chairs the board.

- 50.7 percent of churches see their board as being primarily in charge, while 46.8 percent viewed the church staff as being primarily in charge.

- More than 60 percent of churches report they "don't have a conflict of interest policy" or "probably have one, but have not reviewed it in a long time." Conversely, only 16.4 percent of churches have a policy and ensure that the policy is followed by requiring staff and board members to complete an annual questionnaire.

The full survey and a downloadable summary infographic are available online at ECFA.org.

Key Federal Tax Limits, Rates, and Other Data			
	2015	2016	2017
Social security:			
SECA (OASDI & Medicare) combined rate for employers and employees	15.3% on wages up to $250,000 married-joint, $125,000 married-separate, and $200,000 all others	15.3% on wages up to $250,000 married-joint, $125,000 married-separate, and $200,000 all others	15.3% on wages up to $250,000 married-joint, $125,000 married-separate, and $200,000 all others
OASDI maximum compensation base	$117,000	$118,500	$127,200
Benefits and contributions:			
Maximum annual contribution to defined contribution plan	$53,000	$53,000	$54,000
Maximum salary deduction for 401(k)/403(b)	$18,000	$18,000	$18,000
401(k) & 403(b) over 50 "catch up" limit	$6,000	$6,000	$6,000
Maximum income exclusion for nonqualified plans in 501(c)(3) organizations (IRC 457)	$18,000	$18,000	$18,000
IRA contribution limit – age 49 and below age 50 and above	$5,500 $6,500	$5,500 $6,500	$5,500 $6,500
Highly compensated employee limit	$120,000	$120,000	$120,000
Maximum annual contribution to health flexible spending arrangements	$2,550	$2,550	$2,600

	2015	2016	2017
Per diem and mileage rates and other transportation:			
Standard per diem: Lowest rates in continental USA	Lodging $83 Meals & Incidentals $46	Lodging $89 Meals & Incidentals $51	Lodging $91 Meals & Incidentals $51
Business auto mileage rate	57.5¢ per mile	54¢ per mile	
Moving & medical auto mileage rate	23¢ per mile	19¢ per mile	
Charitable auto mileage rate	14¢ per mile	14¢ per mile	14¢ per mile
Motorcycle mileage rate	54.5¢ per mile	51¢ per mile	
Airplane mileage rate	$1.29 per mile	$1.17 per mile	
Bicycle commuting rate	$20 per month	$20 per month	
Maximum value of reimbursement of business expenses (other than lodging) without receipt	$75	$75	$75
Luxury automobile value (limit on use of cents-per-mile valuation of company automobile)	$16,000	$16,000	
Monthly limit on free parking	$250	$255	$255
Transit passes/token — monthly tax-free limit	$250	$255	$255
Form 990/990-T/990-N and 1099-MISC threshold:			
Threshold for filing Form 990 (if not otherwise exempt)	Gross receipts ≥$200,000 or Total assets ≥$500,000	Gross receipts ≥$200,000 or Total assets ≥$500,000	Gross receipts ≥$200,000 or Total assets ≥$500,000
Threshold for filing Form 990-EZ (if not otherwise exempt)	Gross receipts <$200,000 Total assets <$500,000	Gross receipts <$200,000 Total assets <$500,000	Gross receipts <$200,000 Total assets <$500,000
Threshold for filing Form 990 electronically	$10 million in total assets and 250 information returns	$10 million in total assets and 250 information returns	$10 million in total assets and 250 information returns
Threshold for required filing Form 990-N	Under $50,000 in annual gross receipts	Under $50,000 in annual gross receipts	Under $50,000 in annual gross receipts
Threshold for required filing Form 990-T	$1,000 annual gross UBI	$1,000 annual gross UBI	$1,000 annual gross UBI
Threshold for required filing of Form 1099-MISC (payment for most personal services)	$600	$600	$600
Quid pro quo:			
Minimum contribution and maximum cost of token	Minimum gift: $52.50 Maximum cost: $10.50	Minimum gift: $53.00 Maximum cost: $10.60	Minimum gift: $53.50 Maximum cost: $10.70
Maximum value of *de minimus* benefit	2% of gift, but not more than $105	2% of gift, but not more than $106	2% of gift, but not more than $107
Other:			
Federal minimum wage per hour	$7.25	$7.25	$7.25
Gift tax annual exclusion	$14,000	$14,000	$14,000
Estate tax annual exclusion	$5,430,000	$5,450,000	$5,490,000

Projected 2017 Filing Dates

January

17 Monthly deposit of Social Security, Medicare and withheld income tax

31 Distribute Form 1099 to recipients

31 Distribute Form W-2 to employees

31 Form 941 due for Social Security, Medicare, and withheld income tax

31 Form 940 for unemployment tax

February

15 Monthly deposit of Social Security, Medicare and withheld income tax

15 Federal tax withholding deductions reset for anyone who has not given you an updated Form W-4

March

1 Paper filing of 1099 with IRS – unless filing electronically (see April 1)

1 Form W-3 and Copy A of all Forms W-2 – unless filing electronically (see April 1)

15 Monthly deposit of Social Security, Medicare and withheld income tax

April

3 Electronic filing of Forms 1099 and W-2 with the IRS

17 Form 990-T due if more than $1,000 in gross receipts of unrelated business income

17 Monthly deposit of Social Security, Medicare and withheld income tax

May

1 Quarterly Form 941 due

15 Form 990 due for calendar year-end organizations (other year-ends 15th day of the 5th month after your year-end)

15 Monthly deposit of Social Security, Medicare and withheld income tax

June

15 Monthly deposit of Social Security, Medicare and withheld income tax

July

17 Monthly deposit of Social Security, Medicare and withheld income tax

August

1 Quarterly Form 941 due

15 Monthly deposit of Social Security, Medicare and withheld income tax

September

15 Monthly deposit of Social Security, Medicare and withheld income tax

October

16 If you had an automatic extension to file individual tax return, it's now due

16 Monthly deposit of Social Security, Medicare and withheld income tax

31 Quarterly Form 941 due

November

15 Monthly deposit of Social Security, Medicare and withheld income tax

December

15 Monthly deposit of Social Security, Medicare and withheld income tax

1 Financial Accountability

- Independent board
- Managing conflicts of interest
- Measuring outcomes
- Compensation review and approval
- Proper stewardship practices

Financial accountability is a term commonly used in association with churches and other Christ-centered nonprofits. What the term means depends on the context, but it may raise some of the following questions:

➤ Does the organization have proper internal controls?

➤ Is there adequate financial oversight of the organization?

➤ Is the organization accountable to an external accreditation organization like ECFA (ECFA.org)?

➤ Does the organization have its financial statements audited, reviewed, or compiled by an independent certified public accountant?

➤ Does the organization measure the outcomes of its programs and communicate those outcomes truthfully to donors?

Financial accountability is based on the principle of stewardship (see pages 12–14 for the biblical basis for financial accountability). A steward-manager exercises responsible care over entrusted funds. Good stewardship rarely occurs outside a system of accountability.

Financial accountability has never been more important than it is today. While excellence in financial accountability is on the rise for many churches and Christ-centered nonprofits, fraud and other financial scandals continue to disgrace organizations and the name of Christ. The tension continues between investing the time and resources in demonstrating strong financial accountability versus utilizing the same resources primarily for programming. Financial accountability and strong programs is not an either/or proposition—it is both!

Adequate financial accountability enhances a Christ-centered organization's opportunities to effectively carry out the Great Commission. Financial accountability is strong evidence

Biblical Basis for Accountability

1 Chronicles 9:27 – They would spend the night stationed around the house of God, because they had to guard it; and they had charge of the key for opening it each morning. (NIV)

Ezra 8:28–29 – I said to them, "You as well as these articles are consecrated to the LORD. The silver and gold are a freewill offering to the LORD, the God of your fathers. Guard them carefully until you weigh them out in the chambers of the house of the LORD in Jerusalem before the leading priests...." (NIV)

Ezra 8:34 – Everything was accounted for by number and weight, and the entire weight was recorded at that time. (NIV)

Job 5:24 – "You will know that your tent is secure; you will take stock of your property and find nothing missing." (NIV)

Psalm 25:21 – May integrity and uprightness preserve me, for I wait for you. (NRSV)

May integrity and honesty protect me, for I put my hope in you. (NLT)

Let integrity and uprightness preserve me, for I wait for You. (NASB)

Psalm 106:3 – Blessed are they who maintain justice, who constantly do what is right. (NIV)

Proverbs 10:9 – Whoever walks in integrity walks securely.... (NRSV)

People with integrity have firm footing. (NLT)

He who walks in integrity walks securely. (NASB)

Proverbs 11:1 – The LORD abhors dishonest scales, but accurate weights are his delight. (NIV)

Proverbs 11:3 – The integrity of the upright guides them, but the unfaithful are destroyed by their duplicity. (NIV)

Proverbs 15:22 – Plans fail for lack of counsel, but with many advisers they succeed. (NIV)

Proverbs 21:5 – The plans of the diligent lead to profit as surely as haste leads to poverty. (NIV)

Proverbs 21:20 – In the house of the wise are stores of choice food and oil, but a foolish man devours all he has. (NIV)

Proverbs 22:3 – A prudent man sees danger and takes refuge, but the simple keep going and suffer for it. (NIV)

Proverbs 27:23 – Be sure you know the condition of your flocks, give careful attention to your herds. (NIV)

Ecclesiastes 8:6 – For there is a proper time and procedure for every matter, though a man's misery weighs heavily upon him. (NIV)

Matthew 18:12 – "If a man owns a hundred sheep, and one of them wanders away, will he not leave the ninety-nine on the hills and go to look for the one that wandered off?" (NIV)

Matthew 21:13 – "It is written," he said to them, "'My house will be called a house of prayer,' but you are making it a 'den of robbers.'" (NIV)

Matthew 25:16 – "The man who had received the five talents went at once and put his money to work and gained five more." (NIV)

Matthew 25:21 – "His master replied, 'Well done, good and faithful servant! You have been faithful with a few things; I will put you in charge of many things. Come and share your master's happiness!'" (NIV)

Luke 1:3 – Therefore, since I myself have carefully investigated everything from the beginning, it seemed good also to me to write an orderly account for you. (NIV)

Luke 8:17 – "For there is nothing hidden that will not be disclosed, and nothing concealed that will not be known or brought out into the open." (NIV)

Luke 14:28–29 – "Suppose one of you wants to build a tower. Will he not first sit down and estimate the cost to see if he has enough money to complete it? For if he lays the foundation and is not able to finish it, everyone who sees it will ridicule him." (NIV)

Luke 16:2 – "So he called him in and asked him, 'What is this I hear about you? Give an account of your management, because you cannot be manager any longer.'" (NIV)

Luke 16:10 – "Whoever is faithful in a very little is faithful also in much." (NRSV)

"Unless you are faithful in small matters, you won't be faithful in large ones." (NLT)

"He who is faithful in a very little thing is faithful also in much." (NASB)

John 3:21 – "But whoever lives by the truth comes into the light, so that it may be seen plainly that what he has done has been done through God." (NIV)

Romans 13:1 – Everyone must submit himself to the governing authorities, for there is no authority except that which God has established. The authorities that exist have been established by God. (NIV)

Romans 13:5–6 – Therefore, it is necessary to submit to the authorities, not only because of possible punishment but also because of conscience. This is also why you pay taxes, for the authorities are God's servants, who give their full time to governing. (NIV)

1 Corinthians 4:2 – Now it is required that those who have been given a trust must prove faithful. (NIV)

1 Corinthians 14:33 – For God is not a God of disorder but of peace. (NIV)

1 Corinthians 14:40 – But everything should be done in a fitting and orderly way. (NIV)

2 Corinthians 8:19 – What is more, he was chosen by the churches to accompany us as we carry the offering, which we administer in order to honor the Lord.... (NIV)

2 Corinthians 8:20–21 – We want to avoid any criticism of the way we administer this liberal gift. For we are taking pains to do what is right, not only in the eyes of the Lord but also in the eyes of men. (NIV)

2 Corinthians 8:21 – We intend to do what is right not only in the Lord's sight but also in the sight of others. (NRSV)

We are careful to be honorable before the Lord, but we also want everyone else to know we are honorable. (NLT)

We want to do what pleases the Lord and what people think is right. (CEV)

2 Corinthians 13:1 – Every matter must be established by the testimony of two or three witnesses. (NIV)

Galatians 6:9 – So let us not grow weary in doing what is right. (NRSV)

So let's not get tired of doing what is good. (NLT)

Let us not lose heart in doing good, for in due time we will reap if we do not grow weary. (NASB)

Ephesians 4:16 – From him the whole body, joined and held together by every supporting ligament, grows and builds itself up in love, as each part does its work. (NIV)

Colossians 2:5 – For though I am absent from you in body, I am present with you in spirit and delight to see how orderly you are and how firm your faith in Christ is. (NIV)

1 Thessalonians 5:21 – Test everything. Hold on to the good. (NIV)

1 Timothy 6:20 – Timothy, guard what has been entrusted to your care. (NIV)

1 Peter 4:10 – Each one should use whatever gift he has received to serve others, faithfully administering God's grace in its various forms. (NIV)

(CEV) – Contemporary English Version
(NASB) – New American Standard Bible
(NIV) – New International Version
(NLT) – New Living Translation
(NRSV) – New Revised Standard Version

of organizational integrity. Accountability and integrity are foundational elements in keeping the financial wheels of an organization functioning smoothly. This all begins with a prioritization of these concepts by your board and staff.

How can your church or nonprofit demonstrate strong financial accountability? There is not one "how-to" guide that applies to all organizations. The size, type, and complexity of an organization dictate specific approaches. Consider the following:

➤ Most churches with an average attendance of less than 750 do not have financial statements prepared by an independent CPA. Yet, they are well-served to have an internal audit committee composed of church members who review key aspects of the financial records.

➤ Most nonprofit ministries with annual revenues of $3 million have an annual audit conducted by an independent CPA. However, additional procedures beyond the audit are often appropriate to ensure adequate checks and balances.

➤ An independent audit for a nonprofit organization with $25 million or more in annual revenues is just a starting point. An internal audit staff is often employed to enhance financial accountability.

Drawing on the wise counsel of those who have expertise in the area of financial accountability, a Christ-centered organization can prepare its own blueprint and be an example of how proper stewardship may be provided over funds provided by God. For more resources, visit ECFA.org and ECFA.church.

Independent Board

The importance of an independent board cannot be overemphasized. A lack of independent board oversight can impact the accountability and effectiveness of the organization. In contrast, the independent board will determine the organization's mission, set long-range goals, provide fiduciary oversight, establish adequate board policies, and ensure consistent adherence to these policies.

To demonstrate board independence, a majority of the board should be other than employees or staff

Key Issue

Boards should develop a cyclical pattern of self-evaluation. The purpose of self-assessment is to individually and collectively improve board performance. It can take a variety of formats, from soliciting feedback from individual board members about their contributions to the board's performance, to evaluating the effectiveness of time spent together as a board.

or those related by blood or marriage. Even when employee membership on the board is slightly less than a majority, the independence of the board may be jeopardized, especially if the majority of members in attendance at particular meetings are not independent. Employees often lack independence and objectivity in dealing with many board-level matters. While the organization's top leader is sometimes a member of an organization's board of directors, other staff members are generally not members of the board.

Finding a proper balance between the board and the staff leadership of a church or other nonprofit organization is fundamental. When the top leader is too strong, it may be difficult for the board to provide adequate governance over the charity. Conversely, where the top leader is weak, boards or one or more board members often inappropriately move in and take over.

Does your board have robust discussions on key issues? Are the values and policies of the organization clearly articulated? Are annual evaluations, based on predetermined goals, made of the organization's leader? Does the board evaluate itself as rigorously as it evaluates the organization's leader?

A board should meet at least semiannually, and many boards will meet more frequently. Each board should determine the appropriate number of

> **Caution**
>
> Integrity requires that a board member or other insider disclose a potential conflict of interest to the board. The individual should refrain from voting on the transactions involving a related issue and not be present during the voting.

meetings based on the nature of the organization. However, meetings held too frequently often result in the board being overly involved in management issues.

The actions of an organization's board and its committees should be recorded by written minutes, including the signature of the secretary, on a contemporaneous basis (within a reasonable time period after the meeting is held). Organizations filing the Form 990 must document whether minutes are contemporaneously kept by boards and committees with the authority to act for the board.

The actions of an organization's board often include the approval and revision of policies. These policies should be reflected in the board policy manual, with the manual updated as appropriate. *Good Governance for Nonprofits*, by Fredric L. Laughlin and Robert C. Andringa, is an excellent guide for preparing board policy manuals.

Managing Conflicts of Interest

The potential for a conflict of interest arises in situations in which a person is responsible for promoting one interest at the same time he or she is involved in a competing interest. If this person exercises the competing interest over the fiduciary interest, a conflict of interest has occurred.

Related-party transactions occur between two or more parties with interlinking relationships. These transactions should be disclosed to the governing board and evaluated to ensure they are made on a sound economic basis. The organization may decide to pursue any related-party transactions that are clearly advantageous to the organization.

Undertake *significant* transactions with related parties only in the following situations:

> ➤ The organization's board approves the transaction as one that is in the best interest of the organization.

Sample Conflict of Interest Policy Statement

All directors, trustees, officers, agents, and key employees of this organization shall disclose all real or apparent conflicts of interest that they discover or that have been brought to their attention in connection with this organization's activities. "Disclosure" shall mean providing properly, to the appropriate person, a written description of the facts comprising the real or apparent conflicts of interest. An annual disclosure statement shall be circulated to trustees, officers, and certain identified agents and key employees to assist them in considering such disclosures, but disclosure is appropriate and required whenever conflicts of interest may occur. The written notices of disclosures shall be filed with the board chair or such other person designated to receive such notifications. At the meeting of the governing body, all disclosures of real or apparent conflicts of interest shall be noted for the record in the minutes.

An individual trustee, officer, agent, or employee who believes that he or she or an immediate member of his or her immediate family might have a real or apparent conflict of interest, in addition to filing a notice of disclosure, must abstain from

(1) participating in discussions or deliberations with respect to the subject of the conflict (other than to present factual information or to answer questions),

(2) using his or her personal influence to affect deliberations,

(3) making motions,

(4) voting,

(5) executing agreements, or

(6) taking similar actions on behalf of the organization where the conflict of interest might pertain by law, agreement, or otherwise.

A person with a real or apparent conflict of interest will be excused from all discussions or deliberations with respect to the subject of the conflict.

A member of the governing body or a committee thereof, who, having disclosed a conflict of interest, nevertheless shall be counted in determining the existence of a quorum at any meeting in which the subject of the conflict is discussed. The minutes of the meeting shall reflect the individual's disclosure, the vote thereon, and the individual's abstention from participation and voting.

The board chair shall ensure that all directors, trustees, officers, agents, employees, and independent contractors of the organization are made aware of the organization's policy with respect to conflicts of interest.

Sample Conflict of Interest Disclosure
Annual Reporting Statement

Certification

I have read and understand the Conflict of Interest Policy. I hereby declare and certify the following real or apparent conflict(s) of interest:

Disclosure Statement

_____

_____

_____

_____

_____

_____

(If necessary, attach additional documentation.)

I agree to promptly inform the board upon the occurrence of each event that could potentially result in my involvement in (or implication in) a conflict of interest.

_____   _____
           Date   Signature

                                          _____
                                                Title

➤ Related parties are excluded from the discussion and approval of related-party transactions.

➤ There are competitive bids or comparable valuations.

➤ The audited financial statements of the organization fully disclose related-party transactions.

Even when all of the above precautions are observed with respect to a related-party transaction, the church or nonprofit organization may be at risk to criticism from donors, the media, or other members of the public. This risk may be so significant that it overshadows all of the benefits of the transaction.

Example 1: An organization purchases insurance coverage through a firm owned by a board member. This is a related-party transaction. The transaction might be approved if the cost of the insurance is disclosed, the purchase is subject to proper approvals, the price is equal to or below the competition's, the purchase is in the best interests of the organization, and the related party is not present at the meeting when the decision is made.

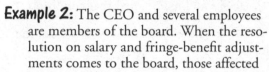

Warning

Information concerning prospective and current board members may reveal potential conflicts that will disqualify the individual. If a conflict is sufficiently limited, the individual may simply need to abstain from voting on certain issues. If the conflict of interest is material, the election or reelection of the individual may be inappropriate.

Example 2: The CEO and several employees are members of the board. When the resolution on salary and fringe-benefit adjustments comes to the board, those affected by the resolution should not discuss and vote on the matter. The CEO and employees should also absent themselves from the meeting to avoid even the appearance of a conflict of interest.

Example 3: A nonprofit board considers a significant investment through a brokerage firm in which a board member has a material ownership interest. This investment might be approved if it is in the best interest of the nonprofit organization, is consistent with its investment policies, and meets its conflicts of interest policy.

Measuring outcomes

Donors and supporters of churches and nonprofits are increasingly focusing on results. Leaders of organizations and their boards need to know whether their programs are providing the intended results. It is not only important to demonstrate effectiveness but to improve it. Measuring outcomes is sometimes called outcome based evaluation (OBE) and managing for results.

Measuring outcomes enables organizations to define and use specific indicators to continually measure how well services or programs are providing desired results. Armed with this information, nonprofit leaders can better develop budgets, allocate resources, and improve services. A sound outcome measurement program includes a process to measure outcomes plus the use of that information to help manage and improve services and organizational outcomes.

Understanding the terminology of outcomes measurement is fundamental:

➤ **Inputs.** These are the resources that a program or organization commits to an effort. For example, time is a crucial input. Staff is another.

➤ **Program.** The program is made up of the products and services an organization applies to a situation. It is the intervention that adds value, brings new information, teaches a skill, expands knowledge, or otherwise influences that situation in some way, directly or indirectly. Program examples include classes and workshops, counseling and performing.

➤ **Output.** This is what the program or organization produces; it is the product. Meals service to the disabled and needy, beds filled in a homeless shelter, and listeners and readers reached are all outputs.

➤ **Outcome.** An outcome is the direct, intended beneficial effect on the stakeholder or interest the organization and programs exist to serve. For example, for a housing and homeless program, an outcome would be the number of clients who were placed in sustainable housing situations and maintained that condition.

"If the program is what we do, and the output is the product of what we do, the outcome is what happens because of that product."[1]

Identifying what will be measured is a key element in measuring outcomes. As someone has said, it is better to measure the right elements imprecisely than to measure the wrong elements with great precision. Measuring the wrong elements may lead to the "law of unintended results."

Compensation Review and Approval

An annual review of a church or nonprofit leader's compensation package is important, particularly when leadership compensation reaches more significant levels. Satisfying the following requirements creates a rebuttable presumption or "safe harbor" that the compensation for an organization's leader is reasonable:

➤ determine comparable pay for similar positions,

➤ make compensation decisions in an independent setting (the individual whose compensation is being considered should be recused from the decision-making process), and

➤ document gross pay and fringe benefits.

The review should focus on all elements of pay, taxable and nontaxable, and an objective evaluation of responsibilities, goals reached, and available resources. A comparison with positions in other organizations may be helpful. National salary surveys may provide meaningful data.

> **Caution**
>
> Reasonable salary and fringe benefits should be carefully documented, especially for the highest paid employees of a charity. The intermediate sanction regulations provide penalties for "excess benefit transactions." Examples of such transactions include unreasonable salaries or bonuses to key employees and excessive travel expenses or other perks.

---

[1] *The Nonprofit Outcomes Toolbox*, Robert Mark Penna (John Wiley & Sons, Inc., Hoboken, New Jersey), 19.

With increased scrutiny of nonprofit salaries by the media, the government, and the public (see chapter 3), it is important that compensation amounts be accurately documented. Gross pay may include the following elements (some taxable and some tax-free or tax-deferred): cash salary; fair rental value of a house, including utilities, provided by the organization; cash housing or furnishings allowance; tax-deferred payments; value of the personal use of organization-owned aircraft or vehicle; value of noncash goods and services; and cash bonuses.

Proper Stewardship Practices

Communications with givers

All statements made by an organization in its stewardship appeals about the use of a gift must be honored. The giver's intent may be shaped by both the organization's communication of the appeal and by any giver instructions with the gift. Any note or correspondence accompanying the gift or conversations between the giver and donee representatives may indicate giver intent, restricting the use of the gift to the intended purpose. If a donor responds to a specific appeal, the assumption is made that the giver's intent is that the funds will be used as outlined in the appeal.

All aspects of a proposed charitable gift should be explained fully, fairly, and accurately to givers. Any limitations on the use of the gift should be clear and complete, both on the response form and in the appeal. These items should be included in the charity's communications to the donor:

➤ **The charity's proposed use of the gift.** Realistic expectations should be communicated regarding what the gift will do within the programs of the ministry.

➤ **Representations of fact.** Any descriptions of the financial condition of the organization or narratives about events must be current, complete, and accurate. References to past activities or events should be appropriately dated. There should be no material omissions, exaggerations of fact, use of misleading photographs, or any other communication tending to create a false impression or misunderstanding.

> ### Key Issue
>
> In deciding whether to support a particular ministry or program, those who donate to Christ-centered organizations rely on the information the ministry provides. Therefore, organizations have the responsibility to represent facts truthfully when communicating with givers.

➤ **Valuation issues and procedures.** If an appraisal is required, the giver should fully understand the procedures and who is responsible to pay for the appraisal.

➤ **Tax consequences and reporting requirements.** While tax considerations should not be the primary focus of a gift, the giver should clearly understand the current and future income, estate, and gift tax consequences, and reporting requirements of the proposed gift. A charitable gift should never be represented as a tax shelter.

➤ **Alternative arrangements for making the gift.** The giver should understand the current and deferred gift options that are available.

➤ **Financial and family implications.** In addition to the tax consequences, the overall financial implications of the proposed gift and the potential impact on family members should be carefully explained.

➤ **Possible conflicts of interest.** Disclose to the giver all relationships that might constitute, or appear to constitute, conflicts of interest. The disclosure should include how and by whom each party is compensated and any cost of managing the gift.

Handling gifts with restrictions by givers

Properly handling donor-restricted gifts is a challenge for many ministries. This is because donor-restricted gifts present a complex combination of accounting, tax, legal, ethical, and other issues.

A donor's written instructions accompanying a gift may provide the basis for a gift restriction. However, in general, a donor's restriction may be either expressed or implied from relevant facts and circumstances. In some instances, the restrictions on donations are driven by the nature of a ministry's appeal. For example, if the appeal describes a project, then any response to the appeal is restricted. In other cases, a donor approaches a ministry desiring to make a restricted gift. Only donors can restrict a gift. In an accounting sense, gift restrictions are either temporary or permanent.

Designations of unrestricted assets or net assets by an organization's governing board do not create restrictions. Designations may be reversed by the board, and they do not result from a donor's contribution. For example, unrestricted assets or net assets do not become restricted merely because a board designates a portion of them to fund future expenditures for a new building.

In certain situations, donors have the power to unrestrict gifts. For example, a donor restricts a gift for a certain project. Later, the ministry asks the donor's permission to redirect the gift for another purpose (unrestricted or restricted) and the donor agrees. The gift is then reclassified from either temporarily or permanently restricted to unrestricted.

Reporting for incentives and premiums

Fundraising appeals may offer premiums or incentives in exchange for a contribution. If the value of the premiums or incentives is not insubstantial, the ministry generally must advise the donor of the fair market value of the premium or incentive and clarify that the value is not deductible for tax purposes either before or after the contribution is made (see pages 171–75 for more detailed information).

Transparency to givers and the public

Churches and other nonprofits should make appropriate disclosures about their governance, finances, programs, and activities. As a demonstration of transparency, a ministry should provide a copy of its current financial statements upon written request. Additionally, many nonprofit organizations are subject to the public disclosure rules requiring charities to provide copies of annual information returns (Form 990) and certain other documents when requested to do so.

Compensation of gift planners

Payment of finders' fees, commissions, or other fees on a percentage basis by a ministry to an outside gift planner or to an organization's own employees as a condition for delivery of a gift is not appropriate under ECFA Standards. Competency-based pay is acceptable when it is paid to employees responsible for an organization's general fundraising program and includes a modest component for achieving broad fundraising goals.

Every effort must be made to keep donor trust. Donor attitudes can be unalterably damaged in reaction to undue pressure and the awareness that a direct commission will be paid to a fundraiser from his or her gift, thus compromising the trust on which the ministry relies.

Acting in the interest of givers

Every effort should be made to avoid accepting a gift from, or entering into a contract with, a prospective donor that would knowingly place a hardship on the donor or place the donor's future well-being in jeopardy.

Fundraisers should recognize that it is almost impossible to properly represent the full interests of the donor and the ministry simultaneously. When dealing with persons regarding commitments on major estate assets, gift planners should seek to guide and advise donors so that they may adequately consider the broad interests of the family and the various organizations they are currently supporting before they make a final decision. Donors should be encouraged to discuss the proposed gift with competent and independent attorneys, accountants, or other professional advisors.

Peer accountability to an oversight organization

ECFA is the only peer accountability organization serving Christ-centered churches and other nonprofits. Founded in 1979, ECFA accredits over 2,100 churches and nonprofit organizations that faithfully demonstrate compliance with established standards for financial accountability, fundraising, and board governance. Members include ministries, denominations, churches, educational institutions, and other tax-exempt 501(c)(3) organizations. Annual revenue of ECFA members exceeds $26 billion.

The ECFA seal is tangible evidence to donors that ECFA member organizations adhere to the highest standards of financial integrity and Christian ethics.

 INTEGRITY***Points***

- **Setting the biblical tone for financial accountability at the top.** Biblical financial accountability starts with the organization's board and top leadership and permeates down through the staff. If the organization is a church, the accountability tone starts with the senior pastor or equivalent leader. If a parachurch organization, it starts with the president, CEO, executive director (or with the person in a similar leadership position).

- **The importance of an independent board.** A majority of independent board members (board members other than staff members or relatives of staff or board members) is vital to ensure the board's action is done without partiality, undue influence, or conflict of interest.

- **Accountability to givers rises with gift restrictions.** When a giver makes an unrestricted gift, the ministry has a general accountability for the funds. However, when a giver places a purpose or time restriction on a gift, the donee charity accepts the responsibility to expend the funds within the limitations of the giver's restrictions.

- **The importance of the work of an independent CPA and/or internal audits.** Churches and other nonprofit organizations of a significant size should annually utilize the services of an independent CPA (annual revenue of $500,000 to $1,000,000 is often considered an appropriate threshold to obtain these services). Large organizations should always have an annual audit. For smaller organizations, an annual review or compilation by an independent CPA may be sufficient. One of the most overlooked CPA services is an "agreed-upon procedures" engagement where the CPA only focuses on certain issues; e.g., bank reconciliations, payroll tax returns, expense reimbursements, or another area that is often troublesome for an organization.

- **Compensation-setting and related-party transactions.** Organizations should establish policies to ensure that compensation-setting and related-party transactions are handled with excellence and integrity. Appropriate policies should require board members without a conflict of interest to set compensation of top leaders and approve related-party transactions only after considering reliable comparability information and documenting the board's review and approval in writing.

CHAPTER 2

Tax Exemption

In This Chapter

- Advantages and limitations of tax exemption
- Tax exemption for churches
- Starting a church or other nonprofit organization
- Unrelated business income

- Private benefit and private inurement
- Filing federal returns
- Postal regulations
- State taxes and fees
- Political activity

Tax exemption for churches and other Christ-centered nonprofits is based on the federal government's recognition that many of the vital contributions to our society's common good are made outside its own agencies in the voluntary or civil society sector. Exempting these organizations from taxes (and additionally, in many instances, providing that contributions to them can be tax-deductible) is a vital governmental means of acknowledging and protecting, instead of burdening and directing, their unique identities and diverse contributions.

And this same characteristic, which exists to some degree in every free society, is acknowledged in biblical theology, which regards not only persons but also a variety of institutions—families, churches, and charities—to have their own independent callings from God to serve their neighbors, beyond the government's responsibility to do good as well as to curb evildoers.

With regard to the many religious organizations that are a large part of civil society, tax-exempt status additionally reflects the government's constitutional commitment to the legitimate separation of church and state. By according churches and other houses of worship automatic recognition of tax-exempt status, the government refrains from illegitimate control of, and intrusion into, the sphere of religion and its institutions, and instead safeguards as it must the free exercise of religion.

To say that government must respect religious charities as well as churches and religious institutions whose freedom it must safeguard is not to say that no government regulation is appropriate. Yet, to be legitimate, such regulation must as far as possible leave the institutions free to chart their own courses and practices.

25

How can your church or other Christ-centered organization obtain federal tax exemption?

> **Churches.** A church is tax-exempt under Section 501(c)(3) of the Internal Revenue Code simply by functioning as a church. While tax law does not define a church, the IRS has developed guidelines that it applies (see page 28). While there is no requirement for a church to file with the IRS for recognition of its tax-exempt status, many churches do so to formally establish this status.

> **Other Christ-centered nonprofits.** A formal filing with the IRS is generally required for other nonprofits to determine if the organization is tax-exempt under federal law.

Can tax-exempt status be lost? Yes. Failure to annually file Form 990, if required, often triggers the loss of tax-exempt status. Participating or intervening in a political campaign or having significant unrelated business activities may also be problematic for an organization's tax-exempt status.

Acquiring and maintaining tax-exempt status not only is vital to churches and other nonprofits, but is also very important to donors who desire a charitable tax deduction for donations made to these organizations.

Advantages and Limitations of Tax Exemption

Tax exemption is available to organizations that meet the requirements of the tax code and are approved by the IRS. This exemption provides relief from federal income tax. This income tax exemption may or may not extend to state and local income taxes. Even if an organization receives tax-exempt status, certain federal taxes may still be imposed. There may be tax due on unrelated business income, excessive compensation, certain "political" activities, and excessive legislative activities.

Tax exemption advantages

Besides the basic exemption from federal income and excise taxes, an organization that is recognized as a charitable organization under the Internal Revenue Code enjoys several advantages:

> Its donors can be offered the benefit of a deduction for charitable contributions.

> It can benefit from using special standard nonprofit mail rates.

> It is in a favored position to seek funding from foundations and other philanthropic entities, many of which will not support organizations other than those recognized as tax-exempt organizations under 501(c)(3).

> It is eligible for government grants available only to entities exempt under 501(c)(3).

Remember

A tax-exempt organization usually means the entity is exempt, in whole or in part, from federal income taxes. The entity may still be subject to social security taxes and certain excise taxes. Nonprofit organizations may be subject to taxes at the state level on income, franchise, sales, use, tangible property, intangible property, and real property.

➤ It often qualifies for exemption not only from state and local income taxes but from property taxes (for property used directly for its exempt function) and certain sales and use taxes as well.

➤ It may qualify for exemption from the Federal Unemployment Tax Act in certain situations.

➤ Its employees may participate in 403(b) tax-sheltered annuities.

➤ It is an exclusive beneficiary of free radio and television public service announcements (PSAs) provided by local media outlets.

➤ If it is a church or a qualified church-controlled organization, it may exclude compensation to employees from the FICA social security base if it meets certain qualifications. The organization must be opposed on religious grounds to the payment of FICA social security taxes. The social security liability shifts to the employees of the electing organizations in the form of SECA social security tax.

Tax exemption limitations

Offsetting the advantages of tax-exempt status are some strict requirements:

➤ Organizations must comply with annual IRS reporting requirements.

➤ Organizations must be engaged "primarily" in qualified charitable or educational endeavors.

➤ There are limitations on the extent to which they can engage in substantial legislative activities or other political activities.

➤ Organizations may not engage in unrelated business activities or commercial activities to an impermissible extent.

➤ There is a prohibition against private inurement or private benefit.

➤ Upon dissolution, organizations' assets must be distributed for one or more exempt purposes.

Tax Exemption for Churches

Tax law and IRS regulations do not define "religious," but the courts have defined "religious" broadly. In part, because of constitutional concerns, some religious organizations are subject to less intrusive reporting and auditing requirements under federal tax law.

The "religious" category includes churches, conventions of churches, associations of churches, church-run organizations (such as schools, hospitals,

Remember

All churches are religious organizations, but not all religious organizations are churches. While many churches have steeples, the definition of a church for IRS purposes is much broader. The term "church" may include religious schools, publishers, television and radio broadcasters, rescue missions, religious orders, and other organizations.

orphanages, nursing homes, publishing entities, broadcasting entities, and cemeteries), religious orders, apostolic groups, integrated auxiliaries of churches, missionary organizations, and Bible and tract societies. IRS regulations define religious worship as follows: "What constitutes conduct of religious worship or the ministration of sacerdotal functions depends on the interests and practices of a particular religious body constituting a church."

Although not stated in the tax law, the IRS generally applies the following 14 criteria to decide whether a religious organization can qualify as a "church":

- ➤ Distinct legal existence
- ➤ Recognized creed and form of worship
- ➤ Definite and distinct ecclesiastical government
- ➤ Formal code of doctrine and discipline
- ➤ Distinct religious history
- ➤ Membership not associated with any other church or denomination
- ➤ Organization of ordained ministers
- ➤ Established places of worship
- ➤ Literature of its own
- ➤ Ordained ministers selected after completing prescribed courses of studies
- ➤ Regular congregations
- ➤ Regular religious services
- ➤ Sunday schools for religious instruction of the young
- ➤ Schools for preparation of its ministers

Churches receive favored status in that they are not required to file either an application for recognition of exemption (Form 1023) or an annual report (Form 990) with the IRS. A church is still subject to filing and disclosing an annual report on unrelated business income (Form 990-T) and Form 5578 for private schools as well as payroll tax, sales tax, and other forms, if applicable. Individuals employed by churches qualify more easily for the special ministerial tax treatments, including a housing allowance.

Because of the highly restrictive requirements of the Church Audit Procedures Act, churches are subject to IRS inquiries or audits only when an appropriate high-level Treasury official makes a reasonable belief determination that a church may not qualify for tax-exempt status. These heightened audit procedures have also recently been extended by the IRS to apply to employment tax-related matters.

Starting a Church or Other Nonprofit Organization

The choice of a nonprofit organizational form is a basic decision. Many churches are unincorporated associations. However, many churches incorporate for the purpose of limiting legal liability. Most other nonprofit organizations are corporations.

While incorporation is usually desirable for churches and other nonprofit organizations, it is generally not mandatory.

Organizations using the corporate form need articles of incorporation and bylaws. An unincorporated organization will typically have similar documents, although the articles may be in the form of a constitution.

> **Key Issue**
>
> If a church or other nonprofit organization wishes to incorporate, it must file articles of incorporation with the appropriate state office. Some states also require the filing of trust documents.

Several planning questions should be asked. If the organization is formed for charitable purposes, is public charity status desired or is a private foundation acceptable? Are any business activities contemplated, and to what degree will the organization be incorporated? Is an attorney competent in nonprofit matters available to help with the preparation of the legal documents? What provisions will the bylaws contain? Who will serve on the board of directors? What name will be used for the organization?

The following materials may provide useful information when starting a church or other nonprofit organization:

irs.gov	Package 1023–Application for Recognition of Exemption with Instructions
irs.gov	Publication 557–Tax-Exempt Status for Your Organization
ECFA.org	12 Steps to Forming a Charitable Organization

Obtaining an employer identification number

All entities, whether exempt from tax or not, must obtain an employer identification number (EIN) by filing IRS Form SS-4. An EIN is required for a church even though churches are not required to file with the IRS for tax-exempt status. This number is not a tax-exempt number, but is simply the organization's unique identifier in the IRS's records, similar to an individual's social security number. An EIN will often be necessary before opening a bank account in the name of the organization.

When an organization is approved by the IRS for exemption from federal income tax (not required for

> **Filing Tip**
>
> The filing for tax-exempt status by a parachurch ministry will determine whether the organization will be recognized as tax-exempt, whether it will be eligible to receive deductible charitable contributions (and sometimes to what extent), and whether the organization will be a public charity or a private foundation.

Form **SS-4**
(Rev. January 2010)
Department of the Treasury
Internal Revenue Service

Application for Employer Identification Number

(For use by employers, corporations, partnerships, trusts, estates, churches, government agencies, Indian tribal entities, certain individuals, and others.)

▶ See separate instructions for each line. ▶ Keep a copy for your records.

OMB No. 1545-0003

EIN

Type or print clearly.

1 Legal name of entity (or individual) for whom the EIN is being requested
Lynn Haven Church

2 Trade name of business (if different from name on line 1)

3 Executor, administrator, trustee, "care of" name

4a Mailing address (room, apt., suite no. and street, or P.O. box)
PO Box 4382

5a Street address (if different) (Do not enter a P.O. box.)
3801 North Florida Avenue

4b City, state, and ZIP code (if foreign, see instructions)
Miami, FL 33014

5b City, state, and ZIP code (if foreign, see instructions)
Miami, FL 33133

6 County and state where principal business is located
Dade County, FL

7a Name of responsible party
Mark Smith, Treasurer

7b SSN, ITIN, or EIN
516-03-9091

8a Is this application for a limited liability company (LLC) (or a foreign equivalent)? . . . . ☐ Yes ☒ No

8b If 8a is "Yes," enter the number of LLC members . . . . ▶

8c If 8a is "Yes," was the LLC organized in the United States? . . . . ☐ Yes ☐ No

9a **Type of entity** (check only one box). **Caution.** If 8a is "Yes," see the instructions for the correct box to check.

☐ Sole proprietor (SSN) _____
☐ Partnership
☐ Corporation (enter form number to be filed) ▶ _____
☐ Personal service corporation
☒ Church or church-controlled organization
☐ Other nonprofit organization (specify) ▶ _____
☐ Other (specify) ▶

☐ Estate (SSN of decedent) _____
☐ Plan administrator (TIN) _____
☐ Trust (TIN of grantor) _____
☐ National Guard ☐ State/local government
☐ Farmers' cooperative ☐ Federal government/military
☐ REMIC ☐ Indian tribal governments/enterprises
Group Exemption Number (GEN) if any ▶

9b If a corporation, name the state or foreign country (if applicable) where incorporated

State	Foreign country

10 **Reason for applying** (check only one box)
☒ Started new business (specify type) ▶ _____
   Church
☐ Hired employees (Check the box and see line 13.)
☐ Compliance with IRS withholding regulations
☐ Other (specify) ▶

☐ Banking purpose (specify purpose) ▶ _____
☐ Changed type of organization (specify new type) ▶ _____
☐ Purchased going business
☐ Created a trust (specify type) ▶ _____
☐ Created a pension plan (specify type) ▶ _____

11 Date business started or acquired (month, day, year). See instructions.
2/01/16

12 Closing month of accounting year

13 Highest number of employees expected in the next 12 months (enter -0- if none).

If no employees expected, skip line 14.

Agricultural	Household	Other
		3

14 If you expect your employment tax liability to be $1,000 or less in a full calendar year **and** want to file Form 944 annually instead of Forms 941 quarterly, check here. (Your employment tax liability generally will be $1,000 or less if you expect to pay $4,000 or less in total wages.) If you do not check this box, you must file Form 941 for every quarter. ☐

15 First date wages or annuities were paid (month, day, year). **Note.** If applicant is a withholding agent, enter date income will first be paid to nonresident alien (month, day, year) . . . . ▶

16 Check **one** box that best describes the principal activity of your business.
☐ Health care & social assistance ☐ Wholesale-agent/broker
☐ Construction ☐ Rental & leasing ☐ Transportation & warehousing ☐ Accommodation & food service ☐ Wholesale-other ☐ Retail
☐ Real estate ☐ Manufacturing ☐ Finance & insurance ☒ Other (specify) **Religious Organization**

17 Indicate principal line of merchandise sold, specific construction work done, products produced, or services provided.

18 Has the applicant entity shown on line 1 ever applied for and received an EIN? ☐ Yes ☒ No
If "Yes," write previous EIN here ▶

Third Party Designee	Complete this section **only** if you want to authorize the named individual to receive the entity's EIN and answer questions about the completion of this form.	
	Designee's name	Designee's telephone number (include area code) ( )
	Address and ZIP code	Designee's fax number (include area code) ( )

Under penalties of perjury, I declare that I have examined this application, and to the best of my knowledge and belief, it is true, correct, and complete.

Name and title (type or print clearly) ▶

	Applicant's telephone number (include area code) ( )
Signature ▶ *Mark Smith* Date ▶ **2/28/16**	Applicant's fax number (include area code) ( )

For Privacy Act and Paperwork Reduction Act Notice, see separate instructions.   Cat. No. 16055N   Form **SS-4** (Rev. 1-2010)

churches), it will receive a "determination letter." This letter does not assign the organization a tax-exempt number.

If an organization is a "central organization" that holds a "group exemption letter," the IRS will assign that group a four-digit number, known as its group exemption number (GEN). This number must be supplied with the central organization's annual report to the IRS (updating its list of included subordinate organizations). The number also is inserted on Form 990 (if required) of the central organization and the subordinate organizations included in the group exemption.

When an organization applies for exemption from state or local income, sales, or property taxes, the state or local jurisdiction may provide a certificate or letter of exemption, which, in some jurisdictions, includes a serial number. This number is often called a "tax-exempt number." This number should not be confused with an EIN.

Application for recognition of tax-exempt status

Although a church is not required to apply to the IRS for tax-exempt status under Section 501(c)(3) of the Internal Revenue Code and is exempt from filing Form 990, it may be appropriate to apply for recognition in some situations:

> **Key Issue**
>
> Approval of tax-exempt status by the IRS is usually effective as of the date of formation of an organization. The effective date determines the date that contributions to the organization are deductible by donors. If an organization is required to alter its activities or substantially amend its charter to qualify, the effective date for tax-exempt purposes will be the date specified in the ruling or determination letter.

➤ National denominations typically file for group exemption to cover all local congregations. A copy of the national body's IRS determination letter may be used by the local group to provide evidence of tax-exempt status.

Independent local churches that are not a part of a national denominational body often file for tax-exempt status to provide evidence of their status. The local congregation may wish to file for group exemption if it is a parent church of other local congregations or separately organized ministries.

➤ If a local congregation ordains, licenses, or commissions ministers, it may be helpful to apply for tax-exempt status. Ministers that are ordained by a local church may be required to provide evidence that the church is tax-exempt. This could be particularly true if the minister files Form 4361, applying for exemption from self-employment tax.

Organizations desiring recognition of tax-exempt status should submit Form 1023 or Form 1023-EZ (see pages 27–28 for churches filing for tax-exempt status). A streamlined For 990-EZ may generally be used by most ministries with gross receipts of $50,000 or less and assets of $250,000 or less.

The IRS must be notified that the organization is applying for recognition of exemption within 15 months from the end of the month in which it was organized. Applications made after this deadline will not be effective before the date on which the application for recognition of exemption is filed. If approved, the IRS will issue a determination letter describing the category of exemption granted.

Organizations that have applied and been approved for tax-exempt status are reflected on the IRS website in the "Exempt Organizations Select Check" section. However, organizations that do not file Form 990, such as churches, will not be listed.

Determination letter request

A user fee of $850 must accompany applications for recognition of tax-exempt status where the applicant has gross receipts that annually exceed $10,000. For an organization that has had annual gross receipts of $10,000 or less during the past four years, the fee is $400. Start-ups may qualify for the reduced fee. Group exemption letter fees are $3,000. Form 8718 should be used to pay the appropriate fee for a determination letter request.

Granting tax exemption

Upon approval of the application for exemption, the IRS will provide a determination letter recognizing that the organizational and operational plans of the nonprofit entitle it to be classified as tax-exempt. The exempt status is usually effective as of the date of formation of the organization, if filing deadlines are met.

Group exemption

An affiliated group of organizations under the common control of a central organization can obtain a group exemption letter. Churches that are part of a denomination are not required to file a separate application for exemption if they are covered by the group letter.

The central organization is required to report annually its exempt subordinate organizations to the IRS. (The IRS does not provide a particular form for this reporting.) The central organization is responsible to evaluate the tax status of its subordinate groups.

Unrelated Business Income

Most Christ-centered ministries are supported primarily from either contributions or revenue from activities directly related to their exempt purposes. Sales of religious books, tuition at schools, and campers' fees are examples of exempt purpose revenue. On the other hand, income from activities not directly related to fulfilling an organization's exempt purposes may be subject to the tax on unrelated business income (UBI).

All income of tax-exempt organizations is presumed to be exempt from federal income tax unless the income is generated by an activity that is

➤ not substantially related to the organization's exempt purpose or function,

➤ a trade or business, and

➤ regularly carried on.

UBI is permitted for tax-exempt organizations. However, these organizations may have to pay tax on income derived from activities unrelated to their exempt purpose. UBI must not comprise a substantial part of the organization's operation. There is no specific percentage limitation on how much UBI is "substantial." However, organizations with 50% to 80% of their activities classified as unrelated have faced revocation of their tax-exempt status.

Filing Tip

Although churches are exempt from filing Form 990 with the IRS, they are still subject to tax on their unrelated business income. Tax law allows churches and other nonprofit organizations to conduct profit-making activities, but it does tax that profit if the income is from an unrelated business activity and none of the exceptions to the tax applies.

Form 990-T must be completed annually to report the source(s) of UBI and related expenses and to compute any tax. UBI amounts are also reportable on Form 990 (if the filing of Form 990 is required). Organizations required to file a Form 990-T will generally also be required to make a state filing related to the UBI. The Form 990-T is subject to the public disclosure rules (see pages 43–50).

Although exempt from filing Form 990, churches must file Form 990-T if they have $1,000 or more of gross UBI in a year. There is a specific deduction of $1,000 in computing unrelated business taxable income. This specific deduction applies to a province of a religious order or a convention or association of churches with respect to each individual church, district, or other local unit.

Unrelated business income consequences

Some church and nonprofit executives are paranoid about UBI to the point that they feel it must be avoided altogether. Some people equate UBI with the automatic loss of exempt status. A more balanced view is to understand the purpose of UBI and to minimize the UBI tax through proper planning.

The most common adverse result of having UBI is that all or part of it may be taxed. A less frequent, but still possible, result is that the organization will lose its tax exemption. It is possible that the IRS will deny or revoke the tax-exempt status of an organization when it regularly derives over one-half of its annual revenue from unrelated activities.

Congress has recognized that some nonprofits may need to engage in unrelated business activities to survive. For example, a nonprofit with unused office space might rent the

Sample Unrelated Business Income Checklist

Determination of whether an activity produces unrelated business taxable income can be made by answering the questions below:

➤ *Is the activity regularly carried on?*

A specific business activity is regularly carried on if it is conducted with a frequency, continuity, and manner of pursuit comparable to the conduct of the same or similar activity by a taxable organization. An activity is regularly carried on if it is conducted

- intermittently the year round, or
- during a significant portion of the season for a seasonal type of business.

However, an activity is not regularly carried on if it is conducted

- on a very infrequent basis (once or twice a year),
- for only a short period of the year, or
- without competitive or promotional efforts.

➤ *Is the activity substantially related to the exempt purposes of the nonprofit?*

To be substantially related, the business activity must contribute importantly to the accomplishment of a purpose for which the nonprofit was granted tax exemption, other than the mere production of income to support such purpose.

➤ *Is the activity conducted with volunteer services?*

Any business activity in which substantially all (85% or more) of the work is performed by volunteers is specifically exempted from unrelated business income tax.

➤ *Is the activity primarily for the convenience of clients, patients, faculty, staff, students, or visitors?*

So-called "convenience" activities are exempt regardless of their nature. Examples are parking lots, food service, bookstores, laundry, telephone service, and vending machines.

➤ *Is the income from the rental of real property?*

Rental income is generally tax-exempt if it does not relate to debt-financed property. But if significant services such as setup, cleaning, and laundry service are also provided, then the income is usually taxable.

➤ *Is the income derived from debt-financed property?*

Examples of income from debt-financed property are dividends, interest, rents, etc., earned from stocks, bonds, and rental property that have been purchased with borrowed money.

space to another organization. Also, nonprofits are expected to invest surplus funds to supplement the primary sources of the organization's income.

A trade or business regularly carried on

A trade or business means any activity regularly carried on which produces income from the sale of goods or services and where there is a reasonable expectation of a profit. To decide whether a trade or business is regularly carried on, the IRS considers whether taxable organizations would carry on a business with the same frequency and continuity. Intermittent activities may escape the "regularly carried on" definition.

Example 1: If a church sells sandwiches at an area bazaar for only two weeks, the IRS would not treat this as the regular conduct of a trade or business.

Example 2: A one-time sale of property is not an activity that is regularly carried on and therefore does not generate unrelated business income unless the property was used in an unrelated business activity.

Example 3: A church is located in the downtown section of a city. Each Saturday, the church parking lot is operated commercially to accommodate shoppers. Even though the business activity is carried on for only one day each week on a year-round basis, this constitutes the conduct of a trade or business. It is subject to the unrelated business income tax.

Substantially related

According to the IRS regulations, a trade or business must "contribute importantly to the accomplishment of the exempt purposes of an organization" if it is to be considered "substantially related." Even if all the profits from a business go to support the work of the nonprofit, the profits may still be taxed.

Example: If a church operates a restaurant and devotes all the proceeds to mission work, the church will not escape taxation on the restaurant's income.

Types of income that may be "related" are

➤ the sale of products made by handicapped individuals as a part of their rehabilitation;

➤ the sale of homes constructed by students enrolled in a vocational training course; and

➤ a retail grocery store operated to provide emotional therapy for disturbed adolescents.

Tours conducted by nonprofits usually create UBI. Tours may be exempt from UBI only if they are strongly educationally oriented, with reports, daily lectures, and so on. Tours with substantial recreational or social purposes are not exempt.

Form **990-T**

Exempt Organization Business Income Tax Return
(and proxy tax under section 6033(e))

OMB No. 1545-0687

2016

For calendar year 2016 or other tax year beginning _____, 2016, and ending _____, 20 _____

Department of the Treasury
Internal Revenue Service

▶ Information about Form 990-T and its instructions is available at *www.irs.gov/form990t.*
▶ Do not enter SSN numbers on this form as it may be made public if your organization is a 501(c)(3).

Open to Public Inspection for 501(c)(3) Organizations Only

A ☐ Check box if address changed

B Exempt under section
☒ 501(C)(3)
☐ 408(e) ☐ 220(e)
☐ 408A ☐ 530(a)
☐ 529(a)

Print or Type

Name of organization (☐ Check box if name changed and see instructions.)
Family Bible Church

Number, street, and room or suite no. If a P.O. box, see instructions.
400 North Sunset Avenue

City or town, state or province, country, and ZIP or foreign postal code
Lemon Grove, CA 92045

D Employer identification number
(Employees' trust, see instructions.)
35-4427081

E Unrelated business activity codes
(See instructions.)
532000

C Book value of all assets at end of year

F Group exemption number (See instructions.) ▶

G Check organization type ▶ ☒ 501(c) corporation ☐ 501(c) trust ☐ 401(a) trust ☐ Other trust

H Describe the organization's primary unrelated business activity. ▶

I During the tax year, was the corporation a subsidiary in an affiliated group or a parent-subsidiary controlled group? . . ▶ ☐ Yes ☒ No
If "Yes," enter the name and identifying number of the parent corporation. ▶

J The books are in care of ▶   Telephone number ▶

Part I	Unrelated Trade or Business Income		(A) Income	(B) Expenses	(C) Net
1a	Gross receipts or sales				
b	Less returns and allowances **c** Balance ▶	**1c**			
2	Cost of goods sold (Schedule A, line 7)	**2**			
3	Gross profit. Subtract line 2 from line 1c	**3**			
4a	Capital gain net income (attach Schedule D)	**4a**			
b	Net gain (loss) (Form 4797, Part II, line 17) (attach Form 4797)	**4b**			
c	Capital loss deduction for trusts	**4c**			
5	Income (loss) from partnerships and S corporations (attach statement)	**5**			
6	Rent income (Schedule C)	**6**			
7	Unrelated debt-financed income (Schedule E)	**7**	79,740	52,301	27,439
8	Interest, annuities, royalties, and rents from controlled organizations (Schedule F)	**8**			
9	Investment income of a section 501(c)(7), (9), or (17) organization (Schedule G)	**9**			
10	Exploited exempt activity income (Schedule I)	**10**			
11	Advertising income (Schedule J)	**11**			
12	Other income (See instructions; attach schedule)	**12**			
13	**Total.** Combine lines 3 through 12	**13**	79,740	52,301	27,439

Part II	Deductions Not Taken Elsewhere (See instructions for limitations on deductions.) (Except for contributions, deductions must be directly connected with the unrelated business income.)		
14	Compensation of officers, directors, and trustees (Schedule K)	**14**	
15	Salaries and wages	**15**	
16	Repairs and maintenance	**16**	
17	Bad debts	**17**	
18	Interest (attach schedule)	**18**	
19	Taxes and licenses	**19**	
20	Charitable contributions (See instructions for limitation rules)	**20**	
21	Depreciation (attach Form 4562) **21**		
22	Less depreciation claimed on Schedule A and elsewhere on return . . **22a**	**22b**	
23	Depletion	**23**	
24	Contributions to deferred compensation plans	**24**	
25	Employee benefit programs	**25**	
26	Excess exempt expenses (Schedule I)	**26**	
27	Excess readership costs (Schedule J)	**27**	
28	Other deductions (attach schedule)	**28**	
29	**Total deductions.** Add lines 14 through 28	**29**	
30	Unrelated business taxable income before net operating loss deduction. Subtract line 29 from line 13	**30**	27,439
31	Net operating loss deduction (limited to the amount on line 30)	**31**	
32	Unrelated business taxable income before specific deduction. Subtract line 31 from line 30 . . .	**32**	27,439
33	Specific deduction (Generally $1,000, but see line 33 instructions for exceptions)	**33**	1,000
34	**Unrelated business taxable income.** Subtract line 33 from line 32. If line 33 is greater than line 32, enter the smaller of zero or line 32	**34**	26,439

For Paperwork Reduction Act Notice, see instructions.   Cat. No. 11291J   Form **990-T** (2016)

The definition of "unrelated trade or business" does not include

➤ activities in which unpaid volunteers do most of the work for an organization;

➤ activities provided primarily for the convenience of the organization's members; or

➤ activities involving the sale of merchandise mostly donated to the organization.

Rental income

Nonprofits often rent facilities, equipment, and other assets for a fee. Rental income usually represents UBI with the following exceptions:

➤ Renting to another nonprofit may be termed "related" if the rental expressly serves the landlord's exempt purposes.

➤ Mailing lists produce UBI, with specific exceptions.

➤ Rental of real estate is excluded from UBI unless the excludable property is acquired or improved with original indebtedness. Rental income from the property becomes UBI to the extent of the ratio of the "average acquisition indebtedness" during the year to the total purchase price. The nonprofit may deduct the same portion of the expenses directly connected with the production of the rental income. Depreciation is allowable using only the straight-line method.

> **Remember**
>
> Nonprofits are normally not taxed on income they receive from renting or leasing real estate, even if the rental activity has nothing to do with their exempt purpose. If the property is financed by debt, however, a portion of the otherwise nontaxable income is typically taxed as debt-financed income.

Debt-financed income

To discourage exempt organizations from borrowing money to purchase passive income items, Congress imposed a tax on debt-financed income. Any property held to produce income is debt-financed property if at any time during the tax year there was acquisition indebtedness outstanding for the property.

Acquisition indebtedness is the outstanding amount of principal debt incurred by the organization to acquire or improve the property:

➤ before the property was acquired or improved, if the debt was incurred because of the acquisition or improvement of the property, or

➤ after the property was acquired or improved, if the debt was incurred because of the acquisition or improvement, and the organization could reasonably foresee the need to incur the debt at the time the property was acquired or improved.

There are exceptions to the debt-financed income rules, including

➤ use of substantially all (85% or more) of any property for an organization's exempt purposes;

➤ use of property by a related exempt organization to further its exempt purposes;

➤ life income contracts, if the remainder interest is payable to an exempt charitable organization;

➤ neighborhood land rule, if an organization acquires real property in its "neighborhood" (the neighborhood restriction does not apply to churches) mainly to use it for exempt purposes within 10 years (15 years for churches).

Activities that are not taxed

Income from the following sources is generally not considered UBI:

➤ **Passive income.** Income earned from most passive investment activities is not UBI unless the underlying property is subject to debt. Types of passive income include

☐ dividends, interest, and annuities;

☐ capital gains or losses from the sale, exchange, or other disposition of property;

☐ rents from real property (some rent is UBI if the rental property was purchased or improved subject to a mortgage);

☐ royalties (however, oil and gas working interest income generally constitutes UBI).

➤ **Volunteers.** Any business where volunteers perform most of the work without compensation does not qualify as UBI. To the IRS, "substantially" means at least 85% of total work performed.

> **Example:** A used-clothing store operated by a nonprofit orphanage where volunteers do all the work in the store would likely be exempt.

> ### Idea
> The use of volunteers to conduct an activity is one of the best ways to avoid tax on what would otherwise be a taxable activity. Intermittent activities may also escape the tax. To decide whether a trade or business is regularly carried on, the IRS considers whether taxable organizations would carry on a business with the same frequency and continuity.

➤ **Convenience.** A cafeteria, bookstore, or residence operated for the convenience of patients, visitors, employees, or students is not a business. Stores, parking lots, and other facilities may be dually used (part related and part unrelated).

➤ **Donated goods.** The sale of merchandise, mostly received as gifts or contributions, does not qualify as UBI. A justification for this exemption is that contributions of property are merely being converted into cash.

➤ **Low-cost items.** Items (costing less than $10.60—2016 adjusted amount) distributed incidental to the solicitation of charitable contributions are not subject to UBI. The amounts received are not considered an exchange for the low-cost articles, and therefore they do not create UBI.

➤ **Mailing lists.** Mailing lists exchanged with or rented to another exempt organization are excluded from UBI, although the commercial sale of the lists will generally create UBI. The structuring of the agreement as a royalty arrangement may make the income exempt from UBI treatment.

Calculating the unrelated business income tax

Income tax rules applicable to businesses, such as depreciation method limitations and rates, apply to the UBI computation. Direct and indirect costs, after proration between related and unrelated activities, may be used to offset income. The first $1,000 of annual net unrelated income is exempt from taxation.

Unrelated business income summary

➤ Be aware of the types of activities that may create UBI in your organization.

➤ Maintain careful records of income and related expenses (both direct and indirect, including depreciation) for any activities that might be considered unrelated to the exempt purpose of your organization. These records should include allocations of salaries and fringe benefits based on time records or, at a minimum, time estimates.

It may be wise to keep a separate set of records on potential unrelated activities. This separate set of records would need to be submitted to the IRS only upon audit.

➤ Be sure that board minutes, contracts, and other documents reflect the organization's view of relatedness of various activities to the exempt purpose of the entity.

➤ If the organization has over $1,000 of gross UBI in a given fiscal (tax) year, file Form 990-T.

Private Benefit and Private Inurement

Tax laws and regulations impose prohibitions on nonprofit organizations concerning private benefit and private inurement. Excise taxes are imposed on "excess benefit transactions" between "disqualified persons" and nonprofits. An excess benefit transaction occurs when an economic benefit is provided by an organization, directly or indirectly, to or for the use of a disqualified person, and the value of the economic benefit provided by the organization exceeds the value of the consideration received by the organization in return for providing the benefit. A disqualified person is any person in a position to exercise substantial influence over the affairs of the organization (often referred to as an "insider").

Private benefit

Nonprofit organizations must serve public, and not private, interests. The private benefit prohibition applies to anyone outside the intended charitable class. The law does allow some private benefit if it is incidental to the public benefits involved. It is acceptable if the benefit to the public cannot be achieved without necessarily benefiting private individuals.

> **Example:** The IRS revoked the exemption of a charity as having served the commercial purposes and private interests of a professional fundraiser when the fundraiser distributed only 3% of the amount collected to the nonprofit organization.

Private inurement

Private inurement is a subset of private benefit. This is an absolute prohibition that generally applies to a distinct class of private interests. These "insiders" may be founders, trustees or directors, officers, managers, or significant donors. Transactions involving these individuals are not necessarily prohibited, but they must be subject to reasonableness, documentation, and applicable reporting to the IRS.

Technically, private inurement is a transfer of resources from a tax-exempt organization to an individual insider that creates a financial benefit for the individual, solely because of that individual's close relationship with the organization and without regard to accomplishing the organization's exempt purposes. In other words, when an individual insider receives something from a nonprofit organization for nothing or even less than what it is worth, private inurement may have occurred. Excessive, and therefore unreasonable, compensation can also result in prohibited inurement. The IRS may ask the following questions to determine if private inurement exists:

➤ Did the expenditure further an exempt purpose, and if so, how?

➤ Was the payment at fair market value, or did it represent reasonable compensation for goods and services?

➤ Does a low- or no-interest loan to an employee or director fall within a reasonable compensation package?

Remember

The most common example of private inurement is excessive compensation. However, the following transactions between a charity and a private individual are other examples of possible private inurement: (1) sale, exchange, or leasing of property; (2) lending of money or other extension of credit; or (3) furnishing of goods, services, or facilities.

Checklist to Document Compensation for a Disqualified Person

1. Name and title: _____Frank Basinger, CEO_____

2. Effective date of contract: _____January 1, 2017_____

3. Duration of contract (one year, two years, etc.): _____one year_____

4. Types of appropriate comparable data relied upon in approving compensation package (check applicable boxes):

    ☒ Compensation paid by similarly situated organizations (taxable and tax exempt)

    ☒ Availability of similar services in the geographical area

    ☐ Independent compensation surveys

5. Explain how comparable data relied upon was obtained: _____The salary data at ECFA.org_____ was relied upon for comparable data.

6. Annual compensation summary:

Cash	Comparable Data	Approved Compensation
• Salary	$ 110,000	$ 95,000
• Bonus or contingent payment (estimate)		5,000
Noncash		
• Deferred compensation	5,000	10,000
• Premiums paid on insurance coverage (life, health, disability, liability, etc.)	20,000	18,000
• Automobile (value of personal use)	4,000	2,000
• Foregone interest on below market loan(s)		
• Other (excluding nontaxable benefits under IRC Sec. 132)	2,000	1,000
Total compensation	$141,000	$131,000

7. Members of authorized body present during discussion of compensation package and vote cast:

Present	In Favor	Opposed
18	16	2

8. Members of authorized body having a conflict of interest with respect to the compensation arrangement and how the conflict was handled (e.g., left room during discussions and votes):

Member	Action re: Conflict
William McIlvain	Absent from board meeting for discussion and vote
Hugh Temple	Absent from board meeting for discussion and vote

9. Date compensation package approved: _____November 10, 2016_____

➤ On an overseas trip for the nonprofit, did the employee (and perhaps a spouse) stay an additional week for a personal vacation and charge the expenses to the organization?

Example 1: An organization lost its exemption when it engaged in numerous transactions with an insider, including the purchase of a 42-foot boat for the personal use of the insider. The insider also benefitted from several real estate transactions, including donations and sales of real property to the organization that were never reflected on its books.

Example 2: A church lost its tax exemption after it operated commercial businesses and paid substantial private expenses of its founders, including expenses for jewelry and clothing in excess of $30,000 per year. The church also purchased five luxury cars for the founders' personal use. None of these benefits were reported as personal income to the founders.

Example 3: A tax-exempt organization transfers an auto to an employee for $1,000. The transfer was not approved by the board and does not constitute a portion of a reasonable pay package. The fair market value of the auto is $10,000. The net difference of $9,000 is not reported to the IRS as compensation. Private inurement has occurred.

Example 4: Same facts as Example 3, except the transfer was approved by the board and properly constituted a portion of the reasonable pay package, and the $9,000 was added to the employee's Form W-2 as compensation. There is no private inurement.

A two-tiered scheme of penalty taxes is imposed on insiders who improperly benefit from excess benefit transactions and on organization managers who are involved in illegal transactions. Sanctions cannot be imposed on the organizations themselves.

A first-tier penalty tax equal to 25% of the amount of the excess benefit is followed by a tax of 200% if there is no correction of the excess benefit within a certain time period. Additionally, there is a 10% penalty on an organization's managers if they knowingly approve an excess benefit transaction.

Filing Federal Returns

Nearly all nonprofit organizations must file an annual return with the IRS (churches, religious orders, and certain foreign missionary organizations are exempt from filing Form 990). The basic filing requirements are as follows:

Form to Be Filed	Conditions
Form 990-N	Gross annual receipts normally $50,000 or less

Form 990	Gross annual receipts over $200,000 or total assets over $500,000
Form 990-EZ	Gross annual receipts less than $200,000 with total assets of less than $500,000
Form 990-T	Any organization exempt under Sec. 501(a) with $1,000 or more gross income from a regularly conducted unrelated trade or business
Form 1120	Any nonprofit corporation that is not tax-exempt
Form 5500	Pension, profit-sharing, medical benefit, cafeteria, and certain other plans must annually file one of several series 5500 Forms

Remember

Form 990 should generally use the same accounting method as the organization uses to keep its books. If the accrual method is used for the books or the audit, use the accrual method on Form 990.

Public inspection of information returns

IRS regulations require the public disclosure of certain documents:

➤ **Materials made available for public inspection.** Nonprofits, other than private foundations, must provide access to the application for tax exemption (Form 1023 or Form 1023-EZ) and any supporting documents filed by the organization in support of its application. These also include any letter or other documents issued by the IRS in connection with the application.

Nonprofits must also provide access to their three most recent information returns. This generally includes Forms 990, 990-T, and schedules and attachments filed with the IRS. There is not a requirement to disclose parts of the information returns that identify names and addresses of contributors to the organization.

➤ **Places and times for public inspection.** Specified documents must be made available without charge at the nonprofit's principal, regional, and district offices during normal business hours. An office is considered a regional or district office only if the aggregate hours per week worked by its paid employees (either full-time or part-time) are 120 or more.

➤ **Responding to requests.** If a person requests copies in person, the request generally must be fulfilled on the day of the request. In unusual circumstances, an organization will be permitted to furnish the copies on the next

Remember

The law requires certain disclosures of financial information. But a general attitude of transparency serves to deter improper diversions of funds and other misdeeds. It also provides a defense to critics and a witness to both believers and nonbelievers.

Form **990**	**Return of Organization Exempt From Income Tax**	OMB No. 1545-0047
	Under section 501(c), 527, or 4947(a)(1) of the Internal Revenue Code (except private foundations)	20**16**
Department of the Treasury Internal Revenue Service	▶ Do not enter social security numbers on this form as it may be made public. ▶ Information about Form 990 and its instructions is at *www.irs.gov/form990*.	**Open to Public Inspection**

A For the 2016 calendar year, or tax year beginning _____, 2016, and ending _____, 20_____

B Check if applicable:	**C** Name of organization **Lifeline Ministries**		**D** Employer identification number
☐ Address change	Doing business as		35 - 7438041
☐ Name change	Number and street (or P.O. box if mail is not delivered to street address)	Room/suite	**E** Telephone number
☐ Initial return	**1212 South Palo Verde**		**480-344-8174**
☐ Final return/terminated	City or town, state or province, country, and ZIP or foreign postal code		
☐ Amended return	**Phoenix, AZ 85035**		**G** Gross receipts $ **1,618,911**
☐ Application pending	**F** Name and address of principal officer:		

H(a) Is this a group return for subordinates? ☐ Yes ☒ No
H(b) Are all subordinates included? ☐ Yes ☐ No
If "No," attach a list. (see instructions)

I Tax-exempt status: ☒ 501(c)(3) ☐ 501(c) ( ) ◀ (insert no.) ☐ 4947(a)(1) or ☐ 527
J Website: ▶
H(c) Group exemption number ▶

K Form of organization: ☒ Corporation ☐ Trust ☐ Association ☐ Other ▶   **L** Year of formation: **1994**   **M** State of legal domicile: **AZ**

Part I Summary

1	Briefly describe the organization's mission or most significant activities: **Lifeline Ministries is an international child sponsoring program. It provides food, education, health care, and spiritual nurture to children in need in 22 countries.**		
2	Check this box ▶ ☐ if the organization discontinued its operations or disposed of more than 25% of its net assets.		
3	Number of voting members of the governing body (Part VI, line 1a)	3	11
4	Number of independent voting members of the governing body (Part VI, line 1b)	4	4
5	Total number of individuals employed in calendar year 2016 (Part V, line 2a)	5	12
6	Total number of volunteers (estimate if necessary)	6	30
7a	Total unrelated business revenue from Part VIII, column (C), line 12	7a	4,100
b	Net unrelated business taxable income from Form 990-T, line 34	7b	(1,875)

		Prior Year	Current Year
8	Contributions and grants (Part VIII, line 1h)	976,624	1,063,877
9	Program service revenue (Part VIII, line 2g)	433,801	489,863
10	Investment income (Part VIII, column (A), lines 3, 4, and 7d)	1,012	608
11	Other revenue (Part VIII, column (A), lines 5, 6d, 8c, 9c, 10c, and 11e) . . .	9,480	10,343
12	Total revenue—add lines 8 through 11 (must equal Part VIII, column (A), line 12)	1,420,917	1,573,691
13	Grants and similar amounts paid (Part IX, column (A), lines 1–3)	10,000	15,000
14	Benefits paid to or for members (Part IX, column (A), line 4)		
15	Salaries, other compensation, employee benefits (Part IX, column (A), lines 5–10)	431,002	452,900
16a	Professional fundraising fees (Part IX, column (A), line 11e)		
b	Total fundraising expenses (Part IX, column (D), line 25) ▶ _____		
17	Other expenses (Part IX, column (A), lines 11a–11d, 11f–24e)	984,903	930,087
18	Total expenses. Add lines 13–17 (must equal Part IX, column (A), line 25) .	1,425,905	1,397,987
19	Revenue less expenses. Subtract line 18 from line 12	5,012	175,704

		Beginning of Current Year	End of Year
20	Total assets (Part X, line 16)	1,625,043	2,043,015
21	Total liabilities (Part X, line 26)	1,610,412	1,852,680
22	Net assets or fund balances. Subtract line 21 from line 20	14,631	190,335

Part II Signature Block

Under penalties of perjury, I declare that I have examined this return, including accompanying schedules and statements, and to the best of my knowledge and belief, it is true, correct, and complete. Declaration of preparer (other than officer) is based on all information of which preparer has any knowledge.

Sign Here	▶ *Harold T. Baldwin*	5/15/17
	Signature of officer	Date
	Harold T. Baldwin, President	
	Type or print name and title	

Paid Preparer Use Only	Print/Type preparer's name	Preparer's signature	Date	Check ☐ if self-employed	PTIN
	Firm's name ▶			Firm's EIN ▶	
	Firm's address ▶			Phone no.	

May the IRS discuss this return with the preparer shown above? (see instructions) . . . . ☐ Yes ☐ No

For Paperwork Reduction Act Notice, see the separate instructions.   Cat. No. 11282Y   Form **990** (2016)

Key Issues in Completing the Form 990
CORE FORM 990

Page 1, Parts I and II – Summary Governance and Financial Information. This page is the focal point for the entire Form 990 and the related schedules. All of the information in Part I is carried forward from other sections of the Form.

Readers of the Form 990 (the media, the donor public, researchers, and others) will generally start their review of an organization's Form 990 with this page. Therefore, a nonprofit should be sure the information on this page accurately reflects the organization's information.

- **The organization's mission or most significant activities.** Describing the organization's mission or most important activities in three-plus lines is highly challenging. The key is referencing other information in the Form 990 such as the exempt purpose achievements on page 2, which provides more space to expand on achievements.

- **Board independence.** By comparing the two lines which reflect the number of independent voting members and the number of total voting members, it will be apparent whether the nonprofit has achieved a majority of independent voting board members.

- **Unrelated business income.** The two lines which reflect gross and net unrelated business revenue tell a reader at a glance whether the nonprofit is required to file Form 990-T (required if gross unrelated business revenue is $1,000 or more) and if the unrelated activity produced a positive or negative financial result.

- **Revenue, expenses, and net assets.** A review of these lines will indicate whether a charity has received more revenue than expenses for the current and previous years, the amount paid to professional fundraisers and the total of fundraising expense, and total assets, total liabilities, and net assets for the current and previous years.

Page 2, Part III – Program Service Accomplishments. The key to completing this section is to maximize the potential of describing the organization's achievements for each of its three largest program services, as measured by total expenses incurred. Activities considered of comparable or greater importance, although smaller in terms of expenses incurred (such as activities conducted with volunteer labor), may be reported on Schedule O. A fundraising activity should not be reported as a program service accomplishment unless it is substantially related to the accomplishment of the organization's exempt purposes (other than by raising funds).

You may report the amount of any donated services, or use of materials, equipment, or facilities received or used in connection with a specific program service on the lines for the narrative description of the appropriate program service. However, do not include these amounts in revenue, expenses, or grants reported in lines 4a-4e.

Pages 3 and 4, Part IV – Checklist of Required Schedules. An organization is not required to answer Yes to questions on these pages and complete the schedule to which the question refers if the organization is not required to provide any information in the schedule. Therefore, a minimum dollar threshold for reporting information in a schedule may be relevant in determining whether the organization must answer Yes to a line on these pages.

A few of the questions on these two pages are particularly noted:

- Line 6 should be answered Yes if the organization maintains a donor advised fund or accounts where donors had advisory privileges on the distribution or investment of amounts in such funds or accounts.

- Line 10 should be answered Yes even if the organization only has quasi-endowments (funds functioning as an endowment that are established by the organization itself, often referred to as board-designated quasi endowments).

- Line 20 only applies to hospitals that were required to be licensed, certified, or similarly recognized by a state as a hospital. This definition excludes hospitals operated internationally.

- On Line 29, an organization is required to answer Yes if it received more than $25,000 during the year in value of donations, gifts, grants, or other contributions of property. Contributed services or the use of facilities is not includable on this line.

Page 5, Part V – Activities That May Require Filing of Other Returns. This page is used to document whether the organization completed the appropriate form or complied with certain other tax requirements. It is effectively a checklist for the organization and the IRS.

Page 6, Part VI – Governance, Management, and Disclosure. Some of the most significant questions on this page include:

- **Independent board.** Line 1b asks for the number of voting members that are independent. A member of the governing body is considered independent only if all three of the following circumstances applied at all times during the organization's tax year:

  - The member was not compensated as an officer or other employee of the organization or of a related organization, except in certain situations under a vow of poverty.

  - The member did not receive total compensation or other payments exceeding $10,000 during the organization's tax year from the organization or from related organizations as an independent contractor, other than reimbursement of expenses under an accountable plan or reasonable compensation for services provided in the capacity as a member of the governing body.

  - Neither the member, nor any family member of the member, was involved in a transaction with the organization that is required to be reported in Schedule L, or in a transaction with a related organization of a type and amount that would be reportable on Schedule L if required to be filed by the related organization.

- **Changes in organizational documents.** Line 4 asks whether significant changes in organizational documents were made since the prior Form 990 was filed. The IRS anticipates the reporting of changes in great detail, including changes in:

  - the number of the governing body's voting members;

  - the number, composition, qualifications, authority, or duties of the organization's officers or key employees;

  - the quorum, voting rights, or voting approval requirements of the governing body;

— the policies and procedures contained within the organizing document or bylaws regarding compensation of officers, directors, trustees, or key employees, conflicts of interest, whistle-blowers, or document retention and destruction; and

— the composition or procedures contained within the organizing document or bylaws of an audit committee.

- **Contemporaneous minutes.** Line 8 asks about the contemporaneous documentation of the meetings of the governing body and each committee with authority to act on behalf of the governing body. While many committees do not have the standing authority to act on behalf of the governing body, it is a best practice for all committees to keep contemporaneous documentation of meetings. This practice will serve an organization well, because boards occasionally delegate responsibility to a committee to act with respect to a certain issue.

- **Providing the Form 990 to the governing body.** Line 11a asks whether the Form 990 was provided to the governing board before it was filed, and requires each organization to describe the process (if any) used to review Form 990.

- **Conflicts of interest.** Lines 12a, b, and c delve into the conflict of interest topic. The questions relate to family and business relationships among officers, directors, and key employees; whether the organization has a written conflict of interest policy; whether the policy requires officers, directors, and key employees to disclose annually interests that could raise conflicts; and whether and how the organization regularly and consistently monitors and enforces compliance with the policy.

- **Whistle-blower policy.** Line 13 asks whether the organization has a written whistle-blower policy. Such a policy is important to prevent retaliation against employees who report suspected illegal activities. Retaliation could violate both federal and state law.

- **Document retention and destruction policy.** Line 14 asks whether an organization has a written document retention and destruction policy. This, too, is important because federal law prohibits the destruction of documents under certain circumstances, particularly if they are relevant to a pending investigation or lawsuit. Establishment and compliance with a written document retention and destruction policy minimizes the likelihood that documents will be destroyed in violation of law, and it may protect an organization from sanctions for destruction of documents in accordance with its policy.

- **Executive compensation.** Lines 15a and b ask for the description of the process the organization uses to approve compensation of the organization's CEO and other officers and key employees; and whether the organization is following the "safe harbor" procedure for approving compensation of "disqualified persons." This procedure includes approval by independent directors or committee members, review of comparable data, and contemporaneous substantiation of the deliberation and decision by the board or committee.

- **Joint venture policy.** Lines 16a and b ask whether organizations that participate in a joint venture have a written procedure ensuring evaluation of the joint venture in light of income tax exemption requirements.

- **Disclosure of documents.** Line 18 asks how the organization makes its Form 1023, Form 990, and Form 990-T available for public inspection. Line 19 asks whether, and if so, how, articles of incorporation, bylaws, conflict of interest policy, and financial statements are made available to the public. The tax code does not require this second group of documents to be published by the organization. However, articles of incorporation and amendments are public record documents, and many nonprofits are required to file their articles of incorporation, bylaws, and audited financial statements with some state offices that regulate charitable solicitations.

Page 7, Part VII – Compensation of Disqualified Persons and Highest Paid Independent Contractors. Organizations are required to list the following officers, directors, trustees, and employees of the organization whose reportable compensation from the organization and related organizations exceeded the following thresholds:

- current officers, directors, and trustees (no minimum compensation threshold)

- current key employees (over $150,000 of reportable compensation)

- current five highest compensated employees other than officers, directors, trustees, or listed key employees (over $100,000 of reportable compensation)

- former officers, key employees, and highest compensated employees (over $100,000 of reportable compensation, with special rules for former highest compensated employees)

- former directors and trustees (over $10,000 of reportable compensation in the capacity as a former director or trustee)

Independent contractors must be listed that received more than $100,000 in compensation for services. The amount paid to the independent contractors must be shown in column (C) whether or not the amount was reported on Form 1099-MISC.

Page 9, Part VIII – Revenue Statement. A few of the key reporting requirements on this page include:

- Fundraising event contributions. This data must now be broken out on line 1c.

- Sales of assets other than inventory. Attachments are not required to reflect the detail of the sale of assets and the sale of securities.

Page 10, Part IX – Functional Expense Statement. There are a number of new expense categories included on the functional expense statement.

"Other expenses" (line 24) should include only expenses not required to be itemized in lines 1–23.

Page 12, Part XII – Financial Statements and Reporting. Key questions in this section include:

a. Financial statements compiled, reviewed, or audited by an independent accountant.

b. Audit committee. The form asks if there is an audit committee. It does not ask if the audit committee is composed of independent members.

OBSERVATIONS ON CERTAIN SCHEDULES

Schedule D – Supplemental Financial Statements. Schedule D requires detailed information on donor-advised funds and endowment funds, even including quasi-endowment funds.

Schedule F – Activities Outside the U.S. Specific reporting of foreign activity is limited to foreign bank accounts and offices located outside the country, where the organization is required to provide the country in which the account or office is located, and checking a box if foreign grants are included in the reported amounts.

The form requires information about foreign activities from organizations that conduct fundraising, grant making, trade or business, or exempt activities outside the United States, or have accounts, offices, employees, or other agents outside the country by region.

Schedule I – Grants and Other Assistance to Organizations, Governments, and Individuals in the U.S. All of the information relating to grants and other assistance to persons inside the U.S. is reported in this schedule. (Foreign grants are reported on the form's Schedule F.) There is a $5,000 per grant filing threshold.

Schedule J – Compensation. This Schedule asks more in-depth questions regarding highly compensated individuals than are asked on the core form. The questions are clearly designed to uncover potentially abusive compensation arrangements.

If the reporting organization is required to complete Schedule J, it first must answer questions, contained in Part I of the Schedule, regarding compensation of all of the individuals it listed on the core form.

Schedule M – Noncash Contributions. In order to collect information from organizations receiving significant amounts of noncash contributions, and specific types of such items, Schedule M collects aggregate annual information on the types of noncash property an organization receives.

Organizations that must file Schedule M are asked if they have a gift acceptance policy that requires the review of any "non-standard contributions." A "non-standard contribution" is a noncash gift that is not used in the organization's activities, for which there is no market in which the gift can be readily liquidated, and whose value is "highly speculative or difficult to ascertain."

Although the definition of a "non-standard contribution" is narrow, organizations should have gift acceptance policies that guide executives regarding the circumstances under which the organization will accept noncash gifts. This is particularly important with respect to gifts of real estate (which may hold environmental cleanup liabilities) and of securities and other business interests that are not publicly traded.

Schedule O – Supplemental Information to Form 990. This form provides an opportunity to explain the organization's operations or responses to various questions. It is a series of blank pages on which to continue explanation from other parts of the form and include information typically included as notes to the current form.

business day. When the request is made in writing, the organization must provide the requested copies within 30 days. If the organization requires advance payment for reasonable copying and mailing fees, it can provide copies within 30 days of the date it is paid, instead of the date of the request.

➤ **Fees for providing copies.** Reasonable fees may be charged by nonprofits for copying and mailing documents. The fees cannot exceed the amounts charged by the IRS (based on fees listed in the Freedom of Information Act)— currently, for noncommercial requesters, 10 cents per page for black-and-white pages, and 20 cents per page for color pages. Organizations are also allowed to charge actual postage costs incurred in providing the copies.

➤ **Documents widely available.** A nonprofit organization does not have to comply with requests for copies if it has made the appropriate materials widely available. This requirement is satisfied if the document is posted on the organization's web page on the Internet or in another database of similar materials.

> **Filing Tip**
>
> As with all tax returns, nonprofits are required by law to provide complete and accurate information on these annual returns. The IRS makes all Forms 990 available to a nonprofit organization, Philanthropic Research, which posts them at guidestar.org.

Reporting substantial organizational changes

An organization's tax-exempt status remains in effect if there are no material changes in the organization's character, purposes, or methods of operation. Significant changes should be reported by letter to the IRS soon after the changes occur and reported on Form 990 if appropriate.

> **Example:** An organization received tax-exempt status for the operation of a religious radio ministry. Several years later, the organization decided to add a facility for homeless children. This change would likely be considered to be material and should be reported to the IRS.

Change in accounting methods

A nonprofit organization may adopt any reasonable method of accounting to keep its financial records that clearly reflects income. These methods include the cash receipts and disbursements method; the accrual method; or any other method (including a combination of methods) that clearly reflects income.

An organization that wishes to change from one method of accounting to another generally must secure the consent of the IRS to make that change. Consent must be obtained both for a general change of method and for any change of method with respect to one or more particular items. Thus, a nonprofit organization that generally uses the cash method, but uses the accrual method with respect to publications for which it maintains inventories, may change its method of accounting by adopting the accrual method for all purposes. But the organization must secure the IRS's consent to do so.

To obtain the consent of the IRS to change an accounting method, the organization should file IRS Form 3115, Application for Change in Accounting Method.

Change of fiscal years

Generally, an exempt organization may change its fiscal year simply by timely filing Form 990 with the appropriate Internal Revenue Service Center for the "short year." The return for the short year should indicate at the top of page 1 that a change of accounting period is being made. It should be filed no later than the 15th day of the fifth month following the close of the short year.

If neither Form 990 nor Form 990-T must be filed, the ministry is not required to notify the IRS of a change in the fiscal year, with one exception. The exception applies to exempt organizations that have changed their fiscal years within the previous ten calendar years. For this exception, Form 1128 must be filed with the IRS.

Other IRS forms commonly used

➤ **Form 5578.** Form 5578 (see page 115) must be completed and furnished to the IRS to provide information regarding racial nondiscrimination policies of private schools, but only for those organizations not already required to file and report this information on Form 990, Schedule E. Form 5578 must be filed for schools operated by a church, including preschools.

➤ **Forms 8717 and 8718.** Nonprofits wishing IRS private letter rulings on employee plans or on exempt organization information must include the new Form 8717 or 8718, respectively, with the appropriate fees.

➤ **Form 8282.** If a nonprofit donee sells or otherwise disposes of gift property for which an appraisal summary is required on Form 8283 within three years after receipt of the property, it generally must file Form 8282 with the IRS. See chapter 7 for more information on these reporting rules.

➤ **Employee and nonemployee payments.** As an employer, a nonprofit organization must file federal and state forms concerning payment of compensation and the withholding of payroll taxes. Payments to nonemployees may require the filing of information returns. See chapters 5 and 6 for more coverage of these requirements.

Postal Regulations

Churches and other nonprofits may qualify to mail at special standard nonprofit mail rates (formerly called bulk third-class). The application (Form 3624) is available at the post office where you wish to deposit the mail (see page 53 for a sample of Form 3624). The following information must be provided (some items apply only if the organization is incorporated):

➤ description of the organization's primary purpose, which may be found in the articles of incorporation or bylaws;

➤ evidence that the organization is nonprofit, such as a federal (and state) tax exemption determination letter; and

➤ materials showing how the organization actually operated in the previous 6 to 12 months, such as program literature, newsletters, bulletins, and any other promotional materials.

The U.S. Postal Service offers rate incentives to nonprofit mailers that provide automation-compatible mail. Automated mail must be readable by an Optical Character Reader (OCR). Contact your local post office for more information.

State Taxes and Fees

Separate filings are often necessary to obtain exemption from state income tax. The requirements vary from state to state. In some states it is also possible to obtain exemption from licensing fees and sales, use, franchise, and property taxes.

A nonprofit organization may be required to report to one or more states in relation to its exemption from or compliance with state income, sales, use, or property taxation. Many states accept a copy of Form 990 as adequate annual reporting for tax-exempt status purposes. Annual reporting to the state in which the organization is incorporated is normally required even if there is no requirement to file Form 990 with the IRS. Check with the offices of the secretary of state and attorney general to determine required filings.

Caution

Do not send a list of major contributors to the state unless it is specifically required. While this list is not open to public inspection with respect to the federal filing, it may not be confidential for state purposes.

Property taxes

Church property is generally exempt from property tax. Whether real estate of a nonprofit organization is exempt from property tax usually depends on its use and ownership. Many states restrict the exemption of church property to property used for worship. It is also important to note that not all religious organizations are churches. Contact the office of the county tax assessor or collector to determine what property tax exemptions are available.

Caution

An initial (and perhaps annual) registration of the property with the proper state authorities is generally necessary to record exempt property. The initial purchase of real estate with notification of state authorities is usually not sufficient to exempt property from tax.

UNITED STATES POSTAL SERVICE ®

Application Number:

**Application to Mail at
Nonprofit Standard Mail Prices**

Section A - Application *(Please read section B on page 2 before completion.)*

Part 1 *(For completion by applicant)*

- All information entered below must be legible so that our records will show the correct information about your organization.
- The complete name of the organization must be shown in item 1. The name shown must agree with the name that appears on all documents submitted to support this application.
- A complete address representing a physical location for the organization must be shown in item 2. If you receive mail through a Post Office™ box, show your street address first and use alternate address for the box.

- The applicant named in item 7 must be the individual submitting the application for the organization and must be a responsible official of the organization. Printers and mailing agents may not sign for the organization.
- No additional organization categories may be added in item 9. To be eligible for the Nonprofit Standard Mail prices, the organization must qualify as one of the types listed.
- The applicant must sign the application in item 15.
- The application must be submitted to the Post Office in item 14 and on the date shown in item 17.

No application fee is required. *(All information must be complete and typewritten or printed legibly.)*

1. Complete Name of Organization *(If voting registration official, include title)*
   Chapel Hill Charity

2. Street Address of Organization *(Include apartment or suite number)*
   300 South Hillcrest Avenue

3. City, State, ZIP+4® Code
   Athens, GA 45701

4. Alternate Mailing Address

5. Alternate City, State, ZIP+4® Code

6. Telephone *(Include area code)*
   614-832-9061

7. Name of Applicant *(Must represent applying organization)*
   Lewis Foster

8. Email Address

9. Type of Organization *(Check only one)*

   [X] (01) Religious   [ ] (03) Scientific   [ ] (05) Agricultural   [ ] (07) Veterans   [ ] (09) Qualified political committee *(Go to item 12)*

   [ ] (02) Educational   [ ] (04) Philanthropic   [ ] (06) Labor   [ ] (08) Fraternal   [ ] (10) Voting registration official *(Go to item 12)*

   Not all nonprofit organizations are eligible for the Nonprofit Standard Mail prices. Domestic Mail Manual® 703.1 lists certain organizations (such as business leagues, chambers of commerce, civic improvement associations, social and hobby clubs, governmental bodies, and others) that, although nonprofit, do not qualify for the Nonprofit Standard Mail prices.

10. Is this a for-profit organization or does any of the net income inure to the benefit of any private stockholder or individual?   [ ] Yes   [X] No

11. Is this organization exempt from federal income tax? *(If 'Yes,' attach a copy of the exemption issued by the Internal Revenue Service (IRS) that shows the section of the IRS code under which the organization is exempt. Required if exempt. Do not submit State tax exemption information.)*   [X] Yes   [ ] No

    Has the IRS denied or revoked the organization's federal tax exempt status? *(If 'Yes,' attach a copy of the IRS ruling to this PS Form 3624.)*   [ ] Yes   [X] No

    From your IRS exemption letter, check off the box corresponding to the section under which the organization is exempt:

    [X] 501(c)(3)   [ ] 501(c)(5)
    [ ] 501(c)(8)   [ ] 501(c)(19)
    [ ] Other 501(c) (____) *(See statement in item 9 above)*

12. Has this organization previously mailed at the Nonprofit Standard Mail prices? *(If 'Yes,' list the Post Office locations where mailings were most recently deposited at these prices and provide the nonprofit authorization number, if known.)*   [ ] Yes   [X] No

13. Has your organization had Nonprofit Standard Mail privileges denied or revoked? *(If 'Yes,' list the Post Office (city and state) where the application or authorization was revoked and provide the nonprofit authorization number, if known.)*   [ ] Yes   [X] No

14. Post Office (not a station or branch) where authorization requested and bulk mailings will be made *(City, state, ZIP Code™).*   **Athens, GA 45701**

I certify that the statements made by me are true and complete. I understand that anyone who furnishes false or misleading information on this form or who omits material information requested on the form may be subject to criminal sanctions (including fines and imprisonment) and/or civil sanctions (including multiple damages and civil penalties). I further understand that, if this application is approved, a postage refund for the difference between the regular Standard Mail and Nonprofit Standard Mail prices may be made for only mailings entered at regular Standard Mail prices at the Post Office identified above while this application is pending, provided that the conditions set forth in Domestic Mail Manual 703.1 and 703.1.9 are met.

15. Signature of Applicant
    Lewis E. Foster

16. Title
    Manager

17. Date
    1/20/16

Part 2 *(For completion by postmaster at originating office when application filed)*

1. Signature of Postmaster *(Or designated representative)*

2. Date Application Filed With Post Office *(Round stamp)*

PS Form **3624**, April 2012 *(Page 1 of 3)* PSN 7530-02-000-9014

PRIVACY NOTICE: See our privacy policy on www.usps.com

Parsonages may be exempt from real estate tax in certain jurisdictions. This is true though there may be several ministers on the staff of one church and therefore multiple parsonages. If the pastor owns the parsonage instead of the church, the parsonage is usually subject to property tax.

Church parking lots are usually exempt if properly recorded. It may be possible to obtain an exemption for vacant land. Property tax exemption of church camps and recreation facilities often comes under attack because of income that may be generated through their use. Property partially used for church use and partially leased to a third-party for-profit entity generally results in the proration of the tax exemption.

Sales taxes

There are presently five states (Alaska, Delaware, Montana, New Hampshire, and Oregon) with no sales tax law. In some states, a nonprofit organization is exempt from sales tax as a purchaser of goods used in ministry. It is generally necessary to obtain recognition of sales tax exemption from the state revenue department. Some states will accept a federal tax exemption as sufficient for a state sales tax exemption.

Even if an organization is exempt from paying sales tax, purchases used for the private benefit of the organization's members or employees are not eligible for exemption.

When a nonprofit organization sells goods to others, a sales tax may or may not be applicable. There are some indications that states may begin a stricter enforcement of laws on the books that allow them to impose sales tax on sales by nonprofit organizations. Occasional dinners and sales of goods at bazaars are typically exempt from sales tax.

Sales by a nonprofit within the state where the nonprofit is located are sometimes taxable. Sales to customers located outside of the state, or interstate sales, may not be subject to sales tax. A 1992 Supreme Court case cleared the way for Congress to decide whether states can require organizations to collect state sales taxes on out-of-state mail-order purchases. Until Congress acts, nonprofits may continue to ship publications and other taxable materials into states where they have no employees or other significant contacts without having to collect taxes.

When a nonprofit organization operates a conference or convention outside of its home state, it is often possible to obtain sales tax exemption for purchases made within the state where the meeting is held. Sales of products at the convention would generally be covered under sales tax laws without an approved exemption.

Political Activity

Churches and other organizations exempt from federal income tax under section 501(c)(3) of the Internal Revenue Code are prohibited from participating or intervening, directly or indirectly, in any political campaign on behalf of or in opposition to any candidate for public office. Even activities that encourage people to vote for or against a particular candidate on the basis of nonpartisan criteria violate the political campaign prohibition law.

To avoid violating the political campaign provisions of the law:

➤ Do not use a rating program to evaluate candidates.

➤ Do not endorse a candidate, or a slate of candidates, directly or indirectly through a sermon, speech, newsletter, or sample ballot.

➤ Do not publish a candidate's statement.

➤ Do not publish the names of candidates who agree to adhere to certain practices.

➤ Do not publish candidate responses to a questionnaire that evidences a bias on certain issues. Classifying particular candidates as too conservative or too liberal is an improper rating system.

➤ Do not publish responses to an unbiased questionnaire focused on a narrow range of issues.

Warning

If a church or 501(c)(3) organization participates in even one political campaign activity (no matter how small the occasion), it can potentially lose its tax-exempt status. The organization must not be involved or participate in the campaign of the individual seeking public office.

➤ Do not raise funds for a candidate or provide support to a political party.

➤ Do not provide volunteers, mailing lists, publicity, or free use of facilities unless all parties and candidates in the community receive the same services.

➤ Do not pay campaign expenses for a candidate.

➤ Do not publish or distribute printed or oral statements about candidates.

➤ Do not display campaign literature on the organization's premises.

If the IRS finds that an organization has engaged in these activities, the organization could lose its exempt status. Also, the IRS may assess an excise tax on the amount of the funds spent on the activity.

Forums or debates may be conducted to educate voters at which all candidates are treated equally, or a mailing list may be rented to candidates on the same basis as it is made available to others. Organizations may engage in voter registration or get-out-the-vote activities. However, it is wise to avoid defining a target group by political or ideological criteria (e.g., encouraging individuals to vote who are "registered Republicans").

INTEGRITY*Points*

- **The church audit potential.** Very few churches are audited each year. The number of churches audited is low because approval of an appropriate high-level IRS official is required to open a church tax inquiry. This is the protection provided in the tax law in recognition of the separation of church and state. However, this audit restriction does not apply to a church that is not filing or paying payroll taxes.

  The danger is for churches that conduct their financial operations beyond the bounds of the law in the belief the church will never be audited. Integrity requires compliance with the law even if the IRS never calls.

- **The danger of "excess benefit transactions."** Excess benefit transactions (as defined on page 40) are often overlooked by churches and other charities. The "insider" involved in the transaction can be subjected to a penalty of up to 225%.

  An excess benefit transaction can be as simple as providing a taxable fringe benefit and not reflecting it as taxable income to a senior pastor, executive director, president, CEO, or other insider. It could be as easy as transferring equipment from a nonprofit organization to an insider at less than fair market value and failing to treat the amount as taxable income to the recipient.

- **The challenge of the Form 990.** Most charities other than churches must annually file Form 990.

  The staff of very few charities have the ability to accurately file the Form 990. At a minimum, a charity should have the Form 990 reviewed by their external CPA or attorney. Better yet is to have the Form 990 prepared by an external professional. After the Form 990 is filed with the IRS, it is soon posted (minus Schedule B) on the Internet by GuideStar. So, an improperly prepared Form 990 soon becomes available for anyone in the world to see. A poorly prepared Form 990 reflects negatively on the charity.

3 Compensating Employees

The three primary challenges for churches and nonprofits in the area of compensating employees are

➤ **Determining the appropriate level of compensation.** Compensating employees too little can create issues for employees covered by the Fair Labor Standards Act. And, compensating employees excessively may jeopardize an organization's tax-exempt status in limited situations. While no absolute limits have been placed on compensation amounts, appropriate total compensation should be determined, taking into consideration reliable comparability data, as well as the skills, talents, education, experience, performance, and knowledge.

➤ **Documenting and reporting compensation.** The approval of the compensation, including fringe benefits, of the ministry's top leader should be contemporaneously documented. The taxable portions of compensation and fringe benefits should be reported to the appropriate taxing authorities.

➤ **Maximizing the tax advantages of certain fringe benefits.** Compensation may be maximized by effectively structuring fringe benefits. The tax-free or tax-deferred features of certain fringe benefits can significantly increase an employee's take-home pay without expending additional ministry funds.

Reasonable Compensation

Employees of churches and nonprofit organizations may receive reasonable compensation for their services. Excessive compensation can result in private inurement and may jeopardize the tax-exempt status of the organization. Reasonable compensation is based on what would ordinarily be paid for like services by a like organization under similar circumstances.

The intermediate sanction regulations impose penalties when excessive compensation or benefits are received by certain key employees and other individuals. These penalties may be avoided if the compensation arrangement was approved by an independent board that (1) was composed entirely of individuals unrelated to and not subject to the control of the employee involved in the arrangement, (2) obtained and relied upon appropriate data as to comparability, and (3) adequately documented the basis for its determination.

Compensation of church and nonprofit leaders should be reviewed by the board or other governing body on an annual basis.

Housing and the Housing Allowance

Housing for nonministers

Housing provided to nonminister employees by a church or nonprofit organization for its convenience, as a condition of employment, and on its premises is

➤ exempt from income tax and FICA tax withholding by the church, and

➤ excluded from wages reporting by the church and employee.

If these criteria are not met, the fair rental value should be reported as compensation on Form W-2 and is subject to withholding and FICA taxation.

Housing for ministers

The 2017 edition of the *Zondervan Minister's Tax & Financial Guide* includes a thorough discussion of the availability of the housing allowance for ministers serving local churches. Ordained, commissioned, or licensed ministers not serving local churches may qualify as "ministers" for federal tax purposes in the situations described below.

➤ **Denominational service.** This category encompasses the administration of religious denominations and their integral agencies, including teaching or administration in parochial schools, colleges, or universities that are under the authority of a church or denomination.

The IRS uses the following criteria to determine if an institution is an integral agency of a church:

☐ Did the church incorporate the institution?

☐ Does the corporate name of the institution suggest a church relationship?

☐ Does the church continuously control, manage, and maintain the institution?

☐ If it dissolved, will the assets be turned over to the church?

☐ Are the trustees or directors of the institution appointed by, or must they be approved by, the church, and may they be removed by the church?

Sample Housing Allowance Resolutions

Parsonage Owned by or Rented by a Church

Whereas, The Internal Revenue Code permits a minister of the gospel to exclude from gross income "the rental value of a home furnished as part of compensation" or a church-designated allowance paid as a part of compensation to the extent that actual expenses are paid from the allowance to maintain a parsonage owned or rented by the church;

Whereas, Nelson Street Church compensates the senior minister for services in the exercise of ministry; and

Whereas, Nelson Street Church provides the senior minister with the rent-free use of a parsonage owned by (rented by) the church as a portion of the compensation for services rendered to the church in the exercise of ministry;

Resolved, That the compensation of the senior minister is $2,500 per month, of which $600 per month is a designated housing allowance; and

Resolved, That the designation of $600 per month as a housing allowance shall apply until otherwise provided.

Home Owned or Rented by a Minister

Whereas, The Internal Revenue Code permits a minister of the gospel to exclude from gross income a church-designated allowance paid as part of compensation to the extent used for actual expenses in owning or renting a home; and

Whereas, Nelson Street Church compensates the senior minister for services in the exercise of ministry;

Resolved, That the compensation of the senior minister is $3,500 per month, of which $1,250 per month is a designated housing allowance; and

Resolved, That the designation of $1,250 per month as a housing allowance shall apply until otherwise provided.

Evangelists

Whereas, The Internal Revenue Code permits a minister of the gospel to exclude from gross income a church-designated allowance paid as part of compensation to the extent used in owning or renting a permanent home; and

Whereas, Nelson Street Church compensates Rev. John Doe for services in the exercise of ministry as an evangelist;

Resolved, That the honorarium paid to Rev. Doe shall be $1,512, consisting of $312 in travel expenses (with documentation provided to the church), a $500 housing allowance, and a $700 honorarium.

☐ Are annual reports of finances and general operations required to be made to the church?

☐ Does the church contribute to the support of the institution?

➤ **Assignment by a church.** Services performed by a minister for a parachurch organization based upon a substantive assignment or designation by a church may provide the basis for ministerial tax treatment. The housing allowance should be designated by the employing organization, not the assigning church.

> ### Caution
>
> Often, a denomination lists a minister as being assigned to a parachurch ministry, for example, in an annual directory, and the minister believes he or she has been assigned for tax purposes. But effective assignments are rare because of the substantive relationship and ongoing documentation of the assignment that are needed.

The following characteristics must be present for an effective assignment:

☐ There must be a sufficient relationship between the minister and the assigning church to justify the assignment of the minister.

☐ There must be an adequate relationship between the assigning church and the parachurch organization to which the minister is assigned to justify the assignment.

To substantiate the relationship between the minister and the church, the church must determine "if there is sufficient authority, power, or legitimacy for the church to assign this particular minister." Such matters as being the ordaining church, providing ongoing supervision, having denominational affiliation, contributing significant financial support, or being the long-term "home church" would all appear to support this relationship.

In addressing the relationship between the church and the parachurch organization, the church must answer the question of "why should the church assign a minister to this particular ministry?" Essentially, the assignment of the minister must accomplish the church's ministry purposes.

In considering an assignment, it is important to distinguish between the process of assigning and the documentation of the assignment. The process of assigning may include the church's theology, philosophy, and policy of operation—its way of doing ministry. The documentation of the assignment provides evidence that the church is doing ministry through the particular individual assigned. The following are keys to a proper assignment:

☐ A written policy describing the specific requirements for the relationship of the church both to the minister being assigned and to the parachurch organization to which the minister is assigned. This would include the church's theological and policy goals for the assignment.

☐ A formal review to confirm that the minister and the proposed ministry with a parachurch organization qualify.

□ A written assignment coupled with guidelines for supervision of and reporting by the minister and the parachurch organization to the church (see page 89 for a sample board resolution).

□ A periodic (at least annual) formal review of the minister's activities to confirm that the assignment continues to comply with the policy.

➤ **Other service.** If a minister is not engaged in service performed in the exercise of ministry of a local church or an integral agency of a church, or a church does not assign a minister's services, the definition of a qualifying minister becomes much narrower. Tax law and regulations provide little guidance for ministers in this category. However, Tax Court cases and IRS rulings suggest that an individual will qualify for the special tax treatments of a minister only if the individual's services for the employer substantially involve conducting religious worship or performing sacerdotal functions. This definition includes conducting Bible studies and spiritual counseling.

Caution

Many ministers are serving organizations other than local churches or integral agencies of churches and do not have an effective assignment by a church. The employer may be a rescue mission, a youth ministry, a Christian radio or TV station, or a missionary-sending organization. Qualifying for ministerial status is often based on the degree to which the individual is performing sacerdotal functions or conducting religious worship.

How much time constitutes substantial involvement in conducting worship or administering the sacraments? This is difficult to say. However, in two IRS letter rulings, the IRS determined that 5% of the minister's working hours were not sufficient to qualify for tax treatment as a minister.

Based on IRS rulings, it is clear that ministers serving as chaplains in government-owned-and-operated hospitals or in state prisons fall in a special category. They are employees for social security (FICA) purposes but qualify for the housing allowance.

➤ **Individuals not qualifying for ministerial tax treatment.** You do not qualify as a "minister" for federal income tax purposes if you are

□ a theological student who does not otherwise qualify as a minister;

□ an unordained, uncommissioned, or unlicensed individual not performing sacerdotal functions or conducting religious worship;

□ an ordained, commissioned, or licensed minister working as an administrator or on the faculty of a nonchurch-related college or seminary;

□ an ordained, commissioned, or licensed minister working as an executive of a nonreligious, nonchurch-related organization;

□ a civilian chaplain at a Veteran's Administration hospital (the tax treatment of ministers who are chaplains in the armed forces is the same as for other members of the armed forces), and

☐ an ordained, licensed, or commissioned minister employed by a parachurch organization but do not perform sacerdotal functions or conduct religious worship.

➤ **Applying the minister's housing allowance.** Qualified ministers receive preferred treatment for their housing. If a minister has a home provided as part of compensation, the minister pays no income tax on the rental value of the home. If a home is not provided but the minister receives a rental or housing allowance designated in the minister's salary, the minister pays no tax on the allowance if it is used for housing expenses subject to certain limitations.

Every minister should have a portion of salary designated as a housing allowance. For a minister living in organization-owned housing, the housing allowance may be only a modest amount to cover incidental expenses such as maintenance, furnishings, and utilities. But a properly designated housing allowance may be worth thousands of dollars in tax savings for ministers living in their own homes or rented quarters.

The excludable housing allowance for ministers is the lowest of these factors:

☐ **Reasonable compensation.** While the law is clear that compensation must be "ordinary and necessary," applying these guidelines is often not easy. All forms of compensation paid by a nonprofit organization must be considered in determining whether reasonable compensation has been exceeded. This includes salary, bonuses, fringe benefits, and retirement benefits. The amount of time an individual devotes to the position is also a factor. Documentation of comparable salaries for similar positions at similar organizations is important to justify compensation arrangements.

☐ **Amount prospectively and officially designated by the employer.** The allowance must be officially designated before payment by the organization. The designation should be evidenced in writing, preferably by resolution of the appropriate governing body, in an employment contract, or, at a minimum, in the church budget and payroll records.

If the only reference to the housing allowance is in the organization's budget, the budget should be formally approved by the top governing body. However, it is highly preferable for the governing board to use a specific resolution to authorize housing allowance designations.

☐ **Amount used from current ministerial income to provide the home.** Only actual housing-related expenses can be excluded from income.

☐ **The fair rental value of the home including utilities and furnishings.** The

Filing Tip

The designation of a housing allowance for a minister living in church-provided housing is often overlooked. While the largest housing allowance benefits go to ministers with mortgage payments on their own homes, a housing allowance of a few thousand dollars is often beneficial to a pastor in a church-provided home.

IRS has not provided any guidance to assist ministers in determining the fair rental value of the home.

Deferred Compensation

In addition to 403(b) and 401(k) plans, churches and nonprofit organizations have available all the qualified retirement plan options that are available to any for-profit. These must be operated according to their terms and are generally subject to the same nondiscrimination and coverage rules as plans in for-profit organizations.

Churches and nonprofit organizations may defer the compensation of executives, but the amount of the deferral is limited in nonprofit organizations by Internal Revenue Code Section 457. For the year 2016, the annual limitation is $18,000. Salary reduction contributions to a 403(b) or 401(k) plan, however, "count" against the annual limitation. For example, if an employee contributed $18,000 to a 403(b) plan, it would use up the entire $18,000 limitation.

Under Section 457(f) there is the ability to set aside deferred compensation without limitation if it is not "vested." The requirement is that it be subject to "significant risk of forfeiture." This is often established by requiring future years of service for it to vest. When vested, it becomes taxable income at that date.

Setting up the deferred compensation as a 457(f) arrangement requires a written agreement that meets the requirements. The agreement between the employee and employer to defer the income must be made before it is earned. Once it has been earned, it is too late for the employee to request its deferral.

> ### Idea
>
> Occasionally, churches and nonprofit organizations will set up a reserve to pay bonuses to employees at a later date. Such a reserve cannot be "designated" or "subject to an understanding" that it will be used for a specific employee. It avoids current taxation because the organization has not allocated it to specific employees nor paid it over.

Amounts that are deferred are often put into a "Rabbi Trust." A Rabbi Trust is established with an independent trustee, who invests the amounts that have been deferred. The assets may still be used to pay creditors of the organization (in a bankruptcy, for instance), but cannot be reclaimed by the corporation for its operations. Essentially, a Rabbi Trust protects the executive from the board's changing its mind and using the money somewhere else.

403(b) plans

Employees of churches and other nonprofit organizations may have a Section 403(b) salary reduction arrangement based on a written plan. These plans are also called tax-sheltered annuities (TSAs).

Both nonelective and elective employer contributions for a minister to a TSA are excludable for income and social security tax (SECA) purposes. Elective contributions for nonministers are subject to FICA. While permissible, after-tax employee contributions are the exception in TSAs.

See the 2017 edition of the *Zondervan Minister's Tax & Financial Guide* for additional information on TSA contribution limitations.

401(k) plans

A church or nonprofit organization may offer a 401(k) plan to its employees. Under a 401(k) plan, an employee can elect to have the employer make tax-deferred contributions to the plan (up to $18,000 for 2016), of amounts that had been withheld from employee pay.

Maximizing Fringe Benefits

Employer-provided cellphones

As long as an employer has provided a cell phone to an employee primarily for noncompensatory business reasons, it is treated as a fringe benefit. Additionally, an employee's personal use will be treated as a *de minimis* fringe benefit. The net effect is that employer-provided cell phones are not taxable income to employees as long as the phone is not provided primarily for noncompensatory purposes.

While the IRS certainly did not identify all business purposes, if cell phones are provided to promote the morale or goodwill of an employee, this is not a sufficient business purpose and the value would be treated as taxable compensation.

To assist in demonstrating the business purpose for employer-provided cell phones, employers may want to consider adding the business reason as part of an employee's job description, in a written cell phone policy or as part of the employment handbook. Employers should generally avoid considering a cell phone as some type of employment perk or as recruitment incentive, as this may give the appearance of compensatory purposes.

Employers should also consider any security risks that may be caused with the loss of a mobile device such as a cell phone. Some phone systems offer additional location and remote data erasing features that can mitigate the risks associated with losing one of these devices. The accidental release of sensitive ministry information could pose serious risks to an organization or its employees.

> **Tip**
>
> Employers should avoid considering a cell phone as some type of employment perk.

Employer reimbursement for employee-owned cell phones

The IRS has issued separate internal guidance to its field staff to address situations where employers provide a reimbursement for employee-owned cell phones. In this guidance, the

IRS indicates that a similar analysis should be used for reimbursements as if the employer had actually provided a cell phone to an employee. Thus, where employers have substantial business reasons other than providing compensation to employees, then it is possible that this does not result in taxable income to the employee.

In order to be eligible for the nontaxable treatment, the reimbursement must

➤ be for business reasons other than providing compensation to employees,

➤ not exceed actual expenses in maintaining the cell phone, and

➤ not substitute a portion of an employee's wages.

Examples of substantial noncompensatory business reasons for requiring employees to maintain personal cell phones and reimbursing them for their use include, but are not limited to,

➤ employer needing to contact the employee at all times for work-related emergencies, or

➤ employer requiring that the employee be available at times outside of an employee's normal work schedule.

It is not considered reasonable to reimburse an employee for international or satellite phone usage if all the employer's necessary contacts are in the local geographic area where the employee works or where reimbursements deviate significantly from normal use in the employer's work.

Employer-owned laptops or reimbursements

The law covering employer-provided laptops technically requires tracking each use and substantiation of a business purpose for each use as well as accounting for any personal use of the machine. It is likely that the rules over laptops will someday follow the same path as cell phones, given their increased prevalence and decreased cost in recent years. Even though the law has not changed regarding laptops, the nature of using laptops makes the accounting for the personal use unreasonable and administratively impracticable. Very few employers make an allocation for personal use of employer-owned laptops.

Personal use of employer-provided vehicles

Vehicles provided by organizations to employees for business use are often used for personal purposes. The IRS (see IRS Publication 535) treats most types of personal use of an employer-provided vehicle as a noncash fringe benefit and generally requires the fair market value of such use to be included in the employee's gross income (to the extent that the value is not reimbursed to the employer).

If the employee reimburses the employer for the full dollar value of the personal use, it will cost the employee more than if the employer includes the personal use value in the income of the employee.

Example: The personal use value of an automobile provided to a lay employee is determined to be $100; if fully reimbursed, the employee would pay $100 to the employer. If there is no reimbursement, the employer includes the $100 in the employee's income, and the employee will subject to payroll taxes on $100 of income. Assuming a federal income tax rate of 28% and a FICA rate of 7.65%, the total would be $35.65 compared with the $100 cash out-of-pocket chargeback.

➤ **Valuation of personal vehicle use.** There are three special valuation rules, in addition to a set of general valuation principles, which may be used under specific circumstances for valuing the personal use of an employer-provided vehicle. This value must be included in the employee's compensation if it is not reimbursed by the employee.

Under the general valuation rule, the value is based on what the cost would be to a person leasing from a third party the same or comparable vehicle on the same or comparable terms in the same geographic area. The special valuation rules, which are used by most employers, are

☐ **Cents-per-mile valuation rule.** Generally, this rule may be used if the employer reasonably expects that the vehicle will be regularly used in the employer's trade or business, and if the vehicle is driven at least 10,000 miles a year and is primarily used by employees. This valuation rule is available only if the fair market value of the vehicle, as of the date the vehicle was first made available for personal use by employees, does not exceed a specified value set by the IRS. For 2016, this value is $16,000.

The value of the personal use of the vehicle is computed by multiplying the number of miles driven for personal purposes by the current IRS standard mileage rate (54 cents per mile for 2016). For this valuation rule, personal use is "any use of the vehicle other than use in your trade or business."

> **Idea**
>
> Start with a policy that requires a contemporaneous log, with the date and personal miles recorded for all ministry vehicles. The log is the basis for determining the personal vs. business use of the vehicle. Then the employer chooses a valuation rule to determine the value of the personal use for Form W-2 reporting. Simply paying for the gas during personal use does not satisfy these rules.

☐ **Commuting valuation rule.** This rule may be used to determine the value of personal use only where the following conditions are met:

- The vehicle is owned or leased by the employer and is provided to one or more employees for use in connection with the employer's trade or business and is used as such.

- The employer requires the employee to commute to and/or from work in the vehicle for bona fide noncompensatory business reasons. One example of a bona fide noncompensatory business reason is the availability of the vehicle to an employee who is on-call and must have access to the vehicle when at home.

- The employer has a written policy that prohibits employees from using the vehicle for personal purposes other than for commuting or *de minimis* personal use such as a stop for a personal errand on the way home from work.

- The employee required to use the vehicle for commuting is not a "control" employee of the employer. For churches and nonprofit organizations, a control employee for 2016 will generally be any board-appointed, confirmed, or elected officer whose pay is $105,000 or more; a director; or an employee whose pay is $215,000 or more.

The personal use of an employer-provided vehicle that meets the above conditions is valued at $1.50 per one-way commute, or $3.00 per day.

☐ **Annual lease valuation rule.** Under the annual lease valuation rule, the fair market value of a vehicle is determined by referring to an annual lease value table published by the IRS (see below). The annual lease value corresponding to this fair market value, multiplied by the personal use percentage, is the amount to be added to the employee's gross income. If the organization provides the fuel, 5.5 cents per mile must be added to the annual lease value. Amounts reimbursed by the employee are offset.

The fair market value of a vehicle owned by an employer is generally the employer's cost of purchasing the vehicle (including taxes and fees). The fair market value of a vehicle leased by an employer generally is either the manufacturer's suggested retail price less 8%, the manufacturer's invoice plus 4%, or the retail value as reported in a nationally recognized publication that regularly reports automobile retail values.

Again, if the three special valuation rules described above do not apply, the value of the personal use must be determined by using a set of general valuation principles. Under these principles, the value must be generally equal to the amount that the employee would have to pay in a normal business transaction to obtain the same or a comparable vehicle in the geographic area in which that vehicle is available for use.

Lease Value Table

Fair Market Value of Car			Annual Lease Value	Fair Market Value of Car			Annual Lease Value
$0	–	$999	$600	8,000	–	8,999	2,600
1,000	–	1,999	850	9,000	–	9,999	2,850
2,000	–	2,999	1,100	10,000	–	10,999	3,100
3,000	–	3,999	1,350	11,000	–	11,999	3,350
4,000	–	4,999	1,600	12,000	–	12,999	3,600
5,000	–	5,999	1,850	13,000	–	13,999	3,850
6,000	–	6,999	2,100	14,000	–	14,999	4,100
7,000	–	7,999	2,350	15,000	–	15,999	4,350

16,000	–	16,999	4,600		34,000	–	35,999	9,250
17,000	–	17,999	4,850		36,000	–	37,999	9,750
18,000	–	18,999	5,100		38,000	–	39,999	10,250
19,000	–	19,999	5,350		40,000	–	41,999	10,750
20,000	–	20,999	5,600		42,000	–	43,999	11,250
21,000	–	21,999	5,850		44,000	–	45,999	11,750
22,000	–	22,999	6,100		46,000	–	47,999	12,250
23,000	–	23,999	6,350		48,000	–	49,999	12,750
24,000	–	24,999	6,600		50,000	–	51,999	13,250
25,000	–	25,999	6,850		52,000	–	53,999	13,750
26,000	–	27,999	7,250		54,000	–	55,999	14,250
28,000	–	29,999	7,750		56,000	–	57,999	14,750
30,000	–	31,999	8,250		58,000	–	59,999	15,250
32,000	–	33,999	8,750					

Note: The annual lease value (calculated using the above table) is based on four-year terms. In other words, employers should refigure the annual lease value every four years that the vehicle is in service, based on the vehicle's fair market value at the beginning of each four-year cycle.

Employer-provided dependent care assistance plan

A church or nonprofit organization can provide employees with child care or disabled dependent care services to allow employees to work. The amount excludable from tax is limited to the smaller of the employee's earned income, the spouse's earned income, or $5,000 ($2,500 if married filing separately). The dependent care assistance must be provided under a separate written plan that does not favor highly compensated employees and that meets other qualifications.

Dependent care assistance payments are excluded from income if the payments cover expenses that would be deductible by the employee as child and dependent care expenses on Form 2441 if the expenses were not reimbursed. It may be necessary to file Form 2441, even though the dependent care assistance payments are excluded from income, to document the appropriateness of the payments.

Disability insurance

Disability insurance may be provided for church and nonprofit organization employees. Coverage is usually limited to 60% to 75% of the annual salary of each individual. Social security and pension benefits are often offset against disability insurance benefits. Disability insurance premiums may be paid through a flexible benefit plan (FSA) to obtain income tax and social security tax (FICA) savings.

If the organization pays the disability insurance premiums, the premiums are excluded from the employee's income. If the organization pays the premiums (and the employee is the beneficiary) as part of the compensation package, any disability policy proceeds are fully taxable to the employee. This is based on who paid the premiums for the policy covering the year when the disability started. If the premiums are shared between the employer and the employee, then the benefits are taxable in the same proportion as the payment of the premiums.

Compensation-related loans

Some churches and nonprofit organizations make loans to employees. The loans are often restricted to the purchase of land or a residence or the construction of a residence. Before a loan is made, the organization should determine if the transaction is legal under state law. Such loans are prohibited in many states.

If an organization receives interest of $600 or more in a year relating to a loan secured by real estate, a Form 1098 must be provided to the payer (see page 109). For the interest to be deductible as an itemized deduction, an employee loan must be secured by the residence and properly recorded.

If an organization makes loans to employees at below-market rates, the organization may be required to report additional compensation to the employee. If the loan is below $10,000, there is no additional compensation to the borrower. For loans over $10,000, additional compensation is calculated equal to the forgone interest that would have been charged if the loan had been made at a market rate of interest. The market rate of interest is the "applicable federal rate" for loans of similar duration. The IRS publishes these rates monthly. The additional compensation must be reported on Form W-2, Box 1.

There are certain exceptions to the general rules on below-market loans. These exceptions relate to loans secured by a mortgage and employee relocation loans.

Social security tax reimbursement

Churches and nonprofit organizations often reimburse ministers for a portion or all of their self-employment tax (SECA) liability. Reimbursement also may be made to lay employees for all or a portion of the FICA tax that has been withheld from their pay. Any social security reimbursement must be reported as taxable income for both income and social security tax purposes. The FICA reimbursement to a lay employee is subject to income tax and FICA withholding.

Because of the deductibility of the self-employment tax in both the income tax and self-employment tax computations, a full reimbursement is effectively less than the gross 15.3% rate:

Marginal Tax Rate	Effective SECA Rate
0%	14.13%
15	13.07
27	12.22
30	12.01

For missionaries who are not eligible for the income tax deduction of one-half of the self-employment tax due to the foreign earned-income exclusion, the full reimbursement rate is effectively 14.13%.

Property transfers

➤ **Unrestricted.** If an employer transfers property (for example, a car, residence, equipment, or other property) to an employee at no charge, this constitutes taxable income to the employee. The amount of income is generally the fair market value of the property transferred.

➤ **Restricted.** To recognize and reward good work, some churches or nonprofits transfer property to an employee subject to certain restrictions. The ultimate transfer may occur only if the employee lives up to the terms of the agreement. Once the terms are met, the property is transferred free and clear. Property that is subject to substantial risk of forfeiture and is nontransferable is substantially not vested. No tax liability will occur until title to the property is vested with the employee. This is a deferral of tax.

When restricted property becomes substantially vested, the employee must report the transfer as taxable income. The amount reported must be equal to the excess of the fair market value of the property at the time it becomes substantially vested, over the amount the employee pays for the property.

> **Example:** A church transfers a house to the pastor subject to the completion of 20 years of service for the church. The pastor does not report any taxable income from the transfer until the 20th year. This situation will generally require advance tax planning since the pastor could have a substantial tax liability in the year of the transfer.

➤ **Property purchased from employer.** If the employer allows an employee to buy property at a price below its fair market value, the employer must include in income as extra wages the difference between the property's fair market value and the amount paid and liabilities assumed by the employee.

Moving expenses

Moving expenses reimbursed by an employer, based on substantiation, are excludable from an employee's gross income. Amounts are excludable only to the extent they would be deductible as moving expenses, i.e., only the cost of moving household goods and travel, other than meals, from the old residence to the new residence. Distance and timing tests must also be met.

Reimbursements to nonminister employees that do not exceed deductible moving expenses are not subject to withholding. However, excess payments are subject to FICA and federal income tax withholding. Nondeductible reimbursements to minister-employees are only subject to income tax withholding if a voluntary withholding agreement is in force.

Nondeductible payments to minister or nonminister employees must be included as taxable compensation, for income tax purposes, on Form W-2.

> **Example:** A church paid a moving company $2,200 for an employee's move. The employer also reimbursed the employee $350. All of the expenses qualify as deductible moving expenses. The employer should report $350

on Form W-2, only in Box 12, using Code P. The $2,200 of expenses paid directly to the moving company are not reportable.

Gifts

The value of a turkey, ham, or other nominally valued item distributed to an employee on holidays need not be reported as income. However, a distribution of cash, a gift certificate, or a similar item of value readily convertible to cash must be included in the employee's income.

Gifts to certain nonemployees up to $25 per year may be tax-free. Gifts of an advertising nature that cost $4 or less given for use on the organization's premises are excluded from the $25 annual limit.

Workers' Compensation

Workers' compensation insurance coverage compensates workers for losses caused by work-related injuries. It also limits the potential liability of the organization for injury to the employee related to his or her job.

Workers' compensation insurance is required by law in all states to be carried by the employer. A few states exempt churches from workers' compensation coverage, and several states exempt all nonprofit employers. Most states also consider ministers to be employees regardless of the income tax filing method used by the minister, and therefore they must be covered under the workers' compensation policy. Contact your state department of labor to find out how your state applies workers' compensation rules to churches.

Workers' compensation premiums are based on the payroll of the organization with a minimum premium charge to issue the policy. An audit is done later to determine the actual charge for the policy.

Most workers' compensation insurance is purchased through private insurance carriers. A few states provide the coverage and charge the covered organizations.

> **Key Issue**
>
> Even if a church or nonprofit organization is exempt from workers' compensation, the voluntary purchase of the coverage or the securing of additional general liability coverage may be prudent. This is because other types of insurance typically exclude work-related accidents: health, accident, disability, auto, and general liability insurance policies are some examples.

Overtime and minimum pay

The Fair Labor Standards Act (FLSA) provides protection for employees engaged in interstate commerce concerning minimum wages, equal pay, overtime pay, recordkeeping, and child labor (some states even have more restrictive versions of the FLSA). Any employee who makes less than $913 per week, full- or part-time, is generally entitled to overtime pay. Overtime pay is required regardless of whether an employee is paid on an hourly or salary basis. For employees to be exempt from the overtime and minimum wage requirements, they must meet the $913 per week threshold and be paid on a salary basis. In other words, employees paid on an hourly basis do not meet the exemption requirements.

The employees of nonprofit organizations involved in commerce or in the production of goods for commerce are generally considered covered by the provisions of the FLSA. Commerce is defined by the FLSA as "trade, commerce, transportation, transmission, or communication among the several states or between any state and any place outside thereof." Conversely, nonprofits that are not engaged in commerce or fall below the $500,000 annual gross sales volume requirement are generally exempt from the Act.

Are ministers exempt from the Fair Labor Standards Act? Generally, yes under the ministerial exception. This common law doctrine received prominent exposure by the U.S. Supreme Court in its unanimous decision in the *Hosanna Tabor* case. One should note that this doctrine likely applies more broadly than the tax determination of who qualifies as a minister. Organizations should consult with their legal counsel in analyzing this potential exemption.

> **Warning**
>
> There is significant confusion over "compensatory time," or giving time off in lieu of paying overtime. If an employee is covered under the Fair Labor Standards Act, providing compensatory time is not an option. Payment for the overtime must be made in cash.

The FLSA applies to schools regardless of whether they are nonprofit entities operated by religious organizations. However, there are special rules for teachers. Church-operated day care centers and elementary and secondary schools are generally considered subject to the FLSA.

Many local churches and small nonprofits do not meet the $500,000 threshold (see above). However, individual employees are generally covered under the FLSA if they send or receive just a few emails each year across state lines. Therefore, most churches and nonprofits should follow the FLSA regulations as a precaution against possible action by the Department of Labor. Ministers are generally exempt under the professional provisions of this exemption.

The current FLSA minimum wage is $7.25 per hour. (Caution: Several states have established minimum wages that exceed the federal rate.) Teenagers may be paid a training wage of any amount above $4.25 per hour for the first 90 days of employment. Minors under age 14 generally cannot be hired.

Any employee paid over $913 per week must meet the duties test in order to be classified as an exempt employee. The duties tests are divided into employee type categories. These categories are executive, administrative, and professional employees.

Nondiscrimination Rules

To qualify for exclusion from income, many fringe benefits must be nondiscriminatory. This is particularly true for many types of benefits for certain key employees. Failure to comply with the nondiscrimination rules does not disqualify a fringe benefit plan entirely. The benefit is simply fully taxable for the highly compensated or key employees.

The nondiscrimination rules apply to the following types of fringe benefit plans: qualified tuition and fee discounts, eating facilities on or near the employer's premises, educational assistance benefits, dependent care assistance plans, tax-sheltered annuities (TSAs), 401(k) plans, and other deferred compensation plans, group-term life insurance benefits, self-insured medical plans, health savings accounts (including health reimbursement arrangements), and cafeteria plans (including a flexible spending account dependent care plan and a health care flexible spending account).

Fringe benefit plans that limit benefits only to officers or highly compensated employees are clearly discriminatory. An officer is an employee who is appointed, confirmed, or elected by the board of the employer. A highly compensated employee for 2016 is someone who was paid more than $120,000, or if the employer elects, was in the top 20% of paid employees for compensation for the previous year.

Paying Employee Expenses

An accountable plan is a reimbursement or expense allowance arrangement that requires (1) a business purpose for the expenses, (2) employees to substantiate the expenses, and (3) the return of any excess reimbursements.

The substantiation of expenses and return of excess reimbursements must be handled within a reasonable time. The following methods meet the "reasonable time" definition:

➤ The fixed date method applies if

☐ an advance is made within 30 days of when an expense is paid or incurred;

☐ an expense is substantiated to the employer within 60 days after the expense is paid or incurred; and

☐ any excess amount is returned to the employer within 120 days after the expense is paid or incurred.

➤ The periodic statement method applies if

☐ the employer provides employees with a periodic statement that sets forth the amount paid under the arrangement in excess of substantiated expenses;

☐ statements are provided at least quarterly; and

☐ the employer requests that the employee provide substantiation for any additional expenses that have not yet been substantiated and/or return any amounts remaining unsubstantiated within 120 days of the statement.

If employees substantiate expenses and return any unused excess payments to the church or nonprofit organization on a timely basis, payments to the employee for business expenses have no impact on tax reporting. They are not included on Form W-2 for the employee. Although Section 179 expense deductions can be claimed by an employee on their Form 1040, Section 179 amounts are not eligible for reimbursement under an accountable expense reimbursement plan.

The timing of documenting expenses for reimbursement is of utmost importance. Under the fixed date method (see above), the IRS provides a safe harbor of 60 days after the expense is paid or incurred. In other words, the IRS may contest a reimbursement, based on timeliness of submitting the documentation, if the documentation is provided to the employer. Does this mean that the IRS will disallow expenses reimbursed within 61 days? Not necessarily. It simply means 60 days is a safe harbor as a "reasonable time."

> **Idea**
>
> The probability of disability greatly exceeds the probability of death during an individual's working years. Individual or group policies may be purchased. These plans may include a probationary period, which excludes preexisting sickness from immediate coverage, and an elimination period, which specifies the time after the start of a disability when benefits are not payable.

Example: A church approves $50,000 of compensation for the pastor and tells her to let the church know at the end of the year how much she has spent on business expenses, and they will show the net amount on Form W-2. Is this valid? No. The salary must be established separately from expense reimbursements. Further, even if an accountable expense reimbursement plan is used, the annual submission of expense documentation would fail the timeliness test for expenses incurred in all but the last portion of the year.

Per diem allowance

Church and nonprofit employers that help their employees cover business travel expenses have two basic options: (1) The employer can pay employees the precise amount of their expenses, or (2) the employer can opt for convenience and pay a set "per diem" allowance for each day of business travel.

The standard per diem rates for travel within the continental United States (CONUS) are $91 for lodging and $51 for meals and entertainment (based on October 1, 2016, to September 30, 2017). Federal per diem rates for travel outside CONUS, including Alaska, Hawaii, Puerto Rico, the northern Mariana Islands, U.S. possessions, and all other foreign localities, are published by the U.S. Department of State.

Given the efficiency and administrative advantages of the per diem approach, some churches and nonprofits choose to make per diem payments to volunteers within the IRS limits based on location. However, unlike in the case of employees, volunteers must include in income any part of per diem allowances that exceed deductible travel expenses.

Sample Accountable Expense Reimbursement Plan

Whereas, Income tax regulations provide that an arrangement between an employee and employer must meet the requirements of business connection, substantiation, and return of excess payments in order to be considered a reimbursement;

Whereas, Plans that meet the three requirements listed above are considered to be accountable plans, and the reimbursed expenses are generally excludable from an employee's gross compensation;

Whereas, Plans that do not meet all the requirements listed above are considered nonaccountable plans, and payments made under such plans are includable in gross employee compensation; and

Whereas, First Church desires to establish an accountable expense reimbursement policy in compliance with the income tax regulations;

Resolved, That First Church establishes an expense reimbursement policy effective _____, 20___, whereby employees serving the church may receive advances for, or reimbursement of, expenses if

A. There is a stated business purpose of the expense related to the ministry of the church, and the expenses would qualify for deductions for federal income tax purposes if the expenses were not reimbursed;

B. The employee provides adequate substantiation to the church for all expenses; and

C. The employee returns all excess reimbursements within a reasonable time.

Resolved, That the following methods will meet the "reasonable time" definition:

A. An advance is made within 30 days of when an expense is paid or incurred;

B. An expense is substantiated to the church within 60 days after the expense is paid or incurred; or

C. An excess amount is returned to the church within 120 days after the expense is paid or incurred.

Resolved, That substantiation of business expenses will include business purpose, business relationship (including names of persons present), cost (itemized accounting), time, and place of any individual non-lodging expense of $75 or more and for all lodging expenses. Auto mileage reimbursed must be substantiated by a daily mileage log separating business and personal miles. The church will retain the original copies related to the expenses substantiated.

Note: The above resolution includes the basic guidelines for an accountable expense reimbursement plan. If the employer desires to place a dollar limit on reimbursements to be made under the plan employee-by-employee, a separate resolution may be adopted for this purpose.

INTEGRITY*Points*

- **Qualifying for the housing allowance.** Determining which individuals qualify for ministerial status (and, therefore, qualify for a housing allowance designation) can be a challenging issue for the employing church or other nonprofit organization—it's always the employer's decision, not the employee's. It's fairly simple to make this determination for a local church and for religious denominations.

  When we move beyond local churches and denominations, ministerial status is more murky. It requires an understanding of assignment of ministers and perhaps performing significant sacerdotal functions. Then there are ordaining, licensing, or commissioning of ministers by churches and the question of whether these practices are valid. All in all, a high degree of integrity must be applied to this process.

- **Fringe benefits, stewardship, and compliance.** The decision of which fringe benefits to offer staff is often indicative of a charity's stewardship. It isn't just how much an employee is paid; it's also how compensation is paid. Are tax-free and tax-deferred opportunities maximized? And then there is the proper reporting of taxable fringe benefits which reflects a charity's willingness to comply with tax law. For example, providing a vehicle to a key employee is an excellent fringe benefit from the employee's compensation view, but there are compliance issues to be followed with respect to personal miles.

- **Fair Labor Standards Act (FLSA) issues.** The overtime and minimum wage rules included in the FLSA are often overlooked and abused by churches and other charities. Many churches and most other charities are subject to the FLSA. With the Department of Labor's generous interpretation of "interstate commerce," just a few emails sent across state lines each year by an employee will often qualify that employee for FLSA coverage even if the organization is not covered. Another common FLSA abuse is "paying" overtime by giving employees "compensatory" time off. While Congress periodically considers compensatory time off with respect to the FLSA, it has never passed.

4 Health Care

Affordable Care Act

A wave of new tax compliance issues came for churches and nonprofits with the Patient Protection and Affordable Care Act (ACA). The law was passed by Congress in 2010, with the majority of reforms scheduled to be implemented between 2010 and 2016.

The text of the ACA spans over several hundred pages, so an easy or concise summary is practically impossible. The full law, its key provisions, and other compliance resources can be accessed at HealthCare.gov. This chapter offers a summary of some of the ACA's most significant provisions and related issues affecting churches and other nonprofits.

Individual mandate

Since 2014, U.S. citizens and legal residents who do not maintain "minimum essential" health insurance coverage are required to pay penalties. To avoid these penalties, individuals who are not exempt from the law's mandate must obtain health insurance coverage privately, through an employer health plan, or through a government-run exchange program.

In 2016, the annual individual penalty equals the greater of (1) $695 per person ($347.50 per child under 18), up to a maximum of $2,085 per family, or (2) 2.5% of household income over the threshold amount of income required for income tax return filing, up to a maximum of the national premium for a Bronze plan. The full penalty was gradually phased in through a three-year period from 2014 to 2016. After 2016, the amount of the penalty is increased based on cost-of-living adjustments.

Among other general exemptions, two specific exemptions from the individual mandate are based on religious belief: one for membership in a religious sect opposed to accepting insurance benefits, and another for participation in a health care sharing ministry. However, both exemptions are somewhat restrictive, in that they require membership or participation in organizations that substantially predate the passage of the health care law (1950 for the religious conscience exemption and 1999 for the health care sharing ministry exemption).

Employer mandate

Large employers, those with 50 or more full-time equivalent employees (see calculation below) working in the United States, are subject to an Employer Shared Responsibility penalty for failure to offer affordable, qualifying health insurance to employees. Starting in 2015, employers with 100 or more full-time equivalent employees (FTEs) were required to provide coverage to their full-time employees (and their full-time employees' dependents). This provision applies to employers with 50 or more FTEs, beginning in 2016. All large employers (including church and nonprofit employers) will generally face substantial tax penalties if (1) they fail to meet the requirements of the Employer Mandate and (2) at least one of their employees receives a premium tax credit under a government-run exchange program.

If a large employer (1) offers no health insurance coverage at all, (2) offers coverage to fewer than 95% of its full-time employees and their dependents, (3) offers coverage that is unaffordable, or (4) offers coverage that does not measure up to the standards of "minimum essential coverage," the employer will be subject to substantial penalties based on the number of its employees. If an employer offers qualifying coverage to at least 95% of its full-time employees (and their dependents), it will be subject to a penalty for any employee (or dependent) who was not offered coverage and who obtained a premium tax credit from a government-run exchange.

For coverage to be considered "affordable," the employee's share of the insurance premium must be no more than 9.66% (for 2016) of that employee's annual household income. Because an employer will often not know an employee's household income, there are three affordability safe harbors for employers: (1) the Form W-2 wages safe harbor, (2) the rate of pay safe harbor, and (3) the federal poverty line safe harbor. An employer health plan that meets one or more of these safe harbors will be considered affordable coverage, regardless of whether the coverage is actually affordable to an employee.

Full-time equivalent employees calculation

For purposes of the employer mandate, an employee who works an average of 30 hours or more per week, or 130 hours per month, is considered a full-time employee (FTE). An hour of work generally means each hour for which an employee is paid, or entitled to payment, including paid time off. If even for just one month someone meets the definition, the ministry must complete information for the employee for all 12 months.

For purposes of determining whether an employer is a large employer subject to the ACA's employer mandate, the hours worked by all part-time employees in a month must be aggregated and divided by 120 (excluding hours worked by "bona fide volunteers"). The result is then added to the number of full-time employees for the month to determine the total FTEs for the purposes of the employer mandate. Some seasonal workers may be excluded from the calculation. Related entities must aggregate their numbers of FTEs to determine whether they are subject to the employer mandate.

Extension of dependent coverage

Large employers must offer affordable, qualifying health insurance to both their employees and their employees' dependents. The ACA extends dependent coverage to include children under age 26. Individual and employer plans must offer coverage to such children even if the children are (1) married, (2) not living with their parents, (3) attending school, (4) not financially dependent on their parents, or (5) eligible to enroll in another employer's plan.

Employer reporting

The ACA also brought changes to what employers must annually report on their employees' Form W-2s regarding health insurance benefits. Beginning with the 2016 tax year (based on current guidance), employers that provide group health plans are required to report the total costs of coverage (costs paid by the employer and employee) on Form W-2 (filed in 2017) in Box 12 using code DD.

As a form of transition relief while further guidance is pending, only employers that file 250 or more W-2s are subject to this reporting requirement. This change in reporting requirements is meant to help show employees the value of their health care benefits and does not affect tax liability. (Qualified employer-provided coverage remains excludable from an employee's taxable income.)

Large employers (with 50 or more full-time equivalent employees) are required to report information to employees and the IRS regarding offers of employer health coverage and enrollment in employer health coverage using the Forms 1095-C and 1094-C. Form 1095-C reports individual information about each employee, and employers must provide a copy to each full-time employee by February 1 following the applicable tax year. Form 1094-C is a summary and transmittal form to send the IRS with copies of the Forms 1095-C. These forms are due to the IRS by March 1 (March 31 if filing electronically) following the applicable tax year.

Large employers that sponsor self-funded group health plans are required to annually report to their enrolled employees and the IRS whether the health coverage offered constitutes "minimum essential coverage" under the ACA.

Notice of exchange option

All employers subject to the Fair Labor Standards Act are required to provide a notice to current employees of the option to participate in a government-run insurance exchange program. Currently, this notice must be provided to all new employees (both full-time and part-time) no later than fourteen days after they begin working. The Department of Labor offers model forms that can be used to fulfill this requirement.

Small employer tax credit

Some nonprofit organizations are eligible for a small employer tax credit under the ACA. The credit is currently up to 35% of the lesser of (1) the actual cost of providing health care coverage for employees, or (2) maximum costs based on the average premium for small group markets in the state (see Instructions for Form 8941). In essence, the amount of the credit is determined on a sliding scale, with the smallest organizations (those with fewer employees and those paying lower average salaries) receiving the greatest tax credit incentives. The credit is available to eligible employers for two consecutive taxable years (excluding credits taken in any years prior to 2014).

To qualify for the small employer health care tax credit for tax years 2016 and beyond, the tax-exempt organization must have

1. paid premiums on behalf of employees enrolled in a qualified health plan offered through a Small Business Health Options Program (SHOP) Marketplace;

2. provided health insurance for fewer than 25 full-time equivalent employees;

3. paid an average wage of less than $52,000 (annually adjusted for inflation) a year to those employees, and

4. paid at least half of employee health insurance premiums (50% of the cost of single [not family] health care coverage for each of the organization's employees).

Ministers who are considered self-employed for Social Security tax purposes should not be included in an employer's calculation of its full-time equivalent employees, and premiums for health care coverage paid on behalf of ministerial workers should also not be taken into account. Similarly, any compensation paid to these workers for performing services in the exercise of ministry should not be taken into account in a church or nonprofit's average annual wage calculation for purposes of the credit.

Eligible churches and nonprofit organizations must use Form 8941, Credit for Small Employer Health Insurance Premiums, to calculate and file the credit. The amount of the credit is included on line 44f of the Form 990-T, Exempt Organization Business Income Tax Return. Form 990-T must be filed to claim the credit even for organizations that would otherwise not be required to file Form 990-T.

Organizations which met the criteria to claim the credit in prior years, but did not actually claim it, may wish to consult with their CPAs or other tax professionals to determine whether it would be beneficial to file amended returns for those years.

Contraception mandate

For religious organizations, one of the most controversial provisions of the new health care law has been the so-called "contraception mandate." The mandate comes from the ACA and its regulations requiring employers to provide coverage for a variety of preventative care services without the imposition of cost-sharing by employees (no co-pay, no deductible). These include not only traditional contraceptive services for women but also the "morning after" pill and the "week after" pill, which have been strongly opposed by some faith-based organizations as "abortifacient" (abortion-inducing) drugs.

Organizations that may be classified under the tax code as churches, conventions or associations of churches, integrated auxiliaries, and religious orders are exempt from the contraception mandate, while a lesser "accommodation" is provided to other religious nonprofit organizations with objections to providing the required coverage. All of the following criteria established by the Department of Health & Human Services (HHS) must be met for an organization to qualify for the accommodation:

➤ on account of religious objections, oppose providing coverage for some or all of any contraceptive services otherwise required to be covered;

➤ be organized and operated as a nonprofit entity;

➤ hold itself out as a religious organization; and

➤ self-certify that it meets these criteria in accordance with the provisions of the final regulations.

If a religious nonprofit organization meets these requirements, then the organization does not have to contract, arrange, pay, or refer for contraceptive coverage. However, the religious organization must certify its objection to its insurer/third-party administrator or the HHS. This notification triggers mandatory, separately-provided coverage by the objecting organization's insurer or third-party administrator.

Some religious organizations have filed lawsuits in objection to the accommodation, claiming it still infringes upon their religious freedom by making them complicit in the provision of abortifacient drugs. However, these challenges have achieved mixed success in the federal court system.

Following the Supreme Court's decision in *Burwell v. Hobby Lobby Stores, Inc.,* this lesser accommodation was extended to closely-held for-profit entities that meet certain requirements.

Reimbursing Medical Expenses

Securing adequate medical insurance is a high priority for church and other nonprofit employees—and their families. And following closely is the importance of having any medical expenses not covered by insurance reimbursed by the employer or covered tax-free under an employer-sponsored plan.

Medical insurance protects against catastrophic medical expenses. But even the best medical insurance policies generally do not pay all of the insured's medical expenses. These unpaid medical expenses are usually in the form of noncovered items or expenses subject to a deductible or coinsurance (or copayment) clause in a health insurance policy.

Medical expenses that are not eligible for reimbursement under a health insurance plan are deductible on Schedule A as itemized deductions. However, for many employees, receiving an itemized deduction benefit from unreimbursed medical expenses is more of a dream than a reality. There are two major barriers to deducting medical expenses. First, many employees use the standard deduction instead of itemizing deductions on Schedule A. This is especially true for most employees who rent or live in church-provided housing. Second, even for those employees who do itemize their deductions, there is generally a 10% of adjusted gross income limitation.

> **Caution**
>
> Consult with your ministry's professional tax advisors before reimbursing medical expenses for employees. Under changes brought by the Affordable Care Act, non-compliant reimbursements may result in penalties of $100 per employee per day.

> *Example:* If adjusted gross income is $30,000 and unreimbursed medical expenses are $2,000, none of these expenses are beneficial in calculating itemized deductions on Schedule A because the 10% adjusted gross income limitation is $3,000 ($30,000 x 10%).

Medical expense reimbursements to an employee under a qualified cafeteria plan, HSA, FSA, or HRA are not subject to federal (usually 15% to 25%) or state income tax (often 5% or so) or social security tax (15.3% for ministers and 7.65% for nonminister employees). The tax savings can easily run up to 40%.

Reimbursing medical expenses seems simple, but it can be complex because employers must select from the following options:

➤ **Cafeteria plans.** The "cafeteria" (Code Section 125) approach provides a flexible benefits and services program. An employee may choose from a menu of different items and "pay" for them with pre-tax dollars by taking a reduced salary. Frequently, various medical insurance options and health care reimbursements may be items on the menu. A health care reimbursement option in a cafeteria plan may also be called a "health care flexible spending account."

➤ **Health Savings Account (HSA).** HSAs are individual portable, tax-free, interest-bearing accounts (typically held by a bank or insurance company) through which individuals with high-deductible health insurance save for medical expenses. The purpose of an HSA is to pay what basic coverage would ordinarily pay.

Within limits, HSA contributions made by employers are excludable from income tax and social security wages. HSA contributions may also be funded through a salary reduction election. The 2016 annual deductible contribution limits to an HSA are $3,350 for an individual and $6,750 for a family. The limits apply to combined employer and employee contributions and are indexed for inflation. Earnings on amounts in an HSA are not currently taxable, and HSA distributions used to pay for medical expenses are not taxable.

Distributions from HSAs which are not used for qualified medical expenses are subject to an additional tax of 20 percent of the amount includible in gross income.

➤ **Flexible spending account (FSA).** An FSA may be established without any other cafeteria plan options. The tax law is the same as for a regular cafeteria plan, but by providing only one option, the plan and administration may be simpler. It allows an employee to pre-fund medical and dental expenses in pre-tax dollars using a salary reduction election. If an FSA only covers medical expenses, it is commonly referred to as a health care FSA.

FSA plans cannot reimburse for over-the-counter drugs except for insulin. Salary reductions for FSAs, indexed for inflation, were limited to $2,550 for 2016.

➤ **Health reimbursement arrangement (HRA).** Under an HRA (Section 105), an employer may reimburse medical expenses up to a maximum dollar amount for the coverage period. HRAs do not provide a salary reduction election.

All employers (including small employers) are prohibited from providing HRAs or FSAs to their employees without also offering group health plans that meet ACA requirements. Furthermore, employers are not permitted to reimburse the cost of healthcare insurance premiums on either a pre-tax or post-tax basis without also offering a qualifying group health plan. All employers (including small employers) who violate these rules are subject to an excise tax of $100 per employee, per day. ECFA has published a free eBook entitled *The 5 Roads to Healthcare Reimbursements by Churches and Ministries* that provides additional information about this issue (http://www.ecfa.org/Content/Healthcare-Reimbursements-eBook).

COBRA and Medical Continuation Provisions

The Consolidated Omnibus Budget Reconciliation Act of 1985 (COBRA) generally requires covered employers to offer 18 months of group health coverage beyond the time the coverage would have ended because of certain "qualifying events." Premiums are reimbursable by the former employee to the former employer.

Churches are excluded from the COBRA requirements. However, churches may provide continuation benefits similar to COBRA. Other nonprofits are generally subject to COBRA if 20 or more employees are employed during a typical working day.

INTEGRITY*Points*

- **Avoiding Affordable Care Act (ACA) penalties.** Individuals and employers must be mindful of new tax penalties brought by changes in the health care laws. Non-compliance with the individual and employer mandates of the ACA can be costly!

- **ACA reporting.** The ACA institutes a new and robust regimen of reporting for ministries. For the year 2016, with filings due in 2017, Form W-2s issued by employers which provide group health plans must include the total cost of health coverage, including costs paid by the employer and employee.

- **Small employer tax credit.** Although smaller employers are not required under the ACA to provide group health coverage, they may qualify for a helpful tax credit for providing coverage if certain requirements are met.

- **Reimbursing medical expenses.** Provisions of the ACA made the reimbursing of medical expenses much more complex. This is especially true for the reimbursement of health care premiums for personally purchased coverage. As with the ACA mandates, penalties for non-compliance are costly!

- **Communication of COBRA provisions.** Employers who are subject to COBRA are required to notify applicable employees of the option to extend health insurance coverage beyond the time coverage would have ended. Failure to provide these notifications can subject the employer to significant penalties.

5 Employer Reporting

In This Chapter

- Classification of workers
- Reporting compensation
- Payroll tax withholding

- Depositing withheld payroll taxes
- Filing quarterly payroll tax forms
- Filing annual payroll tax forms

The withholding and reporting requirements that employers must comply with are complicated. The special tax treatment of qualified ministers simply adds another level of complexity.

Churches and nonprofit organizations are generally required to withhold federal (and state and local, as applicable) income taxes and social security taxes and to pay employer social security tax on all wages paid to all full-time or part-time employees (except qualified ministers).

Classification of Workers

Whether an individual is classified as an employee or independent contractor has far-reaching consequences. This decision determines an organization's responsibility under the Federal Insurance Contributions Act (FICA), income tax withholding responsibilities, potential coverage under the Fair Labor Standards Act (FLSA) (see pages 71–72), and coverage under an employer's benefit plans. Misclassification can lead to significant penalties.

Questions frequently arise about the classification of certain nonprofit workers. Seasonal workers and those working less than full-time such as secretaries, custodians, and musicians require special attention for classification purposes. If a worker receives pay at an hourly rate, it will be difficult to justify independent contractor status. This conclusion holds true even if the workers are part-time.

Since 1935, the IRS has relied on certain common law rules (pages 87–88) to determine whether workers are employees or independent contractors. Pressure continues to build on Congress and the IRS to provide clearer guidance on who can be an independent contractor and when, especially in light of new employer responsibilities under the health care reform law.

Employees

If a worker is a nonministerial employee, the employer must withhold federal income tax (and state income tax, if applicable) and Federal Insurance Contributions Act (FICA) taxes; match the employee's share of FICA taxes; and, unless exempted, pay unemployment taxes on the employee's wages. In addition, the employer may incur obligations for employee benefit plans such as vacation, sick pay, health insurance, and retirement plan contributions.

Key Issue

The employee vs. independent contractor decision is one of the most fundamental issues facing an employer making payments to workers. If a worker is truly an employee but is treated as an independent contractor, this can result in not withholding the appropriate income and FICA-type social security tax amounts.

"Control" is the primary factor in determining whether an individual is an employee or an independent contractor. Among other criteria, *employees* comply with instructions, have a continuous relationship, perform work personally, work full- or part-time, are subject to dismissal, can quit without incurring liability, are often reimbursed for expenses, and must submit reports.

Independent contractors

If the worker is classified as an independent contractor, quarterly estimated income taxes and social security taxes under the Self-Employment Contributions Act (SECA) are paid by the worker. There is no unemployment tax liability or income or social security tax withholding requirement for independent contractors.

Independent contractors normally set the order and sequence of work, set their hours of work, work for others at the same time, are paid by the job, offer their services to the

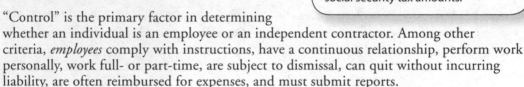

Independent Contractor Status Myths

- *Myth:* A written contract will characterize a person as an independent contractor.

  Fact: It is the substance of the relationship that governs.

- *Myth:* Casual labor or seasonal workers are independent contractors, or their classification is a matter of choice.

  Fact: There is never a choice. The classification is determined by the facts and circumstances.

- *Myth:* If a person qualifies as an independent contractor for federal payroll tax purposes, he or she is automatically exempt for workers' compensation and state unemployment tax purposes.

  Fact: State workers' compensation and unemployment tax laws are often broader, and an individual may actually be covered under these laws even though qualifying as an independent contractor for federal payroll tax purposes.

public, have an opportunity for profit or loss, furnish their own tools, and may do work on another's premises, and there is often substantial investment by the worker.

Common law rules

The IRS generally applies the common law rules to decide if an individual is an employee or self-employed (independent contractor) for income tax purposes. Generally, the individual is an employee if the employer has the legal right to control both the work and how it is done, even if the individual has considerable discretion and freedom of action.

Additionally, the United States Tax Court has applied a modified standard in determining whether a relationship is that of employee or an independent contractor. This is a seven factor test. In ambiguous situations, there is a presumption of an employer-employee relationship by the IRS.

1. **Degree of control.** This is considered the crucial test. The degree of control necessary to find employee status varies with the nature of the services provided by the worker. The emphasis in this test is not on whether there is actual control over how work is accomplished, but rather if there is a right to exert such control.

    The distinction here is whether the employer has more than a right to dictate the result to be accomplished, such as the means and methods to be used in accomplishing the work. If a relationship would extend beyond this result control, then it would be indicative of an employer-employee relationship. Additionally, the fact that a worker is able to set his own hours is not necessarily indicative that it is an independent contractor relationship, but rather it must be considered in the broader context of the entire arrangement.

    > ### Key Issue
    >
    > The amount of control and direction the employer has over a worker's services is the most important issue in deciding whether a worker is an employee or an independent contractor.

2. **Investment in facilities.** The emphasis in this factor is examining who is making the investment in plant, property, or equipment in order to accomplish the work. If the worker is not required to make any investment in order to complete the work, then this would be indicative that there is an employer-employee relationship. Additionally, it should be noted that occasionally working from home and using a personal computer to complete the work may not necessarily be sufficient to be considered an independent contractor. The Tax Court ruled and affirmed this stance especially in cases where this was *de minimis* and voluntary.

3. **Opportunity for profit or loss.** This factor examines whether the worker has an opportunity to profit or loss beyond hourly wages. If there is no such exposure to risk or loss, then this would be indicative of an employer-employee relationship.

4. **Right to discharge.** This factor examines whether the employer has the right to discharge the employee at any time. If this right exists, then this would be consistent with an employer-employee relationship.

5. **Integral part of business.** This factor examines whether the performed work is part of the regular business of the organization paying the compensation. Examples of integral parts of business indicating employee status include filing, photocopying, running errands, and sending mail.

6. **Permanency of the relationship.** This factor examines whether there is sufficient time in which to create some permanence of the relationship, thus indicating employee status. A transitory work relationship may point toward independent contractor status. However, the mere fact that a worker could leave at any time for a better position is not sufficient to establish an independent contractor relationship.

7. **Relationship the parties thought they created.** This factor looks to the parties' intended type of relationship as well as what formalities were followed with respect to the relationship. These formalities include what tax forms were filed. If an independent contractor relationship is intended, then it is important to file Form 1099-MISC for the non-employee compensation paid to the worker.

The classification of ministers

It is important that the organization decide whether the services of ministers employed by the organization qualify for special tax treatment as ministerial services.

Most ordained, commissioned, or licensed ministers serving local churches are eligible for these six special tax provisions with respect to services performed in the exercise of ministry. The IRS and courts apply certain tests to ministers serving local churches, including whether the minister administers the sacraments, conducts worship services, is considered a spiritual leader by the church, and performs management services in the "control, conduct, or maintenance of a religious organization." It may not be necessary for a minister to meet all of these factors to qualify for the special tax treatment. For a complete discussion of this topic, see the 2017 edition of the *Zondervan Minister's Tax & Financial Guide*.

Ordained, commissioned, or licensed ministers not serving local churches may qualify as ministers for federal tax purposes without meeting additional tests if their duties include the following (see also pages 58–61):

➤ Administration of church denominations and their integral agencies, including teaching or administration in parochial schools, colleges, or universities that are under the authority of a church or denomination, and

➤ Performing services for an institution that is not an integral agency of a church pursuant to an assignment or designation by ecclesiastical superiors, but only if the services relate to the assigning church's purposes.

Special Tax Provisions for Ministers

- Exclusion for income tax purposes of the housing allowance and the fair rental value of ministry-owned housing provided rent-free to clergy.

- Exemption of clergy from self-employment tax under very limited circumstances.

- Treatment of clergy (who do not elect social security exemption) as self-employed for social security tax purposes for income from ministerial services.

- Exemption of clergy compensation from mandatory income tax withholding.

- Eligibility for a voluntary income tax withholding arrangement between the minister-employee and the employer.

- Potential double benefit of mortgage interest and real estate taxes as itemized deductions and as housing expenses for housing allowance purposes.

If a church does not assign the minister's services, they will be qualified services only if they substantially involve performing sacerdotal functions or conducting religious worship (including preaching, leading Bible studies, spiritual counseling, etc.).

Sample Board Resolution for Ministerial Assignment

Whereas, _____Name of assigning church_____ recognizes the calling of _____Name of minister assigned_____ as a minister and is (ordained, licensed, or commissioned), and

Whereas, We believe that the assignment of __Name of minister assigned____ will further the efforts and mission of our church and we desire to provide support and encouragement;

Resolved, That _____Name of minister assigned_____ is hereby assigned to _____ _____Name of ministry to which assigned_____ effective_____, 20___ to serve as _____Position Title_____, and

Resolved, That this assignment is made for a period of one year upon which time it will be reviewed and may be renewed, and

Resolved, That this assignment is contingent upon the quarterly submission of activity and financial reports by __Name of minister assigned____ to our church.

Reporting Compensation

Minister-employees

Forms W-2 are annually provided to minister-employees. There is no requirement to withhold income taxes, but they may be withheld under a voluntary agreement. Social security taxes are not withheld.

Nonminister-employees

If an employee does not qualify as a minister for tax purposes, the organization is liable to withhold and pay FICA and income taxes. Certain FICA tax exceptions are discussed below.

Nonemployees

Self-employed recipients of compensation should receive Form 1099-MISC instead of Form W-2 (if the person has received compensation of at least $600 for the year).

Payroll Tax Withholding

FICA social security

Most churches and nonprofit organizations must withhold FICA taxes from their employees' wages and pay them to the IRS along with the employer's share of the tax. Minister-employees are an exception to this rule.

FICA includes both a social security and Medicare tax component. In 2016, employers and employees each pay social security tax at a rate of 6.2% (12.4% total) on the social security wage base of up to $118,500.

The employer and employee also must each pay a 1.45% Medicare tax rate (2.9% total) on all employee wages (unlike social security, there is no wage base limit for Medicare tax). Additionally, under the health care reform law, employers are responsible for withholding an additional 0.9% Medicare tax on all employee wages in excess of $200,000.

Warning

FICA-type social security taxes should never be withheld from the compensation of a qualified minister. Ministers are self-employed for social security purposes, even when performing ministerial duties for a parachurch organization. They must file Schedule SE to compute self-employment social security tax, unless they have opted out of social security.

There are a few exceptions to the imposition of FICA. Generally, wages of less than $100 paid to an employee in a calendar year are not subject to FICA. Services excluded from FICA include

➤ services performed by a minister of a church in the exercise of ministry or by a member of a religious order in the exercise of duties required by such order;

➤ services performed in the employ of a church or church-controlled organization that opposes for religious reasons the payment of social security taxes (see later discussion of filing Form 8274); and

➤ services performed by a student in the employ of a school, college, or university.

Churches and church-controlled organizations opposed to social security taxes

Very few churches and church-controlled organizations are exempt from payment of FICA taxes. An organization must certify opposition for religious reasons to the payment of employer social security taxes.

Organizations in existence on September 30, 1984 were required to file Form 8274 by October 30, 1984 to request exemption from payment of FICA taxes. Any organization created after September 30, 1984 must file before the first date on which a quarterly employment tax return is due from the organization.

Organizations desiring to revoke their exemption made earlier by filing Form 8274 should file Form 941 with full payment of social security taxes for that quarter.

Federal income tax

Most nonprofit organizations are exempt from the payment of federal income tax on the organization's income (see pages 32–39 for the tax on unrelated business income). But they must withhold and pay federal, state, and local income taxes on the wages paid to each employee. Minister-employees are an exception to this rule.

An employee-minister may have a voluntary withholding agreement with a church or nonprofit employer relating to the minister's income taxes (or he or she may file Form 1040-ES, or both). An agreement to withhold income taxes from wages must be in writing. There is no required form for the agreement. A minister may request voluntary withholding by submitting Form W-4 (Employee Withholding Allowance Certificate) to the employer, indicating the additional amount to be withheld in excess of the tax table, or the written request may be in another format.

Caution

Social security taxes (FICA) should never be withheld from the salary of a minister-employee. But under a voluntary withholding agreement for ministers' federal income taxes, additional federal income tax may be withheld sufficient to cover the minister's self-employment tax liability. This withholding must be identified as "federal income tax withheld" (not as social security taxes withheld).

Federal income taxes for all employees (except ministers) are calculated based on the chart and tables shown in IRS Publication 15. State and local income taxes are usually required to be withheld according to state withholding tables.

Form **W-4**	Employee's Withholding Allowance Certificate	OMB No. 1545-0074
Department of the Treasury Internal Revenue Service	▶ Whether you are entitled to claim a certain number of allowances or exemption from withholding is subject to review by the IRS. Your employer may be required to send a copy of this form to the IRS.	20**16**

1 Your first name and middle initial	Last name	2 Your social security number
Walter R.	Knight	511-02-7943

Home address (number and street or rural route)
601 Oakridge Boulevard

City or town, state, and ZIP code
Vinton, VA 24179

3 ☐ Single ☒ Married ☐ Married, but withhold at higher Single rate.
Note: If married, but legally separated, or spouse is a nonresident alien, check the "Single" box.

4 If your last name differs from that shown on your social security card, check here. You must call 1-800-772-1213 for a replacement card. ▶ ☐

5	Total number of allowances you are claiming (from line **H** above **or** from the applicable worksheet on page 2)	5	4
6	Additional amount, if any, you want withheld from each paycheck	6	$
7	I claim exemption from withholding for 2016, and I certify that I meet **both** of the following conditions for exemption.		
	• Last year I had a right to a refund of **all** federal income tax withheld because I had **no** tax liability, **and**		
	• This year I expect a refund of **all** federal income tax withheld because I expect to have **no** tax liability.		
	If you meet both conditions, write "Exempt" here . . . . ▶	7	

Under penalties of perjury, I declare that I have examined this certificate and, to the best of my knowledge and belief, it is true, correct, and complete.

Employee's signature
(This form is not valid unless you sign it.) ▶ *Walter R. Knight*   Date ▶ 1/01/16

8	Employer's name and address (Employer: Complete lines 8 and 10 only if sending to the IRS.)	9 Office code (optional)	10 Employer identification number (EIN)

For Privacy Act and Paperwork Reduction Act Notice, see page 2.   Cat. No. 10220Q   Form **W-4** (2016)

This form must be completed by all lay employees, full- or part-time. Your exemption for 2016 expires February 15, 2017. If a minister completes this form, it can be the basis to determine income tax withholding under a voluntary agreement.

➤ **Form W-4.** All employees, part- or full-time, must complete a W-4 form. (Ministers are an exception to this requirement unless a voluntary withholding arrangement is used.) The withholding allowance information completed on this form gives the basis to determine the amount of income tax to be withheld.

Churches and nonprofits must file all Forms W-4 with the IRS on which employees claim exempt status from withholding (and the employees' wages would normally exceed $200 weekly) or claim more than 10 withholding allowances.

➤ **Form W-7.** Certain individuals who are not eligible for a social security number (SSN) may obtain an individual taxpayer identification number. The following individuals may file Form W-7: (1) nonresident aliens who are required to file a U.S. tax return, (2) nonresident aliens who are filing a U.S. tax return only to claim a refund, (3) individuals being claimed as dependents on U.S. tax returns and who are not eligible to obtain a social security number, (4) individuals being claimed as husbands or wives for exemptions on U.S. tax returns and who are not eligible to obtain an SSN, and (5) U.S. residents who must file a U.S. tax return but are not eligible for an SSN.

Personal liability for payroll taxes

Church and nonprofit officers and employees may be personally liable if payroll taxes are not withheld and paid to the IRS. If the organization has willfully failed to withhold and

Form W-7
(Rev. September 2016)
Department of the Treasury
Internal Revenue Service

Application for IRS Individual Taxpayer Identification Number

➤ For use by individuals who are not U.S. citizens or permanent residents.
➤ See separate instructions.

OMB No. 1545-0074

An IRS individual taxpayer identification number (ITIN) is for federal tax purposes only.

Before you begin:

• **Don't submit** this form if you have, or are eligible to get, a U.S. social security number (SSN).
• Getting an ITIN doesn't change your immigration status or your right to work in the United States and doesn't make you eligible for the earned income credit.

Application Type (Check one box):

[X] Apply for a New ITIN
[ ] Renew an Existing ITIN

Reason you're submitting Form W-7. Read the instructions for the box you check. **Caution:** If you check box **b, c, d, e, f,** or **g,** you must file a U.S. federal tax return with Form W-7 unless you meet one of the exceptions (see instructions).

a [ ] Nonresident alien required to get an ITIN to claim tax treaty benefit
b [ ] Nonresident alien filing a U.S. federal tax return
c [X] U.S. resident alien **(based on days present in the United States)** filing a U.S. federal tax return
d [ ] Dependent of U.S. citizen/resident alien } Enter name and SSN/ITIN of U.S. citizen/resident alien (see instructions) ➤ _____
e [ ] Spouse of U.S. citizen/resident alien
f [ ] Nonresident alien student, professor, or researcher filing a U.S. federal tax return or claiming an exception
g [ ] Dependent/spouse of a nonresident alien holding a U.S. visa
h [ ] Other (see instructions) ➤

Additional information for **a** and **f:** Enter treaty country ➤ _____ and treaty article number ➤ _____

Name (see instructions)	**1a** First name Liam	Middle name Ethan	Last name Martin
Name at birth if different . . ➤	**1b** First name	Middle name	Last name

Applicant's mailing address

2 Street address, apartment number, or rural route number. **If you have a P.O. box, see separate instructions.**
1200 Palm Street
City or town, state or province, and country. Include ZIP code or postal code where appropriate.
Sarasota, FL 34234

Foreign (non-U.S.) address (if different from above) (see instructions)

3 Street address, apartment number, or rural route number. **Don't use a P.O. box number.**
121 Maple Run
City or town, state or province, and country. Include ZIP code or postal code where appropriate.
Toronto, ON M5A 2N4

Birth information

4 Date of birth (month / day / year) 6/20/1975	Country of birth Canada	City and state or province (optional) Toronto, ON	**5** [X] Male [ ] Female

Other information

6a Country(ies) of citizenship Canada	**6b** Foreign tax I.D. number (if any)	**6c** Type of U.S. visa (if any), number, and expiration date Religious Workers

6d Identification document(s) submitted (see instructions) [X] Passport [ ] Driver's license/State I.D.
[ ] USCIS documentation [ ] Other _____
Issued by: PC No.: 12345678 Exp. date: 6 / 1 , 2017
Date of entry into the United States (MM/DD/YYYY): 5 / 1 , 2015

6e Have you previously received an ITIN or an Internal Revenue Service Number (IRSN)?
[X] **No/Don't know.** Skip line 6f.
[ ] **Yes.** Complete line 6f. If more than one, list on a sheet and attach to this form (see instructions).

6f Enter ITIN and/or IRSN ➤ ITIN [ ][ ][ ] – [ ][ ] – [ ][ ][ ][ ] IRSN [ ][ ][ ] – [ ][ ] – [ ][ ][ ][ ] and
name under which it was issued ➤ _____
First name   Middle name   Last name

6g Name of college/university or company (see instructions) First Baptist Church
City and state Sarasota, FL   Length of stay 6 months

Sign Here

Keep a copy for your records.

Under penalties of perjury, I (applicant/delegate/acceptance agent) declare that I have examined this application, including accompanying documentation and statements, and to the best of my knowledge and belief, it is true, correct, and complete. I authorize the IRS to share information with my acceptance agent in order to perfect this Form W-7, Application for IRS Individual Taxpayer Identification Number.

Signature of applicant (if delegate, see instructions) *Liam Ethan Martin*
Date (month / day / year) 5 / 1 , 16
Phone number 914-123-1234

Name of delegate, if applicable (type or print)
Delegate's relationship to applicant [ ] Parent [ ] Court-appointed guardian [ ] Power of Attorney

Acceptance Agent's Use ONLY

Signature	Date (month / day / year) / /	Phone	
		Fax	
Name and title (type or print)	Name of company	EIN	PTIN
		Office Code	

For Paperwork Reduction Act Notice, see separate instructions.   Cat. No. 10229L   Form **W-7** (Rev. 9-2016)

pay the taxes, the IRS has the authority to assess a 100% penalty of withheld income and social security taxes.

This penalty may be assessed against the individual responsible for withholding and paying the taxes, even if the person is an unpaid volunteer such as a church treasurer.

Depositing Withheld Payroll Taxes

The basic rules for depositing withheld payroll taxes are as follows:

➤ If your total accumulated and unpaid employment tax (income tax withheld, social security tax withheld and matched by the organization) is less than $2,500 in a calendar quarter, taxes can be paid directly to the IRS when the organization files Form 941. These forms are due one month after the end of each calendar quarter.

➤ If payroll taxes are over $2,500 for a quarter, payroll tax deposits must be made monthly or before the 15th day of each month for the payroll paid during the preceding month. Large organizations with total employment taxes of over $50,000 per year are subject to more frequent deposits.

To determine if an organization is a monthly depositor, you must determine if the accumulated liabilities in the "look-back period" reached a threshold of $50,000. Those with an accumulated liability of $50,000 or less in the look-back period are generally monthly depositors (except those qualifying for quarterly deposits with liabilities of $1,000 or less).

> **Remember**
>
> A new organization (or one filing payroll tax returns for the first time) will be required to file monthly until a "look-back period" is established. A look-back period begins on July 1 and ends on June 30 of the preceding calendar year.

The cost of missing deposit deadlines can be very high. Besides interest, the organization can be hit with penalties at progressively stiffer rates. These range from 2% if you deposit the money within 5 days of the due date to 15% if it is not deposited within 10 days of the first delinquency notice or on the day that the IRS demands immediate payment, whichever is earlier.

Only very small organizations are exempted from depositing electronically: employers with $2,500 or less in quarterly employment taxes that pay their liability when filing their returns. All other coupon users must switch to making deposits by wire using Treasury's Electronic Federal Tax Payment System (EFTPS): www.eftps.gov or call 800-555-3453.

Using EFTPS is free and a convenient way to make federal tax payments online or by telephone, 24/7. To enroll in this system, you merely need your taxpayer identification number, bank account number, and routing number and address and name as they appear on your IRS tax documents. After you enter the requested information online, you will receive your PIN. Call 1-800-982-3526 to get a temporary Internet password. Then you are ready to make a payment online or by telephone.

Form **941 for 2017:** **Employer's QUARTERLY Federal Tax Return**
(Rev. January 2017)   Department of the Treasury — Internal Revenue Service

950117   OMB No. 1545-0029

Employer identification number (EIN)

Name (not your trade name)   **Barnett Ridge Church**

Trade name (if any)

Address   PO Box 517

Number   Street   Suite or room number

Selma   AL   36704

City   State   ZIP code

Foreign country name   Foreign province/county   Foreign postal code

Report for this Quarter of 2017
(Check one.)

- [X] 1: January, February, March
- [ ] 2: April, May, June
- [ ] 3: July, August, September
- [ ] 4: October, November, December

Instructions and prior year forms are available at *www.irs.gov/form941*.

Read the separate instructions before you complete Form 941. Type or print within the boxes.

Part 1: Answer these questions for this quarter.

1	Number of employees who received wages, tips, or other compensation for the pay period including: Mar. 12 (Quarter 1), June 12 (Quarter 2), Sept. 12 (Quarter 3), or Dec. 12 (Quarter 4)	1	0
2	Wages, tips, and other compensation	2	24,811 .
3	Federal income tax withheld from wages, tips, and other compensation	3	4,642 .
4	If no wages, tips, and other compensation are subject to social security or Medicare tax		☐ Check and go to line 6.

		Column 1		Column 2	
5a	Taxable social security wages	16,340 .	× 0.124 =	2,026 .	
5b	Taxable social security tips	.	× 0.124 =	.	
5c	Taxable Medicare wages & tips	16,340 .	× 0.029 =	474 .	
5d	Taxable wages & tips subject to Additional Medicare Tax withholding	.	× 0.009 =	.	

5e	Add Column 2 from lines 5a, 5b, 5c, and 5d	5e	2,500 .
5f	Section 3121(q) Notice and Demand—Tax due on unreported tips (see instructions)	5f	.
6	Total taxes before adjustments. Add lines 3, 5e, and 5f	6	7,142 .
7	Current quarter's adjustment for fractions of cents	7	.
8	Current quarter's adjustment for sick pay	8	.
9	Current quarter's adjustments for tips and group-term life insurance	9	.
10	Total taxes after adjustments. Combine lines 6 through 9	10	7,142 .
11	Qualified small business payroll tax credit for increasing research activities. Attach Form 8974	11	.
12	Total taxes after adjustments and credits. Subtract line 11 from line 10	12	7,142 .
13	Total deposits for this quarter, including overpayment applied from a prior quarter and overpayments applied from Form 941-X, 941-X (PR), 944-X, or 944-X (SP) filed in the current quarter	13	7,142 .
14	Balance due. If line 12 is more than line 13, enter the difference and see instructions	14	0 .
15	Overpayment. If line 13 is more than line 12, enter the difference Check one: ☐ Apply to next return. ☐ Send a refund.		

▶ You MUST complete both pages of Form 941 and SIGN it.   Next ▶

For Privacy Act and Paperwork Reduction Act Notice, see the back of the Payment Voucher.   Cat. No. 17001Z   Form **941** (Rev. 1-2017)

Name (not your trade name)   **Barnett Ridge Church**   Employer identification number (EIN)   35 - 2017883

950217

Part 2: Tell us about your deposit schedule and tax liability for this quarter.

If you are unsure about whether you are a monthly schedule depositor or a semiweekly schedule depositor, see section 11 of Pub. 15.

16 Check one:
- [ ] Line 12 on this return is less than $2,500 or line 12 (line 10 if the prior quarter was the fourth quarter of 2016) on the return for the prior quarter was less than $2,500, and you didn't incur a $100,000 next-day deposit obligation during the current quarter. If line 12 (line 10 if the prior quarter was the fourth quarter of 2016) for the prior quarter was less than $2,500 but line 12 on this return is $100,000 or more, you must provide a record of your federal tax liability. If you are a monthly schedule depositor, complete the deposit schedule below; if you are a semiweekly schedule depositor, attach Schedule B (Form 941). Go to Part 3.

- [ ] You were a monthly schedule depositor for the entire quarter. Enter your tax liability for each month and total liability for the quarter, then go to Part 3.

Tax liability:		
Month 1		2,201 .
Month 2		2,493 .
Month 3		4,448 .
Total liability for quarter		7,142 .

Total must equal line 12.

- [ ] You were a semiweekly schedule depositor for any part of this quarter. Complete Schedule B (Form 941), Report of Tax Liability for Semiweekly Schedule Depositors, and attach it to Form 941.

Part 3: Tell us about your business. If a question does NOT apply to your business, leave it blank.

17 If your business has closed or you stopped paying wages . . . . ☐ Check here, and

enter the final date you paid wages / /

18 If you are a seasonal employer and you don't have to file a return for every quarter of the year . . . ☐ Check here.

Part 4: May we speak with your third-party designee?

Do you want to allow an employee, a paid tax preparer, or another person to discuss this return with the IRS? See the instructions for details.

- [ ] Yes. Designee's name and phone number
- [ ] No.

Select a 5-digit Personal Identification Number (PIN) to use when talking to the IRS.

Part 5: Sign here. You MUST complete both pages of Form 941 and SIGN it.

Under penalties of perjury, I declare that I have examined this return, including accompanying schedules and statements, and to the best of my knowledge and belief, it is true, correct, and complete. Declaration of preparer (other than taxpayer) is based on all information of which preparer has any knowledge.

✗ Sign your name here   *David Baker*   Print your name here   David Baker

Print your title here   Office Manager

Date   4 /15/ 17   Best daytime phone   334-873-1754

Paid Preparer Use Only   Check if you are self-employed . . . ☐

Preparer's name	PTIN
Preparer's signature	Date / /
Firm's name (or yours if self-employed)	EIN
Address	Phone
City	State ZIP code

Page 2   Form **941** (Rev. 1-2017)

File this form to report social security (FICA) and Medicare taxes and federal income tax withheld.

95

Form 941-X: Adjusted Employer's QUARTERLY Federal Tax Return or Claim for Refund
(Rev. April 2015)   Department of the Treasury — Internal Revenue Service   OMB No. 1545-0029

Employer identification number (EIN)   3 5 – 6 3 0 9 2 9 4

Name (not your trade name)   Little Valley Church

Trade name (if any)

Address   4865 Douglas Road
Number   Street   Suite or room number

Springfield   OH   45504
City   State   ZIP code

Foreign country name   Foreign province/county   Foreign postal code

Return You Are Correcting ...

Check the type of return you are correcting:

[X] 941
[ ] 941-SS

Check the ONE quarter you are correcting:

[X] 1: January, February, March
[ ] 2: April, May, June
[ ] 3: July, August, September
[ ] 4: October, November, December

Enter the calendar year of the quarter you are correcting:

2016   (YYYY)

Enter the date you discovered errors:

05 / 10 / 2016
(MM / DD / YYYY)

Read the separate instructions before completing this form. Use this form to correct errors you made on Form 941 or 941-SS. Use a separate Form 941-X for each quarter that needs correction. Type or print within the boxes. You MUST complete all three pages. Do not attach this form to Form 941 or 941-SS.

Part 1:   Select ONLY one process. See page 4 for additional guidance.

[X] 1. **Adjusted employment tax return.** Check this box if you underreported amounts. Also check this box if you overreported amounts and you would like to use the adjustment process to correct the errors. You must check this box if you are correcting both underreported and overreported amounts on this form. The amount shown on line 20, if less than zero, may only be applied as a credit to your Form 941, Form 941-SS, or Form 944 for the tax period in which you are filing this form.

[ ] 2. **Claim.** Check this box if you overreported amounts only and you would like to use the claim process to ask for a refund or abatement of the amount shown on line 20. Do not check this box if you are correcting ANY underreported amounts on this form.

Use this form to correct income, social security (FICA), and Medicare tax information reported on Form 941. It may be necessary to issue Form W-2c to employees relating to prior year data. The Form 941-X has three pages.

Filing Quarterly Payroll Tax Forms

Employers must report covered wages paid to their employees by filing Form 941, Employer's Quarterly Federal Tax Return, with the IRS.

Form 941

Church and other nonprofit employers that withhold income tax and both social security and medicare taxes must file Form 941 quarterly. There is no requirement to file Form 941 if your organization has not been required to withhold payroll taxes even if you have one or more employee-ministers. However, if the only employee is a minister and voluntary federal income tax has been withheld, Form 941 must be filed.

Most common errors made on Form 941

The IRS has outlined the most common errors discovered during the processing of Form 941 and the best ways to avoid making these mistakes.

Idea

Do not file more than one Form 941 per quarter even if you deposit payroll taxes monthly. If you have multiple locations or divisions, you must file only one Form 941 per quarter. Filing more than one return may result in processing delays and require correspondence with the IRS.

A checklist for avoiding errors follows:

➤ Do not include titles or abbreviations, such as Dr., Mr., or Mrs.

➤ On line 2, do not include amounts designated as housing allowance for qualified ministers.

➤ Make sure that taxable social security wages and the social security tax on line 5a and the taxable Medicare wages and the Medicare tax on line 5c are reported separately. Most employers will need to complete both lines 5a and 5c.

➤ The preprinted form sent by the IRS should be used. If the return is prepared by a third-party preparer, make certain that the preparer uses exactly the name that appears on the preprinted form that was sent.

➤ Check the math for lines 5d, 10, and 11. Line 11 should always be the sum of lines 3, 5d, and 9.

➤ Make sure the social security tax on line 5a is calculated correctly (social security wages x 12.4%).

➤ Make sure the Medicare tax on line 5c is calculated correctly (Medicare wages x 2.9%).

➤ Be sure to use the most recent Form 941 that the IRS sends. The IRS enters the date the quarter ended after the employer identification number. If the form is used for a later quarter, the IRS will have to contact the employer.

➤ Make sure there is never an entry on both lines 14 and 15. There cannot be a balance due and a refund.

Filing Annual Payroll Tax Forms

Form W-2

By January 31, each employee must be given a Form W-2. Be sure to reconcile the data reflected on Forms W-2, W-3, and 941 before distributing Forms W-2 to employees. If these forms do not reconcile, the IRS generally sends a letter to the employer requesting additional information. For additional help, call 866-455-7438.

Make all entries without a dollar sign or comma but with a decimal point and cents (do not use whole dollars).

Void. Put an X in this box when an error has been made on this W-2.

Box 1 – Wages, tips, other compensation. Items to include in Box 1 (before any payroll deductions) are

➤ total wages paid during the year (including love offerings paid by the church or nonprofit organization to a minister or other employee);

➤ the value of noncash payments, including taxable fringe benefits;

➤ business expense payments under a nonaccountable plan;

➤ payments of per diem or mileage allowance paid for business expense purposes that exceed the IRS-specified rates;

➤ payments made by a church or nonprofit organization to an employee's Individual Retirement Account;

➤ payments for nonexcludable moving expenses;

➤ all other compensation, including taxable fringe benefits ("Other compensation" represents amounts an organization pays to an employee from which federal income tax is not withheld. If you prefer, you may show other compensation on a separate Form W-2.); and

➤ the cash housing allowance or the fair market rental value of housing and utilities, which must be reported as taxable income for lay employees (non-ministerial employees), unless lodging is furnished on the employer's premises and the employee is required to accept the lodging as a condition of employment.

Exclude the following:

➤ the fair rental value of a church-provided parsonage or a properly designated housing allowance for ministers;

➤ auto, business, or qualified moving expense reimbursements paid through an accountable expense plan; and

➤ contributions to 403(b) tax-sheltered annuities or 401(k) plans.

Box 2 – Federal income tax withheld. Enter the total federal income tax withheld according to the chart and tables in IRS Publication 15.

A minister-employee may enter into a voluntary withholding arrangement with the employing organization. Based on Form W-4 or other written withholding request, federal income tax withholding may be calculated from the chart and tables in Publication 15, excluding any housing allowance amount.

The minister may request that an additional amount of income tax be withheld to cover self-employment tax. However, the additional amount withheld is reported as income tax withheld on the quarterly Form 941 and in Box 2 of Form W-2.

An organization that provides additional compensation to the employee-minister to cover part or all of the self-employment tax liability may:

Remember

One of an employer's primary challenges is to determine if all of an employee's compensation is reported on Form W-2. Taxable compensation that is often erroneously omitted includes life insurance premiums paid for the employee (only group-term life up to $50,000 is tax-free) and expense allowances (only expenses reimbursed under an accountable plan are tax-free).

Checklist for Completing Box 1 of Form W-2

Minister Only	Both	Nonminister Only	
	yes		Salary
no		yes	Housing/furnishings allowance (designated in advance)
no		yes	Parsonage rental value
no		yes	Utilities paid by church or nonprofit
	yes		Social security/Medicare "allowance" or reimbursement
	no		Transportation/travel and other business and professional expense reimbursements only if paid under a board-adopted accountable reimbursement plan
	yes		"Reimbursements" if not paid under an accountable reimbursement plan
	yes		Love offerings or cash gifts in excess of $25
	no		Contributions to a tax-sheltered annuity plan
	no		Qualified health/dental/long-term care insurance premiums paid directly or reimbursed by the employer
	no		Group-term life insurance premiums (for up to $50,000 coverage) paid directly by the employer
	no		Excludable moving expense paid for or reimbursed to an employee
	yes		Nonexcludable moving expenses paid for or reimbursed to an employee
	yes		Value of personal and nonbusiness use of organization's vehicle

(Data Included for)

➤ pay the additional compensation directly to the IRS by entering that amount on the organization's Form 941 and in Boxes 1 and 2 of Form W-2, or

➤ pay the additional compensation to the minister, with the minister being responsible for remitting the amounts to the IRS with a Form 1040-ES. If this procedure is followed, the organization reports this amount only as additional compensation on Form 941 and only in Box 1 of Form W-2.

Box 3 – Social security wages. Show the total wages paid (before payroll deductions) subject to employee social security tax (FICA). This amount must not exceed $118,500 in 2016 (the maximum social security tax wage base). Include nonaccountable employee business expenses reported in Box 1. Generally, all cash and noncash payments reported in Box 1 must also be shown in Box 3. Voluntary salary reduction tax-sheltered annuity contributions for nonminister employees are included in Box 3.

Box 3 should be blank for a qualified minister (an individual who meets the ministerial factors of the IRS).

Box 4 – Social security tax withheld. Show the total FICA social security tax (not including the organization's share) withheld or paid by the organization for the employee. The amount shown must equal 6.2% of the amount in Box 3 and must not exceed $7,347 for 2016. Do not include the employer portion of FICA tax (6.2%).

22222	Void ☐	**a** Employee's social security number 517-38-6451	For Official Use Only ▶ OMB No. 1545-0008		
b Employer identification number (EIN) 35-2948039			**1** Wages, tips, other compensation 93800.00	**2** Federal income tax withheld 7000.00	
c Employer's name, address, and ZIP code ABC Charity 2870 North Hull Road Traverse City, MI 49615			**3** Social security wages 95000.00	**4** Social security tax withheld 3990.00	
			5 Medicare wages and tips 95000.00	**6** Medicare tax withheld 1377.50	
			7 Social security tips	**8** Allocated tips	
d Control number			**9**	**10** Dependent care benefits	
e Employee's first name and initial Michael A	Last name Black	Suff.	**11** Nonqualified plans	**12a** See instructions for box 12 E 1200.00	
15550 Cleveland Avenue Traverse City, MI 49615			**13** Statutory employee ☐ Retirement plan ☐ Third-party sick pay ☐	**12b** P 984.73	
			14 Other	**12c**	
				12d	
f Employee's address and ZIP code					

15 State MI	Employer's state ID number 6309294	**16** State wages, tips, etc. 93800.00	**17** State income tax 700.00	**18** Local wages, tips, etc.	**19** Local income tax	**20** Locality name

Form W-2 Wage and Tax Statement **2016**

Copy A For Social Security Administration — Send this entire page with Form W-3 to the Social Security Administration; photocopies are **not** acceptable.

Do Not Cut, Fold, or Staple Forms on This Page

Department of the Treasury — Internal Revenue Service
For Privacy Act and Paperwork Reduction Act Notice, see the separate instructions.
Cat. No. 10134D

Form W-2 must be filed for each employee who received taxable compensation or for whom income tax or FICA-type social security tax was withheld. The example shown above is for a lay employee.

Some organizations pay the employee's share of FICA tax for some or all nonminister employees instead of deducting it from the employee's wages. These amounts paid by the organization must be included in Boxes 1, 3, and total paid to the employee as advance earned income credit payments.

Box 4 should be blank for qualified ministers. Any amount of withholding to meet the minister's SECA tax liability must be reported in Box 2, not in Box 4 or Box 6.

Box 5 – Medicare wages. The wages subject to Medicare tax are the same as those subject to social security tax (Box 3), except there is no wage limit for the Medicare tax.

> **Example:** A *nonminister* employee is paid wages of $120,000. The amount shown in Box 3 (social security wages) should be $118,500, but the amount shown in Box 5 (Medicare wages) should be $120,000. If the wages are less than $117,000, the amounts entered in Boxes 3 and 5 will be the same.

Box 5 should be blank for qualified ministers. Nonqualified moving expense reimbursements and payments for lay employees are included in Box 5.

Box 6 – Medicare tax withheld. Enter the total employee Medicare tax (not your share) withheld or paid by you for your employee. The amount shown must equal 1.45% of the amount in Box 5. Box 6 should be blank for qualified ministers.

Box 9 – Advance EIC payment. Show the total paid to the employee as advance earned income credit payments.

Box 10 – Dependent care benefits. Show the total amount of dependent care benefits under Section 129 paid or incurred by you for your employee, including any amount over the $5,000 exclusion. Also include in Box 1, Box 3, and Box 5 any amount over the $5,000 exclusion.

Box 11 – Nonqualified plans. Enter the total amount of distributions to the employee from a nonqualified deferred compensation plan. Nonqualified plans do not include a tax-sheltered annuity or a "Rabbi Trust." Include an amount in Box 11 only if it is also includible in Box 1 or Boxes 3 and 5.

Box 12 – Additional entries. The following items are most frequently inserted in Box 12 by churches and other nonprofit organizations:

C – If you provided your employee more than $50,000 of group-term life insurance, show the cost of the coverage over $50,000. Also include the amount in Box 1 (also in Boxes 3 and 5 if a lay employee).

DD – Value of employer-provided health coverage. This data is required for employers issuing 250 or more Form W-2s.

E – Section 403(b) voluntary salary reduction agreement to purchase an annuity contract. This amount would not be included in Box 1 for either ministerial or lay employees. This amount would be included in Boxes 3 and 5 for a lay employee.

L – Generally, payments made under an accountable plan are excluded from the employee's gross income and are not required to be reported on Form W-2. But if the organization pays a per diem or mileage allowance, and the amount paid exceeds the amount substantiated under IRS rules, you must report as wages on Form W-2 the amount in excess of the amount substantiated. Report the amount substantiated (the nontaxable portion) in Box 12. In Box 1, show the portion of the reimbursement that is more than the amount treated as substantiated. For lay employees the excess amount is subject to income tax withholding, social security tax, Medicare tax, and possibly federal unemployment tax.

> **Example 1:** An employee receives mileage reimbursement at the rate of 54 cents per mile for 2016 and substantiates the business miles driven to the organization. The mileage reimbursement is not reported on Form W-2.

> **Example 2:** An employee receives a mileage allowance of $2,000 per year and does not substantiate the business miles driven. The $2,000 allowance is includible in Box 1 as compensation for a minister and Boxes 1, 3, and 5 for a lay employee. The business mileage is deductible as a miscellaneous deduction on the employee's Schedule A, subject to limitations.

Payments made to nonminister employees under a nonaccountable plan are reportable as wages on Form W-2 and are subject to income tax withholding, social security tax, Medicare tax, and possibly federal unemployment tax.

101

Payments made to minister-employees under a nonaccountable plan are reportable as wages on Form W-2 and may be subject to income tax withholding under a voluntary agreement, but they are not subject to mandatory withholding or social security (FICA) or Medicare tax.

P – Report nonqualified moving expense reimbursements and payments in Box 1 for either ministerial or lay employees. This amount is also included in Boxes 3 and 5 for lay employees.

R – Employer contributions to an Archer medical savings account.

S – Salary reductions to a savings incentive match plan for employees with a SIMPLE retirement account.

T – Employer payments under an adoption assistance plan.

Y – Deferrals under a section 409A nonqualified deferred compensation plan.

Z – Income under a section 409A nonqualified deferred compensation plan.

Box 13 – Check the appropriate boxes. The box that may apply to employees of churches and nonprofit organizations is the retirement plan box. Mark this check box if the employee was an active participant (for any part of the year) in any of the following: (1) a qualified pension plan described in section 401(a), including a 401(k) plan; (2) an annuity plan described in section 403(a); (3) an annuity contract or custodial account described in section 403(b); or (4) a simplified employee pension (SEP) plan described in section 408(k).

Box 14 – Other. You may use this box for any other information the employer wishes to provide to an employee. Label each item and include information such as health insurance premiums deducted or educational assistance payments.

> **Filing Tip**
>
> The minister's housing allowance could be included in Box 14 with the words "Housing Allowance." However, some employers prefer to provide the minister with a separate statement reflecting the housing allowance amount.

If the organization owns or leases a vehicle for an employee's use, the value of the personal use of the vehicle is taxable income. The value of the use of the vehicle is established by using one of the methods described on pages 66–68. The amount of the personal use must be included in Box 1 (and in Boxes 3 and 5 if a lay employee) or on a separate statement to the employee. The employee is required to maintain a mileage log or similar records to substantiate business and personal use of the vehicle and submit this to the employer. If its use is not substantiated, the employer must report 100% of the use of the vehicle as taxable income.

> **Caution**
>
> Do not include any per diem or mileage allowance or other reimbursements for employee business expenses under an accountable plan in Boxes 1 or 14 if the total reimbursement is less than or equal to the amount substantiated.

If the employee fully reimburses the employer for the value of the personal use of the vehicle, then no value would be reported in either Box 1 or in Box 14. Reimbursement of the amount spent for gas on personal trips does not constitute a reimbursement of the full value of the personal use of the vehicle.

Form W-3

A Form W-3 is submitted to the IRS as a transmittal form with Forms W-2. Form W-3 and all attached W-2s must be submitted to the Social Security Administration Center by February 28 (March 31 if e-filing). No money is sent with Form W-3.

Forms W-2c and W-3c

Use Form W-2c to correct errors on a previously filed Form W-2. Use Form W-3c to transmit corrected W-2c forms to the Social Security Administration. If you are correcting only an employee's name or social security number, you do not have to file Form W-3c with Form W-2c. File Forms W-2c and W-3c as soon as possible after you discover an error. Also provide Form W-2c to employees as soon as possible.

If you are correcting only an employee's name and/or social security number, complete Form W-2c through Box g, as appropriate. Do not complete Boxes 1 through 20.

Wages paid in error in a prior year remain taxable to the employee for that year. This is because the employee received and had use of those funds during that year. The employee is not entitled to file an amended return (Form 1040X) to recover the income tax on these wages. Instead, the employee is entitled to a deduction for the repaid wages on his or her Form 1040 for the year of repayment.

Unemployment taxes

The federal and state unemployment systems provide temporary unemployment compensation to workers who have lost their jobs. Employers provide the revenue for this program by paying federal unemployment taxes, under the Federal Unemployment Tax Act (FUTA), and state unemployment taxes. These are strictly employer taxes, and no deductions are taken from employees' wages.

The current federal unemployment tax law exempts from coverage

➤ services performed in the employment of a church, a convention, or an association of churches, or an organization that is operated primarily for religious purposes (to qualify for exemption, employees must be performing strictly religious duties);

➤ services performed by an ordained, commissioned, or licensed minister of a church in the exercise of ministry or by a member of a religious order in the exercise of duties required by such order;

➤ services performed in the employment of an unincorporated church-controlled elementary or secondary school;

Form W-3

DO NOT STAPLE

a Control number: 33333	For Official Use Only ▶ OMB No. 1545-0008		

b Kind of Payer (Check one): 941 [X], Military [ ], 943 [ ], 944 [ ], CT-1 [ ], Hshld. emp. [ ], Medicare govt. emp. [ ]

Kind of Employer (Check one): None apply [ ], 501c non-govt. [X], State/local non-501c [ ], State/local 501c [ ], Federal govt. [ ]

Third-party sick pay (Check if applicable) [ ]

Field	Value	Box	Value
c Total number of Forms W-2	20	1 Wages, tips, other compensation	243987.00
d Establishment number		2 Federal income tax withheld	39142.00
e Employer identification number (EIN)	35-2948039	3 Social security wages	236431.00
		4 Social security tax withheld	14859.00
f Employer's name	ABC Charity	5 Medicare wages and tips	243987.00
		6 Medicare tax withheld	3538.00
	2970 North Hull Road	7 Social security tips	
	Traverse City, MI 49615	8 Allocated tips	
		9	10 Dependent care benefits
		11 Nonqualified plans	12a Deferred compensation
g Employer's address and ZIP code			
h Other EIN used this year		13 For third-party sick pay use only	12b
15 State MI Employer's state ID number 6309294		14 Income tax withheld by payer of third-party sick pay	
16 State wages, tips, etc.	243987.00	18 Local wages, tips, etc.	
17 State income tax	4387.00	19 Local income tax	
Employer's contact person	Daniel L. Lewis	Employer's telephone number	231-435-2201
		For Official Use Only	
Employer's fax number	231-435-2205	Employer's email address	dlewis@gmail.com

Under penalties of perjury, I declare that I have examined this return and accompanying documents and, to the best of my knowledge and belief, they are true, correct, and complete.

Signature ▶ *Daniel L. Lewis*   Title ▶ Treasurer   Date ▶ 1/31/17

Form **W-3** **Transmittal of Wage and Tax Statements** **2016**   Department of the Treasury Internal Revenue Service

Form W-3 is the "cover sheet" or transmittal form for all Forms W-2.

Form W-2c

DO NOT CUT, FOLD, OR STAPLE THIS FORM

44444	For Official Use Only ▶ OMB No. 1545-0008

a Employer's name, address, and ZIP code	c Tax year/Form corrected	d Employee's correct SSN
Little Valley Church 4865 Douglas Road Springfield, OH 45504	2015 / W-2	404-82-1034

e Corrected SSN and/or name (Check this box and complete boxes f and/or g if incorrect on form previously filed.) [ ]

Complete boxes f and/or g only if incorrect on form **previously filed** ▶

f Employee's **previously reported** SSN

b Employer's Federal EIN 35-6309394

g Employee's **previously reported** name

h Employee's first name and initial: Norman R.   Last name: Tice   Suff.

418 Trenton Street
Springfield, OH 45504
i Employee's address and ZIP code

Note. Only complete money fields that are being corrected (exception: for corrections involving MQGE, see the General Instructions for Forms W-2 and W-3, under Specific Instructions for Form W-2c, boxes 5 and 6).

	Previously reported	Correct information		Previously reported	Correct information
1 Wages, tips, other compensation	10000.00	12500.00	2 Federal income tax withheld	4800.00	2000.00
3 Social security wages	10000.00	12500.00	4 Social security tax withheld	820.00	775.00
5 Medicare wages and tips	10000.00	12500.00	6 Medicare tax withheld	145.00	181.25
7 Social security tips			8 Allocated tips		
9			10 Dependent care benefits		
11 Nonqualified plans			12a See instructions for box 12		
13 Statutory employee / Retirement plan / Third-party sick pay			12b		
14 Other (see instructions)			12c		
			12d		

Form W-2c is used to submit changes to data previously filed on Form W-2.

➤ services performed in the employment of an incorporated religious elementary or secondary school if it is operated primarily for religious purposes and is operated, supervised, controlled, or principally supported by a church or a convention or association of churches; and

➤ services performed in the employment of an elementary or secondary school that is operated primarily for religious purposes and is not operated, supervised, controlled, or principally supported by a church or a convention or association of churches.

States may expand their coverage of unemployment taxes beyond the federal minimum. In many states, exemption is also provided for

➤ services performed in the employ of a separately incorporated church school if the school is operated primarily for religious purposes and is operated, supervised, controlled, or principally supported by a church or convention or association of churches.

Unemployment reporting requirements

Nonprofit organizations that are liable for FUTA taxes are required to file Form 940, or 940-EZ Employer's Annual Federal Unemployment Tax Return, due on January 31, if one of the following tests apply:

➤ You paid wages of $1,500 or more in any calendar quarter in the current or prior year, or

➤ You had one or more employees for at least some part of a day in any 20 or more different weeks in the current or prior year.

Filing Tip

Recent court cases reflect attempts by states to subject religious organizations, including churches, to state unemployment taxes. Except for an Oregon case and a New York case, most courts have held that churches are not subject to state unemployment tax.

Although Form 940 covers a calendar year, you may have to make deposits of the tax before filing the return. Generally, deposit FUTA tax quarterly if your FUTA tax exceeds $500.

The taxable wage base under FUTA is $7,000 for 2016. (The state wage base may be different.) The tax applies to the first $7,000 you pay each employee as wages during the year. For example, if you had only one employee for the year and the salary was $20,000, only $7,000 is subject to FUTA. The gross FUTA tax rate is 6.0% for 2016.

Generally, you can take a credit against your FUTA tax for amounts you paid into the state unemployment funds. This credit cannot be more than 5.4% of taxable wages. The credit is reduced for organizations that have not repaid loans from the federal jobless fund.

Use Form 940 or 940-EZ to report this tax. You may be able to use Form 940-EZ instead of Form 940 if (1) you paid unemployment taxes ("contributions") to only one state, (2) you paid state unemployment taxes by the due date of Form 940 or 940-EZ, and (3) all wages that were taxable for FUTA tax purposes were also taxable for your state's unemployment tax.

INTEGRITY*Points*

- **Worker classification issues.** Classifying workers correctly is very important in the minds of two important federal government agencies: the Department of Labor (DOL) and the IRS. The DOL's interest relates to being sure workers who are employees are classified as such because of the implications for the Fair Labor Standards Act (minimum wage and overtime), workers' compensation, and other fringe benefit purposes. The IRS wants to see Federal income tax and FICA-type social security tax (for lay employees) withheld for all workers who qualify as employees. The employer mandate under the health care reform law will also bring increasing scrutiny to worker classification issues.

   Too often churches and nonprofits make a decision on employee vs. independent contractor based on what the FICA social security cost (and perhaps other paperwork costs) will be for the organization. Actually, the social security cost factor has no relationship to an appropriate employee vs. independent contractor decision. Integrity requires proper evaluation of worker classification to insure workers receive the benefits to which they are entitled.

- **Ministers and social security.** One of the most common mistakes made by churches and nonprofits is to withhold FICA-type social security tax from a qualified minister. The employing organization may inappropriately give a minister a choice (of FICA withholding or paying their own social security). Or the minister may inappropriately request that FICA tax be withheld because it was done this way by his or her previous employer. Unfortunately, there is no choice on this issue.

   Qualified ministers must pay their own social security by completing Schedule SE, filed with their Form 1040. If an employer withholds and matches FICA-type social security tax from the pay of a minister, then it has not correctly reported the minister's taxable compensation, because the matched portion of the FICA tax escapes income tax when it is fully taxable for a minister. Organizations must apply these rules with integrity, sometimes in spite of pressure from employees to do otherwise.

6 Information Reporting

In This Chapter

- General filing requirements
- Reporting on the receipt of funds
- Reporting on the payment of funds

- Summary of payment reporting requirements

Information reporting to the IRS is required for almost all nonprofit organizations. The key issues to consider for information reporting are

> **Classifying payments to workers.** An organization generally makes many payments to individuals providing services to the organization. Some of the recipient individuals are employees and others are independent contractors. The organization must first make a determination as to which workers are independent contractors before proceeding with information reporting with respect to these workers. Payments of $600 or more in a calendar year to an independent contractor triggers filing Form 1099-MISC.

> **Information filing for other payments.** Certain payments other than to independent contractors also trigger information reporting such as payments of interest or royalties and payments to annuitants and nonresident aliens.

> **Information filing for receipt of funds.** The receipt of certain funds qualify for information reporting such as the receipt of interest on mortgages.

General Filing Requirements

Information forms (1098 and 1099) must be provided to the payers/recipients on or before January 31 following the calendar year that the funds were paid or received. Copies of the forms (or electronic media) must be filed with the IRS by February 28 following the year that the funds were paid or received.

An extension of time to file may be requested by filing Form 8809, Application for Extension of Time to File Information Returns, by the due date of the returns.

Form **W-9**
(Rev. December 2014)
Department of the Treasury
Internal Revenue Service

**Request for Taxpayer
Identification Number and Certification**

Give Form to the
requester. Do not
send to the IRS.

1 Name (as shown on your income tax return). Name is required on this line; do not leave this line blank.
Richard K. Bennett

2 Business name/disregarded entity name, if different from above

3 Check appropriate box for federal tax classification; check only **one** of the following seven boxes:
[X] Individual/sole proprietor or single-member LLC
[ ] C Corporation
[ ] S Corporation
[ ] Partnership
[ ] Trust/estate
[ ] Limited liability company. Enter the tax classification (C=C corporation, S=S corporation, P=partnership) ▶
Note. For a single-member LLC that is disregarded, do not check LLC; check the appropriate box in the line above for the tax classification of the single-member owner.
[ ] Other (see instructions) ▶

4 Exemptions (codes apply only to certain entities, not individuals; see instructions on page 3):
Exempt payee code (if any)
Exemption from FATCA reporting code (if any)
(Applies to accounts maintained outside the U.S.)

5 Address (number, street, and apt. or suite no.)
829 Garner Street

6 City, state, and ZIP code
Thomasville, SC 27360

Requester's name and address (optional)

7 List account number(s) here (optional)

Part I Taxpayer Identification Number (TIN)

Enter your TIN in the appropriate box. The TIN provided must match the name given on line 1 to avoid backup withholding. For individuals, this is generally your social security number (SSN). However, for a resident alien, sole proprietor, or disregarded entity, see the Part I instructions on page 3. For other entities, it is your employer identification number (EIN). If you do not have a number, see *How to get a TIN* on page 3.

Note. If the account is in more than one name, see the instructions for line 1 and the chart on page 4 for guidelines on whose number to enter.

Social security number

4 0 3 – 9 9 – 1 2 9 7

or

Employer identification number

Part II Certification

Under penalties of perjury, I certify that:

1. The number shown on this form is my correct taxpayer identification number (or I am waiting for a number to be issued to me); and

2. I am not subject to backup withholding because: (a) I am exempt from backup withholding, or (b) I have not been notified by the Internal Revenue Service (IRS) that I am subject to backup withholding as a result of a failure to report all interest or dividends, or (c) the IRS has notified me that I am no longer subject to backup withholding; and

3. I am a U.S. citizen or other U.S. person (defined below); and

4. The FATCA code(s) entered on this form (if any) indicating that I am exempt from FATCA reporting is correct.

Certification instructions. You must cross out item 2 above if you have been notified by the IRS that you are currently subject to backup withholding because you have failed to report all interest and dividends on your tax return. For real estate transactions, item 2 does not apply. For mortgage interest paid, acquisition or abandonment of secured property, cancellation of debt, contributions to an individual retirement arrangement (IRA), and generally, payments other than interest and dividends, you are not required to sign the certification, but you must provide your correct TIN. See the instructions on page 3.

Sign Here
Signature of U.S. person ▶ *Richard K. Bennett*
Date ▶ 1/2/17

Use this form to obtain the taxpayer identification number in non-employee situations.

Do Not Staple   6969

Form **1096**
Department of the Treasury
Internal Revenue Service

**Annual Summary and Transmittal of
U.S. Information Returns**

OMB No. 1545-0108

20**16**

FILER'S name
ABC Charity

Street address (including room or suite number)
2870 North Hull Street

City or town, state or province, country, and ZIP or foreign postal code
Traverse City, MI 49615

Name of person to contact
Marianne Smith

Telephone number
231-435-2201

Email address
marsmith@msn.com

Fax number
231-435-2205

For Official Use Only

1 Employer identification number	2 Social security number	3 Total number of forms	4 Federal income tax withheld	5 Total amount reported with this Form 1096
35-2946039		10	$	$ 5843.00

6 Enter an "X" in only one box below to indicate the type of form being filed.

7 Form 1099-MISC with NEC in box 7, check ▶ [ ]

W-2G 32	1097-BTC 50	1098 81	1098-C 78	1098-E 84	1098-Q 74	1098-T 83	1099-A 80	1099-B 79	1099-C 85	1099-CAP 73	1099-DIV 91	1099-G 86	1099-INT 92	1099-K 10
[ ]	[ ]	[ ]	[ ]	[ ]	[ ]	[ ]	[ ]	[ ]	[ ]	[ ]	[ ]	[ ]	[ ]	[ ]

1099-LTC 93	1099-MISC 95	1099-OID 96	1099-PATR 97	1099-Q 31	1099-QA 1A	1099-R 98	1099-S 75	1099-SA 94	3921 25	3922 26	5498 28	5498-ESA 72	5498-QA 2A	5498-SA 27
[ ]	[X]	[ ]	[ ]	[ ]	[ ]	[ ]	[ ]	[ ]	[ ]	[ ]	[ ]	[ ]	[ ]	[ ]

Return this entire page to the Internal Revenue Service. Photocopies are not acceptable.

Under penalties of perjury, I declare that I have examined this return and accompanying documents, and, to the best of my knowledge and belief, they are true, correct, and complete.

Signature ▶ *Daniel L. Lewis*
Title ▶ Treasurer
Date ▶ 1/13/17

This form is the "cover sheet" or transmittal form that must accompany all your Forms 1099-MISC and other information forms.

Obtaining correct identification numbers

Organizations required to file information returns with the IRS must obtain the correct taxpayer identification number (TIN) to report real estate transactions, mortgage interest paid to or by the organization, and certain other transactions.

Form W-9, Request for Taxpayer Identification Number and Certification, is used to furnish the correct TIN to the organization and in certain other situations to

Remember

If the recipient does not furnish a completed Form W-9, the church or nonprofit organization is required to withhold 28% of the payment for amounts paid, deposit the withholding with Form 8109 or 8109-B, and report amounts withheld on Form 1099-INT, 1099-MISC, or 1099-R, as applicable.

> ➤ certify that the TIN furnished is correct,

> ➤ certify that the recipient of the income is not subject to backup withholding, or

> ➤ certify exemption from backup withholding.

Reporting on the Receipt of Funds

Receipt of interest on mortgages

Use Form 1098, Mortgage Interest Statement, to report mortgage interest of $600 or more received by an organization during the year from an individual, including a sole proprietor. There is no requirement to file Form 1098 for interest received from a corporation, partnership, trust, estate, or association. A transmittal Form 1096 must accompany one or more Forms 1098.

Reporting on the Payment of Funds

Payments of interest

File Form 1099-INT, Interest Income, for each person to whom an organization paid interest reportable in Box 1 of at least $10 in any calendar year. This form is also required if any federal income tax was withheld under the backup withholding rules (28% is the 2016 rate), regardless of the amount of the payment. In certain instances, the $10 limit increases to $600. There is no requirement to file Form 1099-INT for payments made to a corporation or another tax-exempt organization.

The $10 limit applies if the interest is on "evidences of indebtedness" (bonds and promissory notes) issued by a corporation in "registered form." A note or bond is in "registered form" if its transfer must be effected by the surrender of the old instrument and either the corporation's reissuance of the old instrument to the new holder or its reissuance of a new instrument to the new holder.

9292	☐ VOID	☐ CORRECTED	

PAYER'S name, street address, city or town, state or province, country, ZIP or foreign postal code, and telephone no.	Payer's RTN (optional)	OMB No. 1545-0112	Interest Income
Lancaster Community Church 1425 Spencer Avenue Logansport, IN 46958	**1** Interest income $ 913.00	20**16** Form **1099-INT**	
	2 Early withdrawal penalty $		Copy A
PAYER'S federal identification number RECIPIENT'S identification number 35-7921873	**3** Interest on U.S. Savings Bonds and Treas. obligations $		**For Internal Revenue Service Center**
RECIPIENT'S name James R. Moore	**4** Federal income tax withheld $	**5** Investment expenses $	**File with Form 1096.**
Street address (including apt. no.) 804 Linden Avenue	**6** Foreign tax paid $	**7** Foreign country or U.S. possession	For Privacy Act and Paperwork Reduction Act Notice, see the **2016 General Instructions for Certain Information Returns.**
City or town, state or province, country, and ZIP or foreign postal code Wabash, IN 46992	**8** Tax-exempt interest $	**9** Specified private activity bond interest $	
	10 Market discount $	**11** Bond premium $	
FATCA filing requirement ☐	**12** Bond premium on Treasury obligations $	**13** Bond premium on tax-exempt bond $	
Account number (see instructions) 2nd TIN not. ☐	**14** Tax-exempt and tax credit bond CUSIP no.	**15** State **16** State identification no. $ $	**17** State tax withheld $ $

Form **1099-INT**   Cat. No. 14410K   www.irs.gov/form1099int   Department of the Treasury - Internal Revenue Service

Do Not Cut or Separate Forms on This Page — Do Not Cut or Separate Forms on This Page

Use this form to report certain interest payments to the recipients.

Example 1: Sleepy Hollow Church financed a new church by issuing registered bonds. A 1099-INT form must be provided to each bond investor receiving $10 or more in interest during any calendar year.

If Sleepy Hollow engaged a bond broker to handle the issuance of the bonds, the broker would issue 1099-INT forms. If Sleepy Hollow issued the bonds without using a bond broker, the church would issue the 1099-INT forms.

Example 2: Sleepy Hollow Church borrows funds from church members. The notes are transferable. There is no requirement to return the bonds to the church for reissuance. The $600 limit applies for the issuance of 1099-INT forms for the payment of interest on these notes.

Payments to annuitants

File Form 1099-R for each person to whom an organization made a designated distribution that is a total distribution from a retirement plan or a payment to an annuitant of $1 or more. If part of the distribution is taxable and part is nontaxable, Form 1099-R should reflect the entire distribution.

Example: ABC Charity makes payments of $1,000 during the year to one of its annuitants, Mary Hughes. (Several years earlier, Mary entered into the charitable gift annuity agreement by giving a check to ABC.)

A portion of each annuity payment is a tax-free return of principal, and the remainder is annuity income for Mary. ABC will generally report the entire $1,000 in Box 1 on Form 1099-R and check Box 2b unless ABC determines the taxable amount for the year.

๑ธ๑ธ ☐ VOID ☐ CORRECTED			

PAYER'S name, street address, city or town, state or province, country, and ZIP or foreign postal code	1 Gross distribution $ 1000.00	OMB No. 1545-0119 2016 Form 1099-R	Distributions From Pensions, Annuities, Retirement or Profit-Sharing Plans, IRAs, Insurance Contracts, etc.
ABC Charity 8049 Riverside Blvd. Sacramento, CA 95831	2a Taxable amount $		
	2b Taxable amount not determined [X]	Total distribution ☐	Copy A For
PAYER'S federal identification number	RECIPIENT'S identification number	3 Capital gain (included in box 2a) $	4 Federal income tax withheld $	Internal Revenue Service Center File with Form 1096.
35-0179214				
RECIPIENT'S name Mary Hughes	5 Employee contributions /Designated Roth contributions or insurance premiums $	6 Net unrealized appreciation in employer's securities $	For Privacy Act and Paperwork Reduction Act Notice, see the 2016 General Instructions for Certain Information Returns.
Street address (including apt. no.) PO Box 942	7 Distribution code(s) IRA/SEP/SIMPLE ☐	8 Other $ %	
City or town, state or province, country, and ZIP or foreign postal code El Toro, CA 92609	9a Your percentage of total distribution %	9b Total employee contributions $	
10 Amount allocable to IRR within 5 years $	11 1st year of desig. Roth contrib.	FATCA filing requirement ☐	12 State tax withheld $ $	13 State/Payer's state no.	14 State distribution $ $
Account number (see instructions)	15 Local tax withheld $ $	16 Name of locality	17 Local distribution $ $

Form **1099-R**   Cat. No. 14436Q   www.irs.gov/form1099r   Department of the Treasury - Internal Revenue Service

Do Not Cut or Separate Forms on This Page — Do Not Cut or Separate Forms on This Page

Use this form for retirement or annuity payments.

Form W-4P, Withholding Certificate for Pension or Annuity Payments, should be completed by recipients of income from annuity, pension, and certain other deferred compensation plans to inform payers whether income tax is to be withheld and on what basis.

Payments to nonresident aliens

Payments for personal services made to noncitizens who are temporarily in this country (nonresident aliens) are often subject to federal income tax withholding at a 28% rate. Some payments may be exempt from income tax withholding if the person is from a country with which the United States maintains a tax treaty. A nonresident alien is a person who is neither a U.S. citizen nor a resident of the United States. Salary payments to nonresident aliens employed in the United States are subject to income tax withholding based on the regular withholding tables.

Single, nonrecurring, fixed or determinable payments to nonresident aliens are generally not subject

Caution

Generally, you must withhold 30% from the gross amount paid to a foreign payee unless you can reliably associate the payment with valid documentation that establishes the payee is a U.S. person. If you do not have documentation or if you believe the documentation is unreliable or incorrect, you must follow the presumption rules outlined in IRS Publication 515.

to withholding. Honoraria paid to visiting speakers usually fit this definition. It is not clear if love offerings are subject to withholding.

All payments to nonresident aliens, other than expense reimbursements and amounts reported on Form W-2, must be reported on Forms 1042 and 1042-S. These forms are filed with the IRS Service Center in Philadelphia by March 15 for the previous calendar year, and a copy of Form 1042-S must be sent to the nonresident alien.

Payments of royalties and for other services

An organization must file Form 1099-MISC for each recipient (other than corporations) to whom it has paid

➤ at least $10 in royalties, or

➤ at least $600 in rents (for example, office rent or equipment rent), payments for services (nonemployee compensation), or medical health care payments.

Payments of attorneys' fees to a lawyer or law firm must be included, generally in Box 7, even if the firm providing the legal services is incorporated.

Caution

There is more misunderstanding about the use of the Form 1099-MISC than about most IRS forms. Payments of $600 or more per calendar year to non-corporate providers of services trigger the filing of this form. This form should not be used for employee compensation payments, so typically an organization should not report clergy compensation (or the housing allowance) on this form.

Example: A charity has established a written, nondiscriminatory employee health reimbursement arrangement under which the charity pays the medical expenses of the employee, spouse, and dependents.

If $600 or more is paid in the calendar year to a doctor or other provider of health care services, a Form 1099-MISC must be filed. Amounts paid to an employee under a health reimbursement arrangement (or health care flexible spending account) are not reportable on Form W-2 or 1099-MISC.

Benevolence payments to nonemployees are not reportable on Form 1099-MISC (or any other information form). Benevolence payments to employees are reportable on Form W-2.

Do not include the payment of a housing allowance to a minister on Form 1099-MISC. Advances, reimbursements, or expenses for traveling and other business expenses of an employee are not reportable on Form 1099-MISC. These payments may be reportable on Form W-2 if they do not comply with the accountable expense plan rules.

Advances, reimbursements, or expenses for traveling and other business expenses of a self-employed person are not reportable on Form 1099-MISC if made under an accountable expense reimbursement plan. Under this type of plan, expenses are reimbursed *only* if they are substantiated as to amount, date, and business nature, and any excess reimbursements must be returned to the organization.

On Form 1099-MISC, report all advances, reimbursements, or expenses for traveling and other business expenses of a self-employed person for income tax purposes that are *not* substantiated to the paying organization.

Example 1: ABC Ministry organizes a seminar and engages a speaker. The speaker is paid a $750 honorarium, and ABC reimburses the travel expenses of $200 upon presentation of proper substantiation by the speaker. Form 1099-MISC should be issued to the speaker for $750.

Example 2: Same facts as Example 1, except for the $750 payment, $250 is designated for travel expenses and the speaker substantiates to ABC for the travel. Since the honorarium is $500, after excluding the substantiated payments, and therefore is less than the $600 limit, there is no requirement to issue a Form 1099-MISC to the speaker.

If ABC paid an honorarium to the same speaker during the same calendar year of $100 or more, bringing the total for the year to the $600 level, a Form 1099-MISC should be issued.

Example 3: ABC Ministry contracts for janitorial services with an unincorporated janitorial service and pays $2,000 during the year for this service. ABC should issue a Form 1099-MISC for these payments.

9595	☐ VOID	☐ CORRECTED			
PAYER'S name, street address, city or town, state or province, country, ZIP or foreign postal code, and telephone no. **ABC Charity** **110 Harding Avenue** **Cincinnati, OH 45963**		**1** Rents $ **2** Royalties $	OMB No. 1545-0115 20**16** Form **1099-MISC**	**Miscellaneous Income**	
		3 Other income $	**4** Federal income tax withheld $	**Copy A** **For**	
PAYER'S federal identification number **35-1148942**	RECIPIENT'S identification number **389-11-8067**	**5** Fishing boat proceeds	**6** Medical and health care payments	**Internal Revenue Service Center**	
		$	$	**File with Form 1096.**	
RECIPIENT'S name **Mark A. Mitchell**		**7** Nonemployee compensation	**8** Substitute payments in lieu of dividends or interest	For Privacy Act and Paperwork Reduction Act Notice, see the	
Street address (including apt. no.) **512 Warren Avenue**		$ **2400.00**	$	**2016 General Instructions for Certain Information Returns.**	
		9 Payer made direct sales of $5,000 or more of consumer products to a buyer (recipient) for resale ▶ ☐	**10** Crop insurance proceeds $		
City or town, state or province, country, and ZIP or foreign postal code **Norwood, OH 45212**		**11**	**12**		
Account number (see instructions)	FATCA filing requirement ☐	2nd TIN not. ☐	**13** Excess golden parachute payments $	**14** Gross proceeds paid to an attorney $	
15a Section 409A deferrals $	**15b** Section 409A income $	**16** State tax withheld $ $	**17** State/Payer's state no.	**18** State income $ $	

Form **1099-MISC**   Cat. No. 14425J   www.irs.gov/form1099misc   Department of the Treasury - Internal Revenue Service

Do Not Cut or Separate Forms on This Page — Do Not Cut or Separate Forms on This Page

Use this form to report royalty and nonemployee services payments.

Payments to volunteers

Payments to volunteers that represent a reimbursement under an accountable business expense reimbursement plan for expenses directly connected with the volunteer services are not reportable by the charity to the volunteer. With proper substantiation, unreimbursed volunteer expenses may be claimed as charitable contributions.

Remember

Legislation is almost annually introduced to allow tax-free mileage reimbursements to volunteers at the business mileage rate. To date, this provision has not been enacted.

Payments for auto mileage up to the maximum IRS rate for charitable miles are tax-free for volunteers. When an organization provides liability insurance for its volunteers, the value of the coverage can be excluded from the volunteer's income as a working condition fringe benefit.

Payments to or on behalf of volunteers that are not business expenses are reported on Form W-2 or Form 1099-MISC, depending on whether or not a common law employee relationship exists. When the relationship takes the form of an employer-employee relationship, payments other than expense reimbursement are reported on Form W-2. Payments to nonemployee volunteers for medical, education, or personal living expenses must be reported as nonemployee compensation on Form 1099-MISC. Tax-free payments to volunteers for lodging, meals, and incidental expenses are limited to actual expenses (including use of the charitable mileage rate).

Moving expenses

Qualified moving expenses an employer pays to a third party on behalf of the employee (for example, to a moving company) and services that an employer furnishes in kind to an employee are not reported on Form W-2.

A taxpayer must move at least 50 miles to qualify to deduct moving expenses or receive a tax-free reimbursement. Many ministers move less than 50 miles, which makes the expenses nondeductible and reimbursements by the church fully taxable for both income and social security tax purposes.

Tip

Employer reimbursements of moving expenses are excludable from Form W-2 reporting only to the extent that the expenses would qualify for a moving expense deduction if they had been paid by the employee and not reimbursed. For example, many employees move less than 50 miles. This makes the expenses nondeductible and reimbursements by the employer fully taxable both for income and social security tax purposes.

Racial nondiscrimination

Form 5578, Annual Certification of Racial Nondiscrimination for a Private School Exempt from Federal Income Tax, must be filed by churches and other charities that operate, supervise, or control a private school. The form must be filed by the 15th day of the fifth month following the end of the organization's calendar year or fiscal period. For

Form **5578**
(Rev. August 2013)
Department of the Treasury
Internal Revenue Service

Annual Certification of Racial Nondiscrimination for a Private School Exempt From Federal Income Tax
► Information about Form 5578 and its instructions is at *www.irs.gov/form5578*.
(For use by organizations that do not file Form 990 or Form 990-EZ)

OMB No. 1545-0213

Open to Public Inspection

For IRS Use Only ►

For the period beginning _____ , and ending _____ ,

1a Name of organization that operates, supervises, and/or controls school(s).	**1b** Employer identification number
Fellowship Church	73-0896893

Address (number and street or P.O. box no., if mail is not delivered to street address) | Room/suite
East Main Street

City or town, state, and ZIP + 4 (If foreign address, list city or town, state or province, and country. Include postal code.)
Lamont, KS 66855

2a Name of central organization holding group exemption letter covering the school(s). (If same as 1a above, write "Same" and complete 2c.) If the organization in 1a holds an individual exemption letter, write "Not Applicable."

2b Employer identification number

Address (number and street or P.O. box no., if mail is not delivered to street address) | Room/suite

2c Group exemption number (see instructions under *Definitions*)

City or town, state, and ZIP + 4 (If foreign address, list city or town, state or province, and country. Include postal code.)

3a Name of school. (If more than one school, write "See Attached," and attach a list of the names, complete addresses, including postal codes, and employer identification numbers of the schools.) If same as 1a, write "Same."
Fellowship Christian School

3b Employer identification number, if any
Same

Address (number and street or P.O. box no., if mail is not delivered to street address) | Room/suite
Same

City or town, state, and ZIP + 4 (If foreign address, list city or town, state or province, and country. Include postal code.)
Same

Under penalties of perjury, I hereby certify that I am authorized to take official action on behalf of the above school(s) and that to the best of my knowledge and belief the school(s) has (have) satisfied the applicable requirements of sections 4.01 through 4.05 of Rev. Proc. 75-50, 1975-2 C.B. 587, for the period covered by this certification.

Ralph Winzeler
(Signature)

Ralph Winzeler, Superintendent
(Type or print name and title.)

5/26/16
(Date)

For Paperwork Reduction Act Notice, see instructions.   Cat. No. 42658A   Form **5578** (Rev. 8-2013)

organizations that must file Form 990, there is no requirement to file Form 5578 since the information is included in Schedule E.

The "private school" definition includes preschools; primary, secondary, preparatory, and high schools; and colleges and universities, whether operated as a separate legal entity or an activity of a church.

Immigration control

The Immigration Reform and Control Act (IRCA) prohibits all employers from hiring unauthorized aliens, imposes documentation verification requirements on all employers, and provides an "amnesty" program for certain illegal aliens. The law also prohibits employers with three or more employees from discriminating because of national origin. An I-9 Form (see pages 7 and 116) must be completed and retained on file by all employers for each employee. The form must be available for inspection at any time. Form I-9 may be obtained by calling 800-375-5283 or at http://uscis.gov/files/form/i-9.

The Form I-551, Alien Registration Card (Green Card), issued after August 1, 1989, is the exclusive registration card issued to lawful permanent residents as definitive evidence of identity and U.S. resident status.

Employment Eligibility Verification
Department of Homeland Security
U.S. Citizenship and Immigration Services

USCIS
Form I-9
OMB No. 1615-0047
Expires 03/31/2016

▶START HERE. Read instructions carefully before completing this form. The instructions must be available during completion of this form. Employers CANNOT specify which document(s) they will accept from an employee. The refusal to hire an individual because the documentation presented has a future expiration date may also constitute illegal discrimination.

ANTI-DISCRIMINATION NOTICE: It is illegal to discriminate against work-authorized individuals. Employers CANNOT specify which

Section 1. Employee Information and Attestation (Employees must complete and sign Section 1 of Form I-9 no later than the first day of employment, but not before accepting a job offer.)

Last Name (Family Name)	First Name (Given Name)	Middle Initial	Other Names Used (if any)
Hendricks	Fred	W.	

Address (Street Number and Name)	Apt. Number	City or Town	State	Zip Code
408 Forest Avenue		Cincinnati	OH	45980

Date of Birth (mm/dd/yyyy)	U.S. Social Security Number	E-mail Address	Telephone Number
06-12-1959	5 1 4 - 4 2 - 9 0 8 7	fhend@hotmail.com	513-641-5950

I am aware that federal law provides for imprisonment and/or fines for false statements or use of false documents in connection with the completion of this form.

I attest, under penalty of perjury, that I am (check one of the following):

☒ A citizen of the United States

☐ A noncitizen national of the United States (See instructions)

☐ A lawful permanent resident (Alien Registration Number/USCIS Number):

☐ An alien authorized to work until (expiration date, mm/dd/yyyy): _____ Some aliens may write "N/A" in this field.
(See instructions)

For aliens authorized to work, provide your Alien Registration Number/USCIS Number OR Form I-94 Admission Number:

1. Alien Registration Number/USCIS Number: _____

OR

2. Form I-94 Admission Number: _____

If you obtained your admission number from CBP in connection with your arrival in the United States, include the following:

Foreign Passport Number: _____

Country of Issuance: _____

Some aliens may write "N/A" on the Foreign Passport Number and Country of Issuance fields. (See instructions)

3-D Barcode
Do Not Write in This Space

Signature of Employee:	Date (mm/dd/yyyy):
Fred W. Hendricks	01/03/2016

Preparer and/or Translator Certification (To be completed and signed if Section 1 is prepared by a person other than the employee.)

I attest, under penalty of perjury, that I have assisted in the completion of this form and that to the best of my knowledge the information is true and correct.

Signature of Preparer or Translator:	Date (mm/dd/yyyy):

Last Name (Family Name)	First Name (Given Name)

Address (Street Number and Name)	City or Town	State	Zip Code

STOP Employer Completes Next Page **STOP**

Form I-9 03/08/13 N

Page 7 of 9

Section 2. Employer or Authorized Representative Review and Verification

(Employers or their authorized representative must complete and sign Section 2 within 3 business days of the employee's first day of employment. You must physically examine one document from List A OR examine a combination of one document from List B and one document from List C as listed on the "Lists of Acceptable Documents" on the next page of this form. For each document you review, record the following information: document title, issuing authority, document number, and expiration date, if any.)

Employee Last Name, First Name and Middle Initial from Section 1: Hendricks, Fred W.

List A	OR	List B	AND	List C
Identity and Employment Authorization		Identity		Employment Authorization

	List B	List C
Document Title:	Driver's License	Birth Certificate
Issuing Authority:	Ohio	Ohio
Document Number:	514-42-9087	
Expiration Date (if any)(mm/dd/yyyy):	6/30/16	

Document Title:
Issuing Authority:
Document Number:
Expiration Date (if any)(mm/dd/yyyy):

Document Title:
Issuing Authority:
Document Number:
Expiration Date (if any)(mm/dd/yyyy):

3-D Barcode
Do Not Write in This Space

Certification

I attest, under penalty of perjury, that (1) I have examined the document(s) presented by the above-named employee, (2) the above-listed document(s) appear to be genuine and to relate to the employee named, and (3) to the best of my knowledge the employee is authorized to work in the United States.

The employee's first day of employment (mm/dd/yyyy): _____ (See instructions for exemptions.)

Signature of Employer or Authorized Representative	Date (mm/dd/yyyy)	Title of Employer or Authorized Representative
David L. Brown	01/31/2016	Business Manager

Last Name (Family Name)	First Name (Given Name)	Employer's Business or Organization Name
Brown	David L.	Fairfield Church

Employer's Business or Organization Address (Street Number and Name)	City or Town	State	Zip Code
110 Harding Avenue	Cincinnati	OH	45960

Section 3. Reverification and Rehires (To be completed and signed by employer or authorized representative.)

A. New Name (if applicable) Last Name (Family Name)	First Name (Given Name)	Middle Initial	B. Date of Rehire (if applicable) (mm/dd/yyyy):

C. If employee's previous grant of employment authorization has expired, provide the information for the document from List A or List C the employee presented that establishes current employment authorization in the space provided below.

Document Title:	Document Number:	Expiration Date (if any) (mm/dd/yyyy):

I attest, under penalty of perjury, that to the best of my knowledge, this employee is authorized to work in the United States, and if the employee presented document(s), the document(s) I have examined appear to be genuine and to relate to the individual.

Signature of Employer or Authorized Representative:	Date (mm/dd/yyyy):	Print Name of Employer or Authorized Representative:

Form I-9 03/08/13 N

Page 8 of 9

This form must be completed and retained on file by all employers for employees hired after November 6, 1986. (For more information on completing this form, go to www.uscis.gov.)

Summary of Payment Reporting Requirements

Below is an alphabetical list of some payments and the forms necessary to report them. It is not a complete list of payments, and the absence of a payment from the list does not suggest that the payment is exempt from reporting.

Types of Payment	Report on Form
Advance earned income credit	W-2
Annuities, periodic payments	1099-R
* Attorneys' fees	1099-MISC
** Auto, personal use of employer-owned vehicle	W-2
Auto reimbursements (nonaccountable plan):	
Employee	W-2
Nonemployee	1099-MISC
Awards:	
Employee	W-2
Nonemployee	1099-MISC
Bonuses:	
Employee	W-2
Nonemployee	1099-MISC
Cafeteria/flexible benefit plan	5500, 5500-C, or 5500-R
Christmas bonuses:	
Employee	W-2
Nonemployee	1099-MISC
Commissions:	
Employee	W-2
Nonemployee	1099-MISC
Compensation:	
Employee	W-2
Nonemployee	1099-MISC
Dependent care payments	W-2
Director's fees	1099-MISC
Education expense reimbursement (nonaccountable plan):	
Employee	W-2
Nonemployee	1099-MISC
Employee business expense reimbursement (nonaccountable plan)	W-2

Types of Payment	Report on Form
Fees:	
Employee	W-2
Nonemployee	1099-MISC
Group-term life insurance (PS 58 costs)	W-2 or 1099-R
Interest, mortgage	1098
Interest, other than mortgage	1099-INT
Long-term care benefits	1099-LTC
Medical expense reimbursement plan (employee-funded)	5500, 5500-C, or 5500-R
Mileage (nonaccountable plan):	
Employee	W-2
Nonemployee	1099-MISC
Mortgage interest	1098
Moving expense:	
*** Employee	W-2
Nonemployee	1099-MISC
Prizes:	
Employee	W-2
Nonemployee	1099-MISC
Real estate proceeds	1099-S
Rents	1099-MISC
Royalties	1099-MISC
Severance pay	W-2
Sick pay	W-2
Supplemental unemployment	W-2
Vacation allowance:	
Employee	W-2
Nonemployee	1099-MISC

* The exemption from reporting payments made to corporations does not apply to payments to a lawyer or a law firm for legal services, even if the provider of the legal services is incorporated.

** Or, the value may be reported on a separate statement to the employee.

*** Qualified moving expenses paid directly to an employee must be reported on Form W-2, only in Box 12, using Code P.

 **INTEGRITY*Points***

- **Obtaining a completed Form W-9.** The proper completion of forms in the 1099 series all starts with obtaining a completed Form W-9 before the applicable payments are made by the church or nonprofit. Unless the Form W-9 is obtained before payments are made, it may be very difficult to obtain the form at a later date and could complicate the filing of the appropriate 1099 form. Integrity requires having procedures to obtain a Form W-9 at the beginning of the relationship with a recipient of certain charity payments.

- **Reporting of payments to independent contractors.** Because there is generally no tax to withhold, it is easy for a church or nonprofit to overlook the filing of Form 1099-MISC. When an organization fails to file a required Form 1099-MISC, it may be inadvertently giving an independent contractor a license to not report taxable income. Integrity requires the proper filing of Form 1099-MISC and all other forms in the 1099 series, if applicable.

- **Reporting of payments to noncitizens.** Churches and other nonprofits often make payments to individuals who are not U.S. citizens and are temporarily in the U.S. The proper reporting to the IRS is often overlooked. For example, payments might be made by a church to a national worker (noncitizen) visiting the church to report on the effectiveness of gifts made by a church to an international mission field.

  While reimbursements made under an accountable expense reimbursement plan are not reportable, other payments must be reported on Form 1042-S, and some payments are even subject to federal income tax withholding. Integrity requires organizations to understand the rules relating to payment to noncitizens before the payments are made.

One does not have to look far to find examples of organizations that have suffered because their financial records and reporting systems were deficient. Sound financial records are invaluable to churches and other nonprofit organizations in these three ways:

➤ **Helps board and staff make well-informed decisions.** Only from a quality set of financial records may good reports be prepared which reflect the financial condition of the organization. These reports are vital to allow the board and staff to assess the overall financial health of the organization, determine financial trends, measure financial outcomes, and project future budgetary needs. Informed decisions may only be made based on solid financial records.

➤ **Helps the organization to keep running smoothly.** Without a sound accounting system, it will not be possible for an organization to keep on track financially. Quality financial records keep order from turning into chaos. Imagine the challenges that would face an organization if its records did not clearly reflect its liabilities, if it did not know how much had been expended of a donor's temporarily restricted gift, or if the accounting records had not been reconciled to the bank statement. Yes, a smoothly running organization requires good accounting records.

➤ **Helps the organization demonstrate financial accountability.** Churches and nonprofit organizations must demonstrate accountability in a variety of ways. Church members anticipate at least annual financial data on the church's operations. Most nonprofit organizations other than churches must file Form 990 and perhaps Form 990-T with the Internal Revenue Service. Grant funders anticipate appropriate reporting on the use of grant funds. Accountability to the organization's board is a given. Good financial records are the basis for accountability to all constituents.

Recordkeeping of Income and Expenses

A good chart of accounts is the starting point for recording income and expenses. Finding the balance between too few and too many accounts in the chart is the key. Too few accounts will restrict reporting capabilities; too many accounts leads to cumbersome recording processes and excessive time spent in analyzing and reconciling accounts. A sample chart of accounts for a church is reflected on page 121, and it could be adapted for other organizations.

Ensuring the income of an organization is handled with adequate internal controls to safeguard these assets is very important. Offerings are the financial lifeblood of churches, and these funds must be handled with care. Pages 140-44 reflect key guidelines for handling church offerings. Many of these principles apply to handling gifts for other nonprofits and income of various types.

One of the most important principles of disbursing funds is to pay almost all expenses by check. The use of a petty cash fund should be the only exception to payment by check. Cash from a deposit should never be used to pay expenses.

Use preprinted, consecutively numbered checks. All spoiled checks should be marked "void" and kept on file with the canceled checks.

In some instances, it may be wise to require two signatures on every check or on checks over a certain amount. In other situations, one signature may be

> ### Caution
>
> Checks should not be written until near the time when funds are available to cover them. Some organizations write checks when bills are due without regard to available cash. Checks are held for days, weeks, or sometimes months until they are released for payment. This is an extremely confusing practice that makes it very difficult to determine the actual checkbook balance.

appropriate. The level of controls over the funds will help determine if more than one signature is necessary. Access to a checking account should generally be limited to no more than two or three individuals. A church pastor should not have access to the checking account. Checks should never be signed and delivered to anyone without completing the payee and the amount.

The use of check request forms, including the approval by the appropriate person, is often a good expense-control procedure. Large organizations often use a formal purchase order system. In either case, oral requests for funds should not be permitted.

Every check should have some type of written document to support it—an invoice, petty cash receipt, payroll summary, and so on (a sample cash expense report is shown on page 123). If such support is not available for some valid reason, a memo should be written to support the expenditure. For example, an honorarium paid to a visiting speaker would not be supported by an invoice but should be documented by indicating the date of the speaking engagement and the event.

Occasionally, it may be necessary to advance funds before supporting documentation is available (for example, a travel advance for future travel). In these instances, a system must be devised to ensure documentation is provided on a timely basis and any excess funds are returned.

Sample Chart of Accounts for a Church

Note: Fund numbers could be used as a prefix to the account numbers

Assets (100)

101	Cash and cash equivalents
110	Prepaid expenses
120	Short-term investments
	Land, buildings, and equipment
160	Church buildings
161	Parsonage
162	Furnishings
180	Long-term investments

Liabilities (200)

201	Accounts payable
210	Notes payable
220	Long-term debt

Revenues and Support (300)

	Contributions
301	Regular offerings
302	Sunday school offerings
303	Missions offerings
304	Building fund offerings
319	Other offerings
	Investment income
321	Interest income
322	Rental income
	Other income
331	Tape sales
335	Other sales
339	Other income

Expenses (400–500)

	Salaries and wages
401	Salary including cash housing allowance
402	Social security (SECA) reimbursement
	Benefits
411	Pension
412	Tax-deferred payments (TSA)
413	Social security (FICA)
414	Medical expense reimbursement
415	Insurance premiums

	Supplies
421	Postage
422	Literature and printing
423	Office supplies
424	Maintenance supplies
425	Food
426	Kitchen supplies
427	Flowers
439	Other supplies
	Travel and entertainment
441	Auto expense reimbursements
442	Vehicle rental
449	Other travel expense
450	Continuing education
	Insurance
461	Workers' Compensation
462	Health insurance
463	Property insurance
469	Other insurance
	Benevolences
471	Denominational budgets
479	Other benevolences
	Services and professional fees
481	Speaking honoraria
482	Custodial services
483	Legal and audit fees
489	Other fees
	Office and occupancy
491	Rent
492	Telephone
493	Utilities
494	Property taxes
499	Other office and occupancy
500	Depreciation
510	Interest expense
	Other
591	Banquets
592	Advertising

Suffix digits may be used to indicate the functional expense category, such as

- 10	Program expenses	- 16	Youth
- 11	Pastoral	- 17	Singles
- 12	Education	- 18	Seniors
- 121	Sunday school	- 20	Management and general
- 122	Vacation Bible school	- 21	Church plant
- 123	Camps and retreats	- 22	Parsonages
- 13	Music and worship	- 23	Office
- 14	Missions	- 30	Fundraising
- 15	Membership and evangelism		

Cash Count Summary

March 6 _____, 20 16

	Sunday School	Sunday A.M.	Sunday P.M.	Received During Week	TOTAL
Coins	83.12	21.82	10.42		115.36
Currency	320.00	431.00	108.00		859.00
Checks	25.00	1,855.00	360.00	185.00	2,425.00
TOTALS	428.12	2,307.82	478.42	185.00	3,399.36

Breakdown by Type of Gift

	Sunday School	Sunday A.M.	Sunday P.M.	Received During Week	TOTAL
Regular Tithes and Offerings		1,942.82	368.42	140.00	2,451.24
Sunday School	428.12				428.12
Building Fund		85.00	50.00	15.00	150.00
Missions		100.00	30.00	20.00	150.00
Other Designated Funds:					
Benevolence Fund		40.00			40.00
School Project		30.00	10.00		40.00
Choir Robes		50.00			50.00
Youth Trip		40.00	20.00	10.00	70.00
Parking Lot		20.00			20.00
TOTALS	428.12	2,307.82	478.42	185.00	3,399.36

Counted by: _Mike Anderson_
Helen David
Bob Walle

Deposited on: March 7 _____, 20 16

Contributions by Donor

March 6 _____, 20 16 (X) A.M. ( ) P.M. ( ) _____

Name of Contributor	Regular Tithes & Offerings	Sunday School	Building Fund	Missions	Other Description	Other Amount
Wilson, M/M Mark	50.00		10.00	20.00		
Young, Frank	35.00					
Jackson, Ellen	60.00		15.00			
Avery, Lori	40.00					
Floyd, M/M Mike	100.00	10.00			Benevolence	40.00
Long, M/M Harold	45.00		5.00	10.00		
Martin, Mary	75.00			20.00		
Ross, M/M Steve	80.00					
Harris, M/M Joe	65.00		5.00		School Project	30.00
York, Kelly	50.00					
Walker, Peggy	30.00					
Franklin, M/M Bob	75.00	5.00		15.00		
Gilles, Don	40.00		10.00			
Shields, Lou	200.00					
White, M/M Ron	80.00		20.00			
Howe, Art	100.00		20.00		Choir Robes	50.00
Plunkett, M/M Stan	60.00	10.00				
Robbins, Nancy	75.00				Youth Trip	40.00
Lyon, M/M Bill	50.00			5.00		
Clark, M/M David	80.00		20.00			
Bowers, James	40.00				Parking Lot	20.00
Burr, Cindy	60.00	10.00				
TOTALS	1,490.00	25.00	105.00	80.00		180.00

CASH EXPENSE REPORT

Name: **Pastor Frank Morris**

Address: **3801 North Florida Avenue**

Miami, FL 33168

Period Covered: From: **7/1/16** To: **7/14/16**

| DATE | TRAVEL | | | | | | | | OTHER * | | ACCOUNT to |
	City	Purpose of Travel	Brkfast	Lunch	Dinner	Snack	Lodging	Trans.	Description	Amount	be Charged
7/2/16									Lunch w/Bob Cox	18.21	644-002
7/6/16	Atlanta, GA	Continuing Ed. Sem.		10.80	13.40	2.10	90.50	265.08	Tips	8.00	644-010
7/6/16	" "	" " "	6.40								644-010
7/6/16									Lunch w/Al Lane	12.80	641-002
7/14/16									Lunch w/Sam Lee	11.12	641-002
	TOTAL CASH EXPENSES		6.40	10.80	13.40	2.10	90.50	265.08		50.13	

*If this is entertainment, please use the entertainment worksheet on the back of this form.

Frank Morris 7/16/16
Signature (person requesting reimbursement)   Date

Bob Davis 7/16/16
Approved by   Date

Total cash expenses	438.41
Personal auto business mileage (Complete worksheet on the back of this form.)	114.48
212 miles X **54¢** per mile	
Less travel advance	(300.00)
Balance due	252.89
Refund due organization	

PERSONAL AUTO BUSINESS MILEAGE

Date	Purpose/Destination	Miles	Account to be charged
7-01-16	Calls/Valley View Rest Home	23	638-000
7-02-16	Brown Funeral Home/Harold Boone	18	"
7-03-16	Calls/Various Homes	20	"
7-06-16	Calls/Memorial Hospital	15	"
7-05-16	Kiwanis Speaker/Pat's Cafeteria	25	"
7-07-16	Calls/Various Homes	10	"
7-08-16	Calls/St. Luke's Hospital	17	"
7-09-16	Calls/Cannon Nursing Home	12	"
7-10-16	Calls/Various Homes	8	"
7-12-16	Calls/Memorial Hospital	15	"
7-15-16	Ministerial Convention/Webb City	36	"
	TOTAL MILES TRAVELED	199	

To mileage summary on page one

ENTERTAINMENT WORKSHEET
(Expenses paid in behalf of individual(s) other than the person filing this expense report.)

Date	Persons Entertained	Purpose of Entertainment	Place	Amount
7-03-16	M/M Bob Cox	Prospective Members	Olive Garden	18.21
7-06-16	Al Lane	Discuss Ch. Bldg Plans	Chi-Chi's	12.80
7-14-16	Sam Lee	Church Goals w/Bd. Chair	Damon's	11.12
		TOTAL AMOUNT SPENT		42.13

To "other" expense column on page one

Accounting Records

Accounting systems differ in shape, size, complexity, and efficiency. The objectives of the system should be to measure and control financial activities and to provide financial information to an organization's governing body, a congregation, and donors. In choosing the accounting records for your organization, the most important consideration is the ability of the individual(s) keeping the records.

Cash and accrual methods

Most small-to-medium-size churches and nonprofit organizations use the cash or modified cash basis of accounting. These methods do not conform to generally accepted accounting principles (GAAP). When the accrual basis of accounting is required for audit purposes, the cash basis is often used throughout the year with the conversion to accrual at year-end.

Advantages of cash method

Under the cash method, revenue is recorded only when cash is received, and expenses are recorded when they are paid. For example, office supplies expense is shown in the month when the bill is paid, even though the supplies were received and used in the previous month. Pledges are not recorded as receivables, and the revenue from pledges is recorded as the cash is received.

The primary advantage of the cash method is its simplicity. It is easier for non-accountants to understand and keep records on this basis. When financial statements are required, the treasurer just summarizes the transactions from the checkbook stubs or runs the computer-prepared financial statements with fewer adjusting entries required. For smaller organizations, the difference between financial results on the cash and on the accrual basis are often not significantly different.

Advantages of accrual method

Many organizations use the accrual method of accounting when the cash basis does not accurately portray the financial picture. Under the accrual method, revenue is recorded when earned. For example, a church charges a fee for the use of the fellowship hall for a wedding. Under accrual accounting, the revenue is recorded in the month earned even though the cash might not be received until a later month.

Under accrual accounting, expenses are recorded when incurred. For example, telephone expense is recorded in the month when the service occurs although the bill may not be paid until the next month.

> **Idea**
>
> Even when obtaining an accrual basis audit, you can keep your books on the cash basis during the year and record journal entries on the last day of the year to convert to accrual. Too many organizations struggle to keep their books on the accrual basis (recording accounts receivable, accounts payable, etc.) when their financial life would be much simpler if the cash basis were used.

Generally accepted accounting principles for nonprofit organizations require the use of accrual basis accounting. Organizations that have their books audited by Certified Public Accountants (CPAs) and want the CPAs to report that the financial statements appear according to "generally accepted accounting principles" (GAAP) must either keep their records on the accrual basis or make the appropriate adjustments at the end of the year to convert to this basis. Financial statements prepared on a cash or other comprehensive basis may qualify under GAAP if the financial statements are not materially different from those prepared on an accrual basis.

Modified cash method

The modified cash method of accounting is a combination of certain features of the cash and accrual methods. For example, accounts payable may be recorded when a bill is received although other payables or receivables are not recorded. The modified cash method portrays the financial picture more accurately than the cash method but not as well as the full accrual method.

Fund accounting

Fund accounting (or accounting by classes of net assets) provides an excellent basis for stewardship reporting. It is a system of accounting in which separate records are kept for resources donated to an organization that are restricted by donors or outside parties to certain specified purposes or uses.

GAAP requires that net assets be broken down into the following three classes, based on the presence or absence of donor-imposed restrictions and their nature:

> **Remember**
>
> Fund accounting does not necessarily require multiple bank accounts. One bank account is all that is usually necessary. However, it may be appropriate to place restricted funds into a separate bank account to ensure that the funds are not inadvertently spent for other purposes.

➤ **Permanently restricted.** These assets are not available for program expenses, payments to creditors, or other organizational needs. An example is an endowment gift with a stipulation that the principal is permanently not available for spending but the investment income from the principal may be used in current operations.

➤ **Temporarily restricted.** These assets may be restricted by purpose or time, but the restrictions are not permanent. An example of the purpose-restricted gift is a gift for a certain project or for the purchase of some equipment. An example of a time-restricted gift is a contribution in the form of a trust, annuity, or term endowment (the principal of the gift is restricted for a certain term of time).

➤ **Unrestricted.** These net assets may be used for any of the organization's purposes. According to accounting standards, "The only limits on unrestricted net assets are broad limits resulting from the nature of the organization and the purposes specified in its articles of incorporation or bylaws."

Donor-imposed restrictions normally apply to the use of net assets and not to the use of specific assets. Only donors or outside parties may "restrict" funds given to a nonprofit organization. The organization's board may not "restrict" monies—they may only "designate" funds. For example, if a donor gives money for a new church organ, the funds should be placed in a restricted fund. If the church board sets funds aside in a debt retirement fund, this is a designated fund, a subdesignation of unrestricted net assets.

Records retention and destruction

Proper maintenance of corporate documents and records is critical from both management and legal aspects. An organization's preparedness for a financial or IRS audit, legal action and/or response, public inquiry, and loss by theft or natural catastrophe, among other things, depends largely on keeping accurate records for as long as necessary.

Sample Record Retention and Destruction Policy

The following is a partial listing of recommended retention times for several types of records. Churches and nonprofit organizations will retain many of these documents on their computer network. These apply to both physical and electronic documents. If no physical copy of an electronic document is retained, the means to "read" the electronic document must also be retained.

Record Type	Retention Period
A. Accounting and Finance	
Accounts payable and accounts receivable ledgers and schedules	7 years
Annual audit reports and financial statements	Permanent
Annual audit records, including workpapers and other documents that relate to the audit	7 years after completion of audit
Bank statements and canceled checks	7 years
Credit card numbers	Full credit card numbers should not be retained any longer than immediate business needs and merchant account agreements dictate
Employee expense reports	7 years
General ledgers	Permanent
Notes receivable ledgers and schedules	7 years
Investment records	7 years after sale of investment
B. Contracts	
Contracts and related correspondence (including any proposal that resulted in the contract and all other documentation)	7 years after expiration or termination

Comment: Some states may require longer retention periods generally, or for specific types of contracts. A local attorney should be consulted.

Record Type	Retention Period

C. Corporate Records

Corporate records (minutes books, signed minutes of the Board and all committees, corporate seals, articles of incorporation, bylaws, annual corporate reports) — Permanent

Licenses and permits — Permanent

D. Electronic Documents

Electronic mail: Retention of emails depends on the subject matter.
- All email—from internal or external sources—is generally deleted after 12 months.
- The organization will archive email for six months after the staff has deleted it, after which time the email will be permanently deleted.
- Staff should not store or transfer organization-related email to non-work-related computers except as necessary or appropriate for organization purposes.

Electronic Documents: Retention of electronic documents (including Microsoft Office, PDF files, etc.) depends on the subject matter.

Web page files - Internet cookies: At all workstations, the Internet browser should be scheduled to delete Internet cookies once per month.

Comment: This section may be the appropriate place to include other policies regarding email retention, usage, or subject matter. Whether the paper or electronic document is the "official document" would be determined by each organization.

E. Payroll Documents

Employee deduction authorizations	4 years after termination
Payroll deductions	Termination + 7 years
W-2 and W-4 forms	Termination + 7 years
Garnishments, assignments, attachments	Termination + 7 years
Payroll registers (gross and net)	7 years
Time cards/sheets	2 years
Unclaimed wage records	6 years

F. Personnel Records

Commissions/bonuses/incentives/awards	7 years
EEO-1/EEO-2 – Employer information reports or filing (whichever is longer)	2 years after superseded
Employee earnings records	Separation + 7 years
Employee handbooks	1 copy kept permanently
Employee personnel records (including individual attendance records, application forms, job or status change records, performance evaluations, termination papers, withholding information garnishments, test results, training and qualification records)	6 years after separation
Employment contracts – individual	7 years after separation
Employment records – correspondence with employment agencies and advertisements for job openings	3 years from date of hiring decision
Employment records – all non-hired applicants (including all applications and resumes – whether solicited or unsolicited, results of post-offer, pre-employment physicals, results of background investigations, if any, related correspondence)	2–4 years (4 years if file contains any correspondence which might be construed as an offer)
Job descriptions	3 years after superseded

Record Type	Retention Period
Personnel count records	3 years
Forms I-9	3 years after hiring, or
	1 year after separation if later

Comment: Many employment and employment tax-related laws have both state and federal law requirements. A local attorney should be consulted.

G. Property Records

Correspondence, property deeds, assessments, licenses, rights of way	Permanent
Property insurance policies	Permanent

H. Tax Records

Tax exemption documents and related correspondence	Permanent
IRS rulings	Permanent
Excise tax records	7 years
Payroll tax records	7 years
Tax bills, receipts, statements	7 years
Tax returns – income, franchise, property	Permanent
Tax workpaper packages – originals	7 years
Sales/use tax records	7 years
Annual information returns – federal and state	Permanent
IRS or other government audit records	Permanent

Comment: Retention period for sales taxes and property taxes are determined by state law. A local accountant or attorney should be consulted.

I. Contribution Records

Records of contributions	7 years
Documents evidencing terms, conditions, or restrictions on gifts	7 years after funds are expended

Financial Reports

In preparing financial reports, there is one basic rule: Prepare different reports for different audiences. For example, a church board would normally receive a more detailed financial report than the church membership. Department heads in a nonprofit organization might receive reports that relate only to their department.

Financial statements should

> ➤ be easily comprehensible so that any person taking the time to study them will understand the financial picture;

> ➤ be concise so that the person studying them will not get lost in detail;

> ➤ be all-inclusive in scope and embrace all activities of the organization;

> ➤ have a focal point for comparison so that the person reading them will have some basis for making a judgment (usually this will be a comparison with a budget or data from the corresponding period of the previous year); and

➤ be prepared on a timely basis (the longer the delay after the end of the period, the longer the time before corrective action can be taken).

Dashboard reports present a quick, comprehensible overview of an organization's financial status (dashboard reports can also reflect other critical measures of organizational performance and mission effectiveness). When dashboard reports present key indicators in consistent formats, board members and staff can readily spot changes and trends in these measurements. Like the dashboard inside a car, these reports often display the equivalent of warning lights that only flare up when there is an impending problem or when certain variables are outside of predetermined limits.

Key Issue

"Dashboard" financial reporting is increasingly used by nonprofits. It gets its name because it's like a financial dashboard—with gauges, redlines, and warning lights. It cuts through the barrage of uninterrupted data and delivers a clear view of the organization's performance. It often includes a visualization of historical information and personalized reports for key staff members.

For additional reading, see the *Accounting and Financial Reporting Guide for Christian Ministries* (Evangelical Joint Accounting Committee, 800-323-9473) and *Financial and Accounting Guide for Not-for-Profit Organizations* by John A. Mattie, John H. McCarthy, and Nancy E. Shelmon (John Wiley & Sons, Inc.).

Statement of financial position

A statement of financial position shows assets, liabilities, and net assets as of the end-of-period date. This statement is also called a balance sheet because it shows how the two sides of the accounting equation (assets minus liabilities equals net assets) "balance" in your organization.

Anything an organization owns that has a money value is an asset. Cash, land, buildings, furniture, and fixtures are examples of assets. Anything the organization owes is a liability. Liabilities might include amounts owed to suppliers (accounts payable) or to the bank (notes payable and other amounts due).

Statement of activity

The statement of activity (also referred to as a statement of revenues and expenses) reflects an organization's support and revenue, expenses, and changes in net assets for a certain period of time. It shows the sources of an organization's income and how the resources were used. The form of the statement will depend on the type of organization and accounting method used. But the statement must present the change in unrestricted, temporarily restricted, permanently restricted, and total net assets.

Many smaller organizations will have several lines for support and revenue such as contributions, sales of products, investment income, and so on. Expenses are often listed by natural classification such as salaries, fringe benefits, supplies, and so on.

Financial Questions for Boards

Financial reporting to the organization's board should answer the following questions:

1. Is our cash flow projected to be adequate? (This question presumes the organization prepares cash flow projections.)

2. What is the trend of cash in terms of number of days or number of months of cash on hand (excluding cash related to temporarily and permanently restricted net assets)? What is the organization's goal in terms of the number of days or months of cash in hand?

3. Do we have sufficient net assets (reserves)? (This question presumes the organization has established goals for net assets so measurement is possible.)

4. Did total net assets increase or decrease, and is this a significant change from last year?

5. Did unrestricted net assets increase or decrease, and is it a significant change from last year?

6. Have any funds related to temporarily or permanently restricted net assets been borrowed for operational or capital needs?

7. Is the financial activity compared with the operating and capital budgets? (This question presumes the organization prepares both operating and capital budgets.)

8. Are there any significant differences between actual and budgeted data? If so:

   a. Why did they occur?

   b. Do they need to be addressed, and if so, how?

9. Are there any significant differences between this year-to-date and prior year-to-date actual data? If so:

   a. Are trends reflected by major revenue categories, e.g., contributions?

   b. Are trends reflected by major expense categories, e.g., salaries and fringe benefits?

10. If investments show major changes, does the Statement of Cash Flows show significant sales or purchases?

11. Were there significant purchases of property or equipment during the year?

12. Has long- and/or short-term debt significantly increased or decreased?

13. Are payroll tax payments up-to-date and always timely made?

14. Are federal, state, and local filings up-to-date, e.g., 941s, W-2s, 1099s, etc.?

15. Are any vendor accounts in over-30-day status?

Organizations desiring to meet GAAP accounting standards must reflect functional expenses (for example, by program, management and general, fundraising, and membership development) in the statement of activity or footnotes. Some organizations will also show expenses by natural classification in the statement of activity or in the footnotes. While the reporting of expenses by natural classification is not generally required under GAAP, readers of the financial statements will often find the additional reporting very helpful.

Common Nonprofit Financial Statement Errors

Statement of Financial Position

- **Omitting net assets by class.** Net assets must be categorized by unrestricted, temporarily restricted, and permanently restricted. When unrestricted net assets are subdivided into components such as net investment in plant, board-designated, and other, a total for all these components must be shown.

- **Reflecting negative balances in the temporarily restricted net asset class.** It is improper to show either a negative total of temporarily restricted net assets or a component of this net asset class, perhaps in a footnote to the financial statements. When the balance in a temporarily restricted account has been totally released, additional expenditures must be charged to the unrestricted class.

Statement of Activities

- **Reporting exchange transactions as temporarily restricted revenue.** All earned income should be reported as unrestricted revenue. Contributions with specific donor restrictions as to time or purpose and investment return relating to the investment of temporarily restricted contributions are the only types of temporarily restricted revenue.

- **Reporting fundraising events, conferences, thrift shops, etc. as a net amount.** It is appropriate to show the two gross numbers (gross proceeds of an activity, less expenses of activity—net revenue from activity) for each activity in the statement of activities. The display of the gross data is typically shown in the revenue section of the statement unless expenses exceed revenue for this activity. In this case, the display is generally shown in the expense section.

- **Failure to recognize all gifts-in-kind revenue.** Examples of revenue that should be reflected include free rent and services provided by another organization.

- **Failure to report qualifying contributed services of volunteers.** All contributed services must be recorded unless the services do not meet the recognition criteria in FASB Accounting Standards Codification 958-605-25-16 or there is no reasonable way to assign a value to the services.

- **Failure to disclose fundraising expense.** Fundraising expenses must be disclosed except in the very rare circumstances where these expenses are immaterial.

- **Failure to properly allocate expenses functionally.** Expenses must be allocated and reported functionally—e.g., program, general and administration, fundraising. Depreciation, interest, and occupancy expenses must be functionally allocated unless the amounts are immaterial.

- **Reporting expenses in either of the restricted classes of net assets.** Although losses may be reported in any class, all expenses should be reported as decreases in unrestricted net assets.

Statement of cash flows

The statement of cash flows provides information about the cash receipts and disbursements of your organization and the extent to which resources were obtained from, or used in, operating, investing, or financing activities. The direct method of presenting a cash flow statement starts by listing all sources of cash from operations during the period and deducts all operating outflows of cash to arrive at the net cash flow. The indirect method begins with the change in net assets and adjusts backwards to reconcile the change in net assets to net cash flows. The Financial Accounting Standards Board (FASB) encourages the use of the direct presentation method.

Statement of functional expenses

A statement of functional expenses provides information about the nature and amount of costs associated with each of the program services and supporting activities (administration, fundraising, etc.) carried out by the organization.

Currently, only voluntary health and welfare organizations must provide a statement of functional expenses as a basic statement. Additionally, many churches and other nonprofits find the use of the statement of functional expenses very helpful in providing information about expenses by their natural classification (e.g., salaries, rent, utilities) either in a separate statement, schedule, or in the notes to the financial statements.

New nonprofit accounting standards

The Financial Accounting Standards Board's (FASB) Accounting Standards Update (ASU) 2016-14, *Presentation of Financial Statements of Not-for-Profit Entities,* was released on August 18, 2016. The standard is effective for annual financial statements issued for fiscal years beginning after December 15, 2017 and for interim periods within fiscal years beginning after December 15, 2018.

Net asset classifications. As a result of the new standard, the three existing classes of net assets (unrestricted, temporarily restricted, and permanently restricted) will now become two:

- Net assets without donor restrictions

- Net assets with donor restrictions

To enhance readers' understanding of the donor restrictions, footnote disclosures will be required to include the timing and nature of the restrictions, as well as the composition of net assets with donor restrictions at the end of the period. The disclosures will continue to show an analysis by time, purpose, and perpetual restrictions.

Underwater endowments. As part of the change to classification of net assets, endowments that have a current fair value that is less than the original gift amount (or amount required to be retained by donor or by law), known as "underwater" endowments, will now be classified in net assets with donor restrictions, instead of the current classification in unrestricted net assets. Expanded disclosures will be required to include the following information:

- The original amount of the endowment

- The NFP's policy relating to spending from these funds

- Whether that policy was followed

Board-designated net assets. At times, an NFP's governing board may make designations or appropriations that result in self-imposed limits on the use of resources without donor restrictions, known as board-designated net assets; enhanced disclosure information will be required on the amounts and purposes of these designations. In addition, the placed-in-service approach will be required when releasing restrictions related to long-lived assets. The option to imply a time restriction and release the restriction over an asset's useful life will no longer be permitted.

Transparency and utility of liquidity information. Quantitative and qualitative information about liquidity will be required for the purpose of providing financial statement users with an understanding of an entity's exposure to risks, as well as how an entity manages its liquidity risk, and information about the availability of assets to meet cash needs for general expenditures within one year of the balance sheet (statement of financial position) date. Presenting a classified balance sheet may be an effective way for organizations to comply with many of the new disclosure requirements.

Reporting financial performance measures. Reporting the change in total net assets for the period continues to be a requirement. In addition, NFPs will also report the amount of change in each of the two classes of net assets in the statement of activities. Presenting an intermediate measure of operations is still allowable; however, disclosures will be enhanced to provide additional information about the items included or excluded from the operating measure.

Presentation of investment expenses. A net presentation of investment expenses against investment return will be required on the face of the statement of activities. External and direct internal investment expenses will be netted against the investment return. A disclosure of the components of investment expense will no longer be required.

Expenses classified by function and nature. An analysis of expenses by both function and natural classification will be required for all NFPs on a separate statement, on the face of the statement of activities, or in the footnotes. While a separate statement of functional expenses is not required, it may be the most effective presentation option for NFPs with more than one program. Investment expenses that have been netted against investment return are

> **Remember**
>
> Independence is the cornerstone of the external CPA. The independent CPA should have no ties to management and no responsibility for governance or finance. The public can place faith in the audit or review function because an independent CPA is impartial and recognizes an obligation of fairness.

not permitted to be included in that analysis. Additional disclosures will also be required regarding specific methodologies used to allocate costs among program and support functions.

Presentation for cash flow information. Under the new standard, NFPs may continue to present cash flows from operations using either the direct or indirect method. However, NFPs will no longer be required to present the indirect method reconciliation if the direct method is used. The intent of this change is to allow an organization to select the presentation method that best serves the needs of the entity, providing greater flexibility in financial reporting.

Budgeting

A budget is an effective tool for allocating financial resources and planning and controlling spending even for smaller organizations. A budget matches anticipated inflows of resources with outflows of resources. Preparing a budget requires considerable effort. It includes looking back at revenue and expense trends. Projected plans and programs must be converted into estimated dollar amounts. Too many organizations budget expenses with some degree of precision and then set the income budget at whatever it takes to cover the total expenses. This is often a disastrous approach.

Separate budgets should be prepared for all funds of an organization. Even capital and debt-retirement funds should be budgeted. The separate budgets are then combined into a unified budget.

Line-item budgets within each fund reflect the projected cost of salaries, fringe benefits, utilities, maintenance, debt retirement, and other expenses. The line-item approach is generally used by a treasurer in reporting to department heads or other responsible individuals.

Program budgets are often presented to the board of a nonprofit organization or a church's membership. In this approach, the cost of a program is reflected rather than the cost of specific line-items such as salaries or fringe benefits.

Audits and Other Related Services

An annual audit, review, or compilation of the financial statements and the disclosure of the financial statements are key components of transparency, both within a church or other nonprofit and to donors and the public. This flows directly from biblical principles: "This is the verdict: Light has come into the world, but men loved darkness instead of light because their deeds were evil. Everyone who does evil hates the light, and will not come into the light for fear that his deeds will be exposed" (John 3:19–20 NIV).

External audits, reviews, and compilations should be performed by an independent CPA who has no impairing relationship to the organization and has maximum objectivity. Internal audits are generally performed by members or those closely associated with the organization.

External services

An **audit** is a formal examination of financial statements intended to assess the accuracy and thoroughness of financial records. An independent CPA performs this procedure on a set of financial statements in order to render an opinion based on the accounting records provided. An unqualified audit opinion states that the financial statements are in conformity with accounting principles generally accepted in the United States (GAAP). Audits are performed according to auditing standards generally accepted in the United States (GAAS). An audit is more expensive than a review or compilation because an opinion on the accuracy of financial statements requires significantly more work than that involved in either a review or a compilation.

A **review** is the performance of limited procedures as a basis for expressing limited assurance on financial statements. Although not as comprehensive as an audit, a review provides some assurance compared to no assurance provided with respect to a compilation. A review report states that: (1) the accountants do not express an opinion on the financial statements, and (2) based on their review, they are not aware of any material modifications that should be made to the financial statements. A review is less expensive than an audit but more expensive than a compilation. In performing this accounting service, the accountant must conform to the American Institute of Certified Public Accountants (AICPA) Statements on Standards for Accounting and Review Services (SSARS).

SSARS requires an engagement letter for compilations; in it, clarify certain requirements and reviews in addition to allowing CPAs to disclose non-independence due to performing internal control procedures.

A **compilation** is the gathering of financial information and the creation of financial statements for an organization. A compilation involves no assurance on the financial statements, as the accountant simply assembles the financial statements for the organization. In performing this accounting service, the accountant must conform to SSARS.

Agreed-upon procedures may be appropriate when an audit, review, or compilation is not required or selected. An independent CPA is engaged to report findings on specific procedures performed on subject matter. For example, an agreed-upon procedures engagement might be performed to evaluate an organization's internal control procedures, cash handling procedures, or worker classification procedures.

A good choice for your CPA firm is one that

➤ is thoroughly knowledgeable about current accounting standards and one that understands your niche of Christ-centered nonprofits,

➤ routinely prepares value-added management letters for its audit clients,

➤ helps you minimize your fees, and

➤ understands your accounting system.

Internal audits

Members of the organization may form an audit committee to perform an internal audit to determine the validity of the financial statements. (Sample internal audit guidelines for churches are shown on pages 140–47.) If the committee takes its task seriously, the result may be significant improvements in internal control and accounting procedures. A key concept of an internal audit is to *test* transactions, not to *review* all the transactions.

Fraud

Internal controls and preventing fraud

Fraud and misuse of givers' funds in churches and nonprofits can create some of the most sensational news. When this happens, it is generally attributed to all nonprofits and churches. Sadly, this causes a diminished witness of the Gospel in the sight of skeptics.

So why don't we just eliminate the possibility of any fraud being committed? The simple answer is that we just cannot. The processes necessary to eliminate all fraud are nothing short of having a small army of employees rotating through different jobs as they separately review each transaction, with checks and balances that would bring any organization to a grinding halt. This would not be effective stewardship. Therefore, our goal should not be to eliminate all fraud but to find a reasonable balance between preventive efforts and risks.

An additional perspective in fraud prevention is to consider what happens when a staff member is subjected to inaccurate accusations of fraud. If the organization has not allowed for adequate controls in this situation, that person may be without any means to disprove the accusations, resulting in a grave injustice to the staff member of a nonprofit or a church.

ECFA has developed a site specifically on fraud awareness, recent news, and prevention at ECFA.org/Fraud.

Understanding why fraud happens

In the aftermath of a fraud discovery, the guilty party often indicates that he or she did not believe they were doing something wrong. In short, this is a result of a progression of rationalizations that has caused the person to believe they are doing something that is appropriate or that would not hurt anyone.

A situation of fraud generally occurs when there are three elements combined:

1. **A need or pressure develops.** A person has either internal or external motivation to acquire additional resources. This could include medical needs, a divorce, or even just trying to impress someone.

2. **An opportunity forms.** A person is presented with an opportunity to acquire funds or assets and they convince themselves they will not get caught. Hardly anyone commits a crime thinking that they would get caught.

3. **A rationalization is created.** A person is able to rationalize away what they are doing so they are comfortable committing the fraud. This could be a perception of being unappreciated, under-compensated, or even thinking it will be only a short-term loan.

When one or more of these three elements are present, it may be just a matter of time until a fraud is committed—the more elements present, the more likely the fraud. Of these three elements, the only one that an organization has control over is the opportunity element.

Different types of fraud

There are generally two types of fraud that are committed: those generated externally and those caused from within an organization. External fraud situations are frequently a type of Ponzi investment scheme. The organization will be offered a handsome rate of return in exchange for depositing or investing the funds with the person for a time. Other examples of external fraud can include external check manipulation, billing scams, and technology related crimes.

Internal fraud can include fraudulent use of checks, manipulation of invoices or expenses, mishandling of cash, mishandling of gifts-in-kind or other assets, misuse of organizational credit cards, and manipulation of computer systems.

As technology continues to make leaps forward, the nature and the types of fraud situations will continue to become more complex and will leverage these technologies.

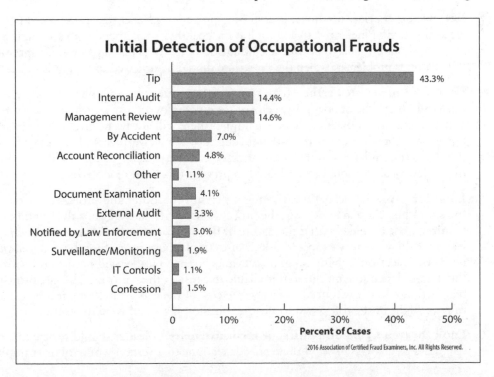

Initial Detection of Occupational Frauds

Detection Method	Percent of Cases
Tip	43.3%
Internal Audit	14.4%
Management Review	14.6%
By Accident	7.0%
Account Reconciliation	4.8%
Other	1.1%
Document Examination	4.1%
External Audit	3.3%
Notified by Law Enforcement	3.0%
Surveillance/Monitoring	1.9%
IT Controls	1.1%
Confession	1.5%

Percent of Cases

2016 Association of Certified Fraud Examiners, Inc. All Rights Reserved.

Organizations should be vigilant in keeping up with these technologies and conduct full due diligence when adopting new technologies to help prevent unknown vulnerabilities. For example, receiving funds or paying funds can exponentially increase transaction complexity and make it much more difficult to identify fraudulent transactions.

How to detect fraud

The latest report from the Association of Certified Fraud Examiners shows that merely relying on one fraud detection tool is ineffective in uncovering fraud. It also highlights the importance of equipping personnel with a means to effectively report suspicions without fear of retribution, especially when job markets may be tight.

The frequency of discovering fraud is also higher, for instance, when an organization's management has taken proactive steps to look for fraud. Management reviews of systems and transactions, internal audits, reconciliations, reviewing documentations, and other monitoring senior staff may conduct will help prevent unnecessary steps in operations as well as enhance fraud prevention and detection. It is important that an organization's leadership sets this example from the top down, rather than trivializing these important steps. Note: Looking for fraud in a public manner on a regular basis is also a good deterrent as it helps decrease the likelihood of an opportunity for fraud, since a person may believe they might get caught.

Looking for fraud can take a variety of forms, and it is helpful if this process is modified periodically to prevent them from being easily anticipated. A leader will want to

➤ **Review and check procedures.** In reviewing processes, a leader may find procedures that are antiquated or ineffective to accomplish the goal they were intended to accomplish. A leader should be able to provide a logical reason for any step in a process. If expressing this reason is problematic, then the procedure should be reviewed to see if it is necessary.

➤ **Look for uncorrected errors.** If an error goes unnoticed by anyone in an office, this could form the opportunity element for an employee, just waiting for pressure and rationalization. As long as we are human there will always be errors that occur; however, if there are errors that are not caught by a review process, this poses a bigger problem. If a leader discovers an uncorrected error, especially a substantial one, then the review process should be evaluated to prevent this from reoccurring.

➤ **Look for gaps.** As a leader is reviewing different procedures and processes, he or she should take a step back from the process and see if there are gaps that could be manipulated. It could be that the nature of the organization has changed in such a way that there are new exposure risks. For example, have procedures been developed to oversee electronic giving programs? It may be that a leader will need to prioritize these gaps depending on the staff available to assist in the controls. The key principle here is that a leader will need to review the cost of the procedure, even if it is just staff time, in light of the risk posed to the organization if a fraud were to occur.

➤ **Look for trends, abnormalities, or inconsistencies.** A leader should review inconsistencies or changes to see if there are correlations to a certain worker. For example, every time a certain pair of workers counts funds, there appears to be a drop in gifts received. These abnormalities can be elusive, but the possibility of fraud should be considered when faced with such situations.

➤ **Look for unwillingness to let others help.** It is fairly common for frauds or errors to be discovered when someone goes on leave or vacation. Frequently fraudsters will avoid being detected by preventing others from getting too close to certain information or even refuse to take vacations for fear that a fraud would be discovered. This is a good reason, among others, to consider job cross-training and mandatory vacations for employees.

How to prevent fraud

As previously discussed, one method in preventing fraud is to look for it. This step and internal controls in general should all be structured to prevent any person from developing the opportunity to commit fraud undetected.

Surveys show that weaknesses creating an opportunity for fraud mostly relate to either not having sufficient controls in place or a lack of leadership to adequately review, update, and test controls to ensure effectiveness. This equates to a double impact for organizations. First, it indicates a vulnerability to fraud opportunities. Second, it's likely that resources have been ineffectively expended in trying to prevent the fraud. It is important for leaders to continually review fraud prevention efforts and to maintain a balance between prevention and program operations. This is a process, not just a one-time event.

The importance of finding an appropriate balance between efficiency and effectiveness of fraud prevention efforts cannot be underestimated. It provides a reasonable assurance that fraud is not happening. Either too many or too few controls for an organization is not prudent management; therefore, controls an organization utilizes must be custom tailored for that organization rather than just utilizing a template. One size does not fit all. The internal control and internal audit guidelines on the following pages are just examples and should be viewed in light of your organization's needs before being adopted.

What to do when you discover fraud

If you are ever in a leadership role when fraud is discovered, it is important that you have a plan ready to keep it from spiraling out of control. Time is of the essence when dealing with a suspicion of fraud as there may be time limitations when pursuing legal recourse or recovering the funds before they or related records disappear. An organization should consider working through the following steps in a timely manner.

1. **Investigate the complaint immediately.**

2. **Report to necessary parties.**

3. **Do not use the press as your first resource.**

4. **Move swiftly to recover any stolen resources.**

5. **Consider protecting other organizations.**

Internal Control and Internal Audit Guidelines

Financial statements

➤ Are monthly financial statements prepared on a timely basis and submitted to the ministry's board?

➤ Do the financial statements include all funds (unrestricted, temporarily restricted, and permanently restricted)?

➤ Do the financial statements include a statement of financial position and statement of activity?

➤ Do the financial statements provide sufficient explanatory notes to provide context for financial data?

➤ Are account balances in the financial records reconciled with amounts presented in financial reports?

Guidelines for Handling Digital Offerings

While thefts of physical offerings are tragic, usually only the cash is lost because it is so difficult for a thief to deposit checks made out to the ministry.

But with digital gifts, there is no challenge of checks to cash—it is as simple as redirecting the flow of the digital funds and covering up the missing funds.

Gifts are flooding in through ministry's websites and other portals, as givers use debit and credit cards, ACH (Automated Clearing House) debits to their bank accounts, electronic checks, charges to their cellular accounts, and even virtual currency, using a variety of devices, including their computers, tablets, and smart phones as well as church giving kiosks.

To understand how to prevent your ministry from being a victim of digital theft, you must first understand the basics of how electronic giving is set up. There are three basic elements in establishing digital giving:

1. **Giving platform.** Typically, the ministry collects credit card information and, depending on the way it's designed, the bank account information through an online giving platform such as GivingKiosk, PushPay, and SecureGive.

   To ensure your giving platform is secure, look for SSL (Secure Sockets Layer) encryption, which establishes an encrypted link, allowing data to be transmitted securely between browsers and web servers (you'll know if you see "https" in the web address instead of just "http").

2. **Payment processor.** The giving platform is in between the giver and the payment processor (also called the merchant account provider), which processes the gift and delivers it to the ministry's financial institution. It is usually a third-party service using a system of computer processes to receive, verify, and accept or decline credit card transactions on behalf of the ministry through secure Internet connections.

3. **Giver management system.** While some giving platforms have the option of processing giving records, most churches host giving records on their own IT systems, which may or may not easily integrate with a giving platform.

Strong internal controls for digital giving include:

❐ **Building a strong, multi-person payment processor relationship.** Digital giving involves interaction with at least one outside vendor—the payment processor. Who should have the initial and ongoing interaction with this and other vendors in the digital giving process?

While one person must initially establish an account with each payment processor, multiple staff should verify the initial set-up, including a high-ranking ministry staffer.

❐ **Limit authorized changes to payment processor accounts.** After initially establishing a payment processor relationship, changes to the account routing number should be limited to high-ranking ministry staff, none of whom participate in the reconciliation of digital funds or have access to the giver management system.

❐ **Set notifications to come any time changes are made to payment processor accounts.** Each payment processor should be requested to immediately notify a high-ranking ministry leader of any change to the bank routing information.

❐ **Verify that the payment processor has internal controls in place.** How do you evaluate the quality of the internal controls employed by your payment-processing vendors? Only by insisting it has a SSAE 16 Type 2 (also commonly referred to as a SOC 1 Type 2) report issued by an independent auditing firm covering its internal controls.

❐ **Require regular payment processor transaction reports.** All payment processor transaction monthly reports should be received by a high-ranking ministry leader, in addition to a staff member more directly involved with the transactions. Use the reports to confirm the proper routing number was used.

❐ **Reconcile digital giving accounts regularly.** A high-ranking ministry official should begin each examination of digital gifts with the following reconciliations:

✓ Bank accounts to payment processor transaction reports. This reconciliation ensures that all digital gifts were deposited in the appropriate bank account.

✓ Giving records to payment processor transaction reports. This reconciliation verifies that all digital gifts are recorded in the giver management system (this is in addition to verifying that all non-digital gifts are recorded).

✓ Giving records to bank accounts. This reconciliation verifies that all digital gifts deposited into bank accounts are reflected in the giving records.

Guidelines for Handling Physical Church Offerings

❐ **Adopt policies to prevent problems.** Written policies are the ounce of prevention that could avoid serious problems at your church. Adopt a series of detailed policies that outline the procedures to be followed from the time the money goes into the offering plate—in worship services, Sunday school classes, other services, received in the mail, or delivered to the church—until the money is deposited in the bank.

❐ **Make accountability and confidentiality dual goals.** Too many churches focus so much on confidentiality that accountability takes too low a priority. True, some confidentiality is sacrificed when good accountability exists. But the church that does not balance confidentiality and accountability is treading on dangerous ground.

❐ **Use confidentiality statements.** Counters should sign a written statement of confidentiality before participating in the counting process. If the commitment of confidentiality is broken, the individual(s) should be removed from the team of counters.

❐ **Always follow the principle of two.** When a church leaves the offering in control of a single person—even for a short time period—before the count has been recorded or the uncounted offering has been dropped at the bank, it is a blatant invitation for problems. When sole access to the offering is allowed, most people will not take any money. However, for some, the temptation may be too great.

❐ **Encourage the use of offering envelopes.** Members should be encouraged to use offering envelopes. The envelopes provide a basis for recording contributions in the church's donor records.

❐ **Have counters complete offering tally sheets.** Tally sheets should be completed that separately account for loose checks and cash that were placed in offering envelopes. Checks or cash placed in blank, unidentified offering envelopes should be recorded with the loose funds. This separation of money serves as a control amount for the later posting to donor records.

❐ **Use a secure area for counting.** For safety of the counting team, confidentiality, and avoidance of interruptions, provide a secure area in which the offering can be counted. (When offerings are significant, consider providing armed security when offerings are transported to the bank.) The counters should have an adding machine, coin wrappers, offering tally sheets, and other supplies. The adding machine should have a tape (instead of a paperless calculator) so the counting team can run two matching adding machine tapes of the offering.

❐ **Deposit all offerings intact.** Offerings should always be counted and deposited intact. Depositing intact means not allowing cash in the offering to be used for the payment of church expenses or to be exchanged for other cash or a check.

If offerings are not deposited intact, an unidentified variance between the count and the deposit could occur. Additionally, if an individual is permitted to cash a check from offering funds, the church may inadvertently provide the person with a canceled check that could be used in claiming a charitable tax deduction.

❐ **Properly identify donor-restricted funds.** All donor restrictions should be carefully preserved during the counting process. These restrictions are usually noted on an offering envelope, but they can take the form of an instruction attached to a check or simply a notation on the check.

❐ **Place offerings in a secure location when they are stored in the church.** If offerings are stored in the church, even for short periods of time, the use of a secure location is important. A safe implies security, while an unlocked desk drawer connotes lack of security. But defining security is often not that easy.

Follow these steps:

✓ Use a safe with two locks.

✓ The head usher and the assist should bag the gifts and seal the bag before it is transported to the safe.

✓ Members of the same family should not transport the offering to the safe or open the safe at the same time.

✓ Require two individuals to open the safe, one with the key and the other with the combination.

✓ No one is permitted to have both the combination and the key to the safe.

✓ Change the combination at regular intervals.

✓ After placing funds in the safe, each individual must sign the safe opening log (names, date, time of opening).

Ideally, offerings are counted during or after the service, and a deposit is made as soon as possible. Alternately, the cash portion of the offering is recorded, and the uncounted offerings are immediately transported to the bank drop box by two people. When these two preferable options are not used, the offerings are generally stored at the church for a period of time on Sunday or perhaps until Monday morning. This process requires a secure storage location, preferably a safe, and highly structured controls over access to locked bank bags and the safe.

❏ **Use proper controls when dropping uncounted funds at the bank.** If your church drops uncounted offerings at the bank, several key principles should be followed:

✓ All individuals transporting funds should have a current background check on file (updated within the last two years).

✓ The funds should be placed in locked bank bags with careful control of the number of persons who have keys to the bags.

✓ Two individuals should transport the funds to the bank.

✓ Two people should pick up the funds from the bank on the next business day, count the funds, and make the deposit.

❏ **Segregate duties when recording individual contributions.** Someone other than a member of the counting team should record individual gifts in donor records. This segregation of duties reduces the possibility of misappropriation of gifts.

➤ **General**

• Are cash handling procedures in writing?

• Has the bank been notified to never cash checks payable to the organization?

• Are procedures established to care for contributions delivered or mailed during the week and on weekends?

➤ **Offering counting**

- Are at least two individuals present when contributions are counted? (The persons counting the money should not include a pastor of a church, the church treasurer, business administrator, controller, or other individuals in supervisory positions.)

- Do money counters verify that the contents of the offering envelopes are identical to the amounts written on the remittance devices (envelopes, postcards, etc.)?

- Are all checks stamped with a restrictive endorsement stamp immediately?

- Are money counters rotated so the same people are not handling the funds at all times?

- Are donor-restricted funds properly identified during the process of counting contributions?

➤ **Depositing of funds**

- Are all funds promptly deposited? Are receipt records compared with bank deposits?

- Are all contributions deposited intact? Contribution monies should not be used to pay cash expenses.

➤ **Restricted funds**

- Arc donations for restricted purposes properly recorded in the accounting records?

- Are restricted funds held for the intended purpose(s) and not spent on operating needs?

Donation records/receipting

➤ Are individual donor records kept as a basis to provide donor acknowledgments for all cash contributions and all other single contributions of $250 or more?

➤ If no goods or services (other than intangible religious benefits) were provided in exchange for a gift, does the receipt include a statement to this effect?

➤ If goods or services (other than intangible religious benefits) were provided in exchange for a gift, does the receipt

- inform the donor that the amount of the contribution that is deductible for federal income tax purposes is limited to the excess of the amount of any money and the value of any property contributed by the donor over the value of the goods and services provided by the organization, and

- provide the donor with a good-faith estimate of the value of such goods and services?

➤ Are the donations reconciled from the weekly contribution counting sheets to the donor records for a selected time period?

Cash disbursements

➤ Are all disbursements paid by check (except for minor expenditures paid through the petty cash fund)?

➤ Is written documentation available to support all disbursements?

➤ Is there an accountable reimbursement plan for expenses?

- Do employees report and substantiate expenses within 60 days of incurring the expense?

- Does the substantiation include original receipts and documentation of the time, place, amount, and purpose of expenditure?

➤ Is a petty cash fund used for disbursements of small amounts? If so, is the fund periodically reconciled and replenished based on proper documentation of the cash expenditures?

➤ If a petty cash fund is used, are vouchers prepared for each disbursement from the fund?

➤ Are prenumbered checks used? Account for all the check numbers, including voided checks.

➤ Are blank checks ever signed in advance? This should never be done.

Information reporting

➤ Has the organization filed Form 990 or received written confirmation that it is exempt from the Form 990 filing requirement?

➤ Has the organization filed Form 990-T for gross unrelated business income over $1,000 per fiscal year, if required?

➤ Were payments made to recipients (other than corporations) of at least $10 in royalties or at least $600 in rents, payments for services, prizes and awards, or medical and health care payments?

- Did the organization obtain Form W-9 for all applicable recipients and file Form 1099-MISC?

➤ Was a Form 1099-INT provided to each recipient of interest totaling $600 or more during the calendar year?

➤ If operating a preschool or private school which is not separately incorporated, did the organization file Form 5578 concerning a statement of racial nondiscrimination with the IRS?

Payroll tax reporting

➤ Does the organization withhold and pay the employee's share of FICA taxes for all nonministerial employees?

➤ Does the organization pay the employer's share of FICA taxes for all nonministerial employees?

➤ Were timely deposits of employment taxes made?

➤ Was a Form 941 filed for each quarter of the previous calendar year?

➤ Were the totals from the four quarterly Forms 941 verified with the totals on Form W-3 prepared at year-end?

➤ Was a Form W-2 given to all persons classified as employees (including ministers) by January 31?

➤ Were Form W-2 and Transmittal Form W-3 provided to the IRS for all persons classified as employees (including ministers) by February 28?

Bank statement reconciliation

➤ Are written bank reconciliations prepared on a timely basis? Test the reconciliation for the last month in the fiscal year. Trace transactions between the bank and the books for completeness and timeliness.

➤ Are there any checks that have been outstanding over three months?

➤ Are there any unusual transactions in the bank statement immediately following year-end? Obtain the bank statement for the first month after year-end directly from the bank for review by the audit committee, or obtain the last bank statement (unopened).

Savings and investment accounts

➤ Are all savings and investment accounts recorded in the financial records? Compare monthly statements to the ledger.

➤ Are earnings or losses from savings and investment accounts recorded in the ledger?

Land, buildings, and equipment records

➤ Are there detailed records of land, buildings, and equipment including date acquired, description, and cost or fair market value at date of acquisition?

➤ Was a physical count of any inventory taken at year-end?

➤ Have the property records been reconciled to the insurance coverages?

Accounts payable

➤ Is there a schedule of unpaid invoices including vendor name, invoice date, and due date?

➤ Are any of the accounts payable items significantly past due?

➤ Are there any disputes with vendors over amounts owed?

Insurance policies

➤ Has a schedule been prepared of insurance coverage in force? Does it reflect effective and expiration dates, kind and classification of coverages, maximum amounts of each coverage, premiums, and terms of payment?

➤ Is workers' compensation insurance being carried as provided by law in most states? Are all employees (and perhaps some independent contractors) covered under the workers' compensation policy?

Amortization of debt

➤ Is there a schedule of debt, such as mortgages and notes?

➤ Have the balances owed to all lenders been confirmed directly in writing?

➤ Have the balances owed to all lenders been compared to the obligations recorded on the balance sheet?

Securities and other negotiable documents

➤ Are any marketable securities or bonds owned? If so, are they kept in a safe-deposit box, and are two signatures required for access?

➤ Have the contents of the safe-deposit box been recently examined and recorded?

Credit cards

➤ Has the organization ensured that its credit card merchant processor and any related systems are secure? A security audit should be available from your processor.

➤ Are there any organization-owned credit cards?

- Is there written documentation for all uses of organization-owned credit cards?

- Has there been an independent review of the organization's use and appropriateness of all organization-owned credit cards?

- Are there any signs of personal use of organization-owned credit cards? This should be avoided. If this should happen, these amounts must be refunded to the organization or added to taxable compensation.

Copyright and licensing issues

➤ Does the organization have a policy of prohibiting the unlawful duplication or use of copyrighted works?

➤ Does the organization pay an annual fee to Christian Copyright Licensing, Inc. for the right to reproduce copyrighted music?

➤ Does the organization have a policy which prohibits the showing of rented or purchased videos without authorization of the copyright owner?

➤ Does the organization post a copyright notice at each photocopy machine?

➤ Does the organization comply with all computer software licensing agreements?

General

➤ Are federal (and state) minimum wage and overtime requirements observed for applicable employees?

➤ If overtime payments are required, has the organization taken steps to avoid paying overtime through compensatory time off?

➤ Is there a record retention policy specifying how long records should be kept?

➤ Are record retention and storage requirements formally considered at year-end?

➤ Do you know the location of the original deed of all property?

➤ Is the organization in full compliance with restrictions imposed by the deed or mortgage?

➤ Did the organization refrain from participating in (directly or indirectly) a particular candidate's political campaign for public office?

INTEGRITY*Points*

- **Handling incoming funds.** The handling of incoming funds by a church or other nonprofit organization is one of the most critical elements of the financial management process. The potential of embezzlement is often high at the point funds are received.

  Sound policies and procedures should be adopted and followed to ensure no funds are lost at the point of entry. Sound internal controls also protect the staff members or volunteers handling the funds. Pastors and ministry leaders should stay far away from handling funds.

- **Choosing an accounting method.** The choice of an accounting method has many implications. Large organizations generally use the accrual basis of accounting throughout the year and use the same approach for budgeting, while smaller organizations often utilize the cash or modified cash basis of accounting. The basis of accounting used for interim financial statements can be changed at year-end by posting a few journal entries. Reverse the entries on the first day of the subsequent accounting year, and the books are back to the previous accounting method. The following are a few of the accounting methods used:

  ○ Cash basis through the year/accrual basis at year-end.

  ○ Modified cash through the year/accrual basis at year-end.

  ○ Cash basis through the year/cash basis at year-end.

  To ensure comparative financial data, it is important that the same approach (accrual, modified cash, or cash) be used on the accounting records throughout the year as is used for budgeting purposes.

8 Charitable Gifts

While most donors care more about the reason for giving than about the potential tax implications, the spirit of giving should never be reduced by unexpected tax results.

A gift is an unconditional transfer of cash or property with no personal benefit to the donor. The mere transfer of funds to a church or charitable nonprofit is not necessarily a gift. For example, when a parent pays the college tuition for a child, there is no gift or charitable deduction despite the tax-exempt educational nature of the organization.

If payments are made to a ministry to receive something in exchange (an "exchange transaction"), the transaction is more in the nature of a purchase. The tax law states that a transfer to a nonprofit is not a contribution when made "with a reasonable expectation of financial return commensurate with the amount of the transfer." When one transfer comprises both a gift and a purchase, only the gift portion is deductible.

The two broad categories of charitable gifts are *outright* gifts and *deferred* gifts. Outright gifts require that the donor immediately transfer possession and use of the gift property to the donee. In deferred giving, the donor also makes a current gift, but the gift is of a future interest. Accordingly, actual possession and use of the gift property by the donee is deferred until the future.

Charitable contributions are deductible if given "to and for the use" of a "qualified" tax-exempt organization to be used under its control to accomplish its exempt purposes. ("Qualified" organizations are churches and other domestic 501(c)(3) organizations.)

The following are three types of gifts commonly given to churches and other nonprofit organizations:

➤ **Gifts without donor stipulations.** Contributions received without donor restriction (e.g., "use where needed most") are generally tax-deductible.

➤ **Personal gifts.** Gifts made through an organization to an individual, where the donor has specified, by name, the identity of the person who is to receive the gift, generally are not tax-deductible.

Charitable gift receipts should not be issued to a donor for personal gifts, and the organization should affirmatively advise donors that the gifts are not tax-deductible.

➤ **Donor-restricted gifts.** Donors often place temporary or permanent restrictions on gifts that limit their use to certain purposes or times. These stipulations specify a use for a contributed asset that is more specific than the broad limits relating to the nature of the organization, the environment in which it operates, and the purposes specified in its articles of incorporation or bylaws (or comparable documents for unincorporated entities). A restricted gift generally results whenever a donor selects a giving option on a response device other than "unrestricted" or "where needed most."

> **Remember**
>
> The practice by nonprofits of raising funds with the gifts preferenced for the support of certain employees of the organization is often called deputized or staff-support fundraising. The IRS acknowledges that deputized fundraising is a widespread and legitimate practice, and contributions properly raised by this method are tax-deductible (see pages 179–82).

If gifts are earmarked for a specific individual, no tax deduction is generally allowed unless the organization exercises adequate discretion and control over the funds and they are spent for program activities of the organization (see pages 176–93 for a discussion of preferred gifts).

Charitable Gift Options

Irrevocable nontrust gifts

➤ **Cash.** A gift of cash is the simplest method of giving. A cash gift is deductible within the adjusted gross income limitations, depending on the type of the recipient organization. Generally the 50% limit applies; for gifts to certain types of organizations, the limit is 30%.

➤ **Securities.** The contribution deduction for stocks and bonds held long-term (12 months or more) is the mean between the highest and lowest selling prices on the date of the gift where there is a market for listed securities. The contribution deduction is limited to cost for securities held short-term.

Example: An individual taxpayer plans to make a gift of $50,000 to a college. To provide the capital, the taxpayer planned to sell stock that had cost $20,000 some years earlier, yielding a long-term capital gain of $30,000. The taxpayer decides to donate the stock instead of donating the proceeds of the sale. The taxpayer qualifies for a contribution deduction of $50,000, and the unrealized gain on the stock is not taxable.

➤ **Real estate.** The contribution deduction for a gift of real estate is based on the fair market value on the date of the gift. If there is a mortgage on the property, the value must be reduced by the amount of the debt.

➤ **Life insurance.** The owner of a life insurance policy may choose to give it to a charitable organization. The deduction may equal one of the following: the cash surrender value of the policy, its replacement value, its tax basis, or its "interpolated terminal reserve" value (a value slightly more than cash surrender value). The deduction cannot exceed the donor's tax basis in the policy.

➤ **Bargain sale.** A bargain sale is part donation and part sale. It is a sale of property in which the amount of the sale proceeds is less than the property's fair market value. The excess of the fair market value of the property over the sales price represents a charitable contribution to the organization. Generally, each part of a bargain sale is a reportable event, so the donor reports both a sale and a contribution.

➤ **Remainder interest in a personal residence or life estate.** A charitable contribution of the remainder interest in a personal residence (including a vacation home) or farm creates an income tax deduction equal to the present value of that future interest.

➤ **Charitable gift annuity.** With a charitable gift annuity, the donor purchases an annuity contract from a charitable organization for more than its fair value. This difference in values between what the donor could have obtained and what the donor actually obtained represents a charitable contribution. The contribution is tax-deductible in the year the donor purchases the annuity.

Idea

The American Council on Gift Annuities suggests charitable gift annuity rates for use by charities and their donors. The latest are available at www.acga-web.org.

➤ **Donor-advised funds.** Donor-advised gifts may be made to a donor-advised fund (DAF). A DAF is defined as a fund or account that is separately identified by reference to contributions of a donor or donors, is owned and controlled by a charitable sponsoring organization, and to which a donor (or any person appointed or designated by the donor) has advisory privileges with respect to the distribution or investment of amounts in the fund.

A donor makes an irrevocable contribution of cash and/or securities to the separate fund or account. The donor is eligible for a tax deduction at the time of the contribution to the DAF even though the DAF may distribute the funds to one or more charities in a subsequent tax year. The donor makes recommendations to the trustees for grants to be made out of his or her separate fund with the DAF. The representatives of the DAF then review these recommended grants to verify whether the target organization is a qualified charity.

The right of a donor to make recommendations to the trustees of a DAF generally does not constitute a restricted gift. However, if a gift to a DAF is restricted by the donor as to purpose or time, with the right to make recommendations as to the eventual charitable recipient(s) of the funds, this gift is temporarily or permanently restricted, based on the nature of the restriction.

Irrevocable gifts in trust

➤ **Charitable remainder annuity trust.** With an annuity trust, the donor retains the right to a specified annuity amount for a fixed period or the lifetime of the designated income beneficiary. The donor fixes the amount payable by an annuity trust at the inception of the trust.

➤ **Charitable remainder unitrust.** The unitrust and annuity trust are very similar with two important differences: (1) the unitrust payout rate is applied to the fair market value of the net trust assets, determined annually, to establish the distributable amount each year, as contrasted to a fixed payment with an annuity trust, and
(2) additional contributions may be made to a unitrust compared to one-time gifts allowable to annuity trusts.

Idea

To set up a charitable remainder trust, a donor places cash or certain assets—such as publicly traded securities or unmortgaged real estate—in a trust that will ultimately benefit a charity. The donor collects payments from the trust and gets an immediate income tax deduction. Before accepting the administration of a charitable remainder trust, a charity should determine if it has the resources to properly administer the trust.

➤ **Charitable lead trust.** The charitable lead trust is the reverse of the charitable remainder trust. The donor transfers property into a trust, creating an income interest in the property in favor of the charitable organization for a period of years or for the life or lives of an individual or individuals. The remainder interest is either returned to the donor or given to a noncharitable beneficiary (usually a family member).

➤ **Pooled income fund.** A pooled income fund consists of separate contributions of property from numerous donors. A pooled income fund's payout to its income beneficiaries is not a fixed percentage. The rate of return that the fund earns each year determines the annual payout.

Revocable gifts

➤ **Trust savings accounts.** A trust savings account may be established at a bank, credit union, or savings and loan. The account is placed in the name of the depositor "in trust for" a beneficiary, a person, or organization other than the depositor.

The depositor retains full ownership and control of the account. The beneficiary receives the money in the account either when the depositor dies or when the depositor turns over the passbook.

➤ **Insurance and retirement plan proceeds.** A nonprofit organization may be named the beneficiary of an insurance policy or retirement plan. The owner of the policy or retirement plan completes a form naming the nonprofit as the beneficiary, and the policy or plan provider accepts the form in writing. The gift may be for part or all of the proceeds.

➤ **Bequests.** By a specific bequest, an individual may direct that, at death, a charity shall receive either a specified dollar amount or specific property. Through a residuary bequest, an individual may give to charity the estate portion remaining after the payment of other bequests, debts, taxes, and expenses.

Percentage Limitations

Charitable deductions for a particular tax year are limited as follows:

➤ Gifts of cash and ordinary income property to public charities and all private operating foundations and certain private foundations are limited to 50% of adjusted gross income (AGI). Any excess may generally be carried forward up to five years.

➤ Gifts of long-term (held 12 months or more) capital gain property to public charities and private operating foundations are limited to 30% of AGI. The same five-year carry-forward is possible.

➤ Donors of capital gain property to public charities and private operating foundations may use the 50% limitation, instead of the 30% limitation, where the amount of the contribution is reduced by all the unrealized appreciation (nontaxed gain) in the value of the property.

➤ Gifts of cash, short-term (held less than 12 months) capital gain property, and ordinary income property to private foundations and certain other charitable donees (other than public charities and private operating foundations) are generally limited to the item's cost basis and 30% of AGI. The carry-forward rules apply to these gifts.

➤ Gifts of long-term (held 12 months or more) capital gain property to private foundations and other charitable donees (other than public charities and private operating foundations) are generally limited to 20% of AGI. There is no carry-forward for these gifts.

➤ Charitable contribution deductions by corporations in any tax year may not exceed 10% of pre-tax net income (taxable income). Excess contributions may be carried forward up to five years.

Gifts That May Not Qualify as Contributions

Some types of gifts do not result in a tax deduction, and no contribution acknowledgment should be provided by the charity in certain situations:

➤ **Earmarked gifts.** When computing one's tax return, most taxpayers know that they cannot count tuition payments as a charitable deduction, even though the check is made out to a charity. In addition, most taxpayers know that their tuition payments are still not deductible if they are paid to a charity with instructions to forward the funds to a certain educational institution. Unfortunately, far too few donors and charities apply the same logic to other similar circumstances.

Some earmarked gifts may qualify for a charitable gift deduction, e.g., a gift earmarked for the building fund. However, other earmarked gifts generally do not meet the requirements of a charitable gift. Here are some examples:

"I realize they have no connection with your ministry, but if I give the ministry $500, will you pass it through to them and give me a charitable receipt?"

"I want to give $10,000 to the ministry so the funds can be passed on to a college to cover the tuition for the pastor's daughter. Will the charity process this gift and give me a receipt?"

Examples like these are donations "earmarked" for individuals. They are also called "conduit" or "pass-through" transactions. These connotations are negative references when used by the IRS and generally denote amounts that do not qualify for a charitable deduction. To be deductible, the charity must have discretion and control over the contribution without any obligation to benefit a designated individual.

> ### Warning
>
> Gifts restricted for projects by donors qualify for a charitable deduction. Gifts preferenced for support under the deputized fundraising concept (see pages 176–80) may qualify for a charitable deduction. But when a donor places too many restrictions on a gift, especially when the donor wants the gift to personally benefit a certain individual, it often does not qualify for a charitable deduction.

A telltale sign of an earmarked gift is when someone says they want to "run a gift through the ministry," "pass a gift through the ministry," or "process a gift through the ministry." Of course, it is possible the donor will not so clearly signal an earmarked gift and use more general terminology. This is why charities should clearly understand the concept of earmarked gifts in addition to an awareness of telltale terminology.

Though the concept in tax law is well-established, it can be hard to apply to specific situations. Several issues may impact the complexities of these gifts:

☐ The donor's motivation may be loving and charitable in a broad sense; they really want to help, and the only problem is their desire for control.

☐ Many organizations are lax in monitoring this area, and the donor may well say, "If your charity won't process this gift for me, I know of another charity that will handle it."

☐ Sometimes the difference between a nondeductible earmarked gift and a deductible restricted gift is not who benefits but only who determines the beneficiary.

However, wise charity leaders will establish and follow clear policies to prohibit donors from passing money through a charity simply to gain a tax benefit.

Though many charitable donations are based on a sense of charity, selflessness, and even love, the IRS believes that people may also have other motivations. The law prevents donors from having undue influence over charities and restricts donors from manipulating a charity into serving noncharitable interests and themselves receiving a deduction for it at the same time.

A special category of earmarked gifts is one in which a donor passes a gift through the charity for the donor's personal benefit. Such gifts often raise issues beyond the loss of a charitable deduction. Examples include

☐ Scholarship gifts passed through a charity for the donor's children (instead of paying tuition) raise allegations of tax fraud.

☐ Gifts by a donor to purchase life insurance on the donor benefiting the donor's family resulted in a law which can cause substantial penalties for both the donor and organization.

Gifts to a church or nonprofit for the support of missionaries or other workers (often called "deputized fundraising") are subject to a different set of guidelines than those generally associated with earmarked gifts. Gifts made under a properly structured deputized fundraising program are generally tax-deductible to the donor (see pages 179–93).

➤ **Strings attached.** A gift must generally be complete and irrevocable to qualify for a charitable deduction. There is usually no charitable deduction if the donor leaves "strings attached" that can be pulled later to bring the gift back to the donor or remove it from the control of the charity.

Example: A donor makes a "gift" of $10,000 to a church. The "gift" is followed or preceded by the sale from the church to the donor of an asset valued at $25,000 for $15,000. In this instance, the $10,000 gift does not qualify as a charitable contribution. It also raises the issue of private inurement relating to the sale by the church.

➤ **Services.** No deduction is allowed for the contribution of services to a charity.

> **Example:** A carpenter donates two months of labor on the construction of a new facility built by your church. The carpenter is not eligible for a charitable deduction for the donation of his time. The carpenter is entitled to a charitable deduction for any donated out-of-pocket expenses including mileage (14 cents per mile for 2016) for driving to and from the project. If the donated out-of-pocket expenses are $250 or more in a calendar year, the carpenter will need an acknowledgment from the church to substantiate the charitable deduction (see page 201 for a sample letter).

Warning

When a person makes a gift of services to a charity, it may be the highest gift that can be made—a gift of one's talents. However, the gift of services does not qualify for a charitable deduction, and it should never be receipted by the charity—only express appreciation. Out-of-pocket expenses related to the gift of services qualify as a charitable gift.

➤ **Use of property.** The gift of the right to use property does not yield a tax deduction to the donor.

> **Example:** A donor provides a church with the rent-free use of an automobile for a year. No charitable deduction is available to the donor for the value of that use. If the donor paid the taxes, insurance, repairs, gas, or oil for the vehicle while it was used by the church, these items are deductible as a charitable contribution based on their cost.

Charitable Gift Timing

A charitable gift is considered made on the date of delivery. This date is important because it determines the tax year in which the gift is deductible, the valuation date, when applicable, and the date for determining whether the gift qualifies for short-term or long-term property, when applicable.

➤ **Checks.** Under the "delivered-when-mailed" rule, if a donor mails a contribution check to a nonprofit organization, the date of the mailing is deemed the date of delivery, if there are no restrictions on the time or manner of payment and the check is honored when presented.

There are two exceptions:

☐ **Postdated checks.** The date of mailing will not make any difference if the check is postdated. A postdated check is not an immediately payable contribution, but it is a promise to pay on the date shown.

☐ **Checks that bounce.** Generally, if a check is dishonored for insufficient funds, the gift will not be deemed to have been made when it was mailed or delivered.

Normally, the date on a U.S. Mail postmark will conclusively establish the date of mailing. A postage meter date may not be sufficient to establish the date of delivery for a gift that is mailed. The "delivered-when-mailed" rule applies to delivery by the U.S. Postal Service, not to private couriers.

Example 1: A donor mails a check with a postmark of December 31, 2016. The charity does not receive the check until January 7, 2017. The charity deposits the check in its bank on January 7, and it clears the donor's bank on January 10. The gift is deductible by the donor in 2016.

Example 2: A donor delivers a check to the charity on December 31, 2016. The donor asks that the check be held for three months. Complying with the donor's request, the charity deposits the check on March 31, 2017. This gift is deductible by the donor in 2016.

Example 3: A donor delivers a check to the charity on January 5, 2017. The check is dated December 31, 2016. The gift is deductible by the donor in 2017.

➤ **Credit cards.** A contribution charged to a credit card is deductible by the donor when the charge is made, even though the credit card charge is not paid until the next year.

➤ **Internet donations.** Donors may instruct their banks via phone, mobile devices, or the Internet to pay contributions to your church or charity. If a donor uses this method to make a donation, it is deductible at the time payment is made by the bank.

IRS Publication 526 (Charitable Contributions) does not provide specific guidance on electronic funds transfers (EFTs) via the Internet or mobile devices. It says "pay-by-phone" arrangements are not deductible when the donor directs the payment but later when the payment is made by the financial institution.

➤ **Pledges.** A pledge is not deductible until payment or other satisfaction of the pledge is made.

➤ **Securities.** A contribution of stock is completed upon the unconditional delivery of a properly endorsed stock certificate to your charity or its agent. If the stock is mailed and is received by the charity or its agent in the ordinary course of the mail, the gift is effective on the date of mailing. If the donor delivers a stock certificate to the issuing corporation or to the donor's broker for transfer to the name of the charity, the contribution is not completed until the stock is actually transferred on the corporation's books.

➤ **Real estate.** A gift of real estate is deductible at the time a properly executed deed is delivered to the charity.

Acknowledging and Reporting Charitable Gifts

Contributors to your church or nonprofit seeking a federal income tax charitable contribution deduction must produce, if asked, a written receipt from the organization for all gifts of cash and other single contributions valued at $250 or more. Strictly speaking, the burden of compliance with the $250 or more rule falls on the donor. In reality, the burden and administrative costs fall on the organization, not the donor.

The IRS can fine a church or nonprofit that deliberately issues a false acknowledgment to a contributor. The fine is up to $1,000 if the donor is an individual and $10,000 if the donor is a corporation.

➤ **Information to be included in the acknowledgment.** The following information must be included in the gift receipt:

☐ the donor's name,

☐ if cash, the amount of cash contributed,

☐ if property, a description, but not the value of the property (if the gift is an auto, boat, or airplane, the charity must generally provide Form 1098-C to the donor—see pages 168–70 for a more detailed discussion),

> **Idea**
>
> Donors are only required to have receipts for single gifts of $250 or more (receipts are required for cash gifts of any amount). Churches often issue gift acknowledgments on a quarterly, semiannual, or annual basis. However, most parachurch ministries issue receipts for every gift, regardless of the amount.

☐ a statement explaining whether the charity provided any goods or services to the donor in exchange for the contribution,

☐ if goods or services were provided to the donor, a description and good-faith estimate of their value and a statement that the donor's charitable deduction is limited to the amount of the payment in excess of that value, and if services were provided consisting solely of intangible religious benefits, a statement to that effect,

☐ if no goods or services were provided to the donor, the acknowledgment must state so,

☐ the date the donation was made, and

☐ the date the acknowledgment was issued.

➤ **When acknowledgments should be issued.** Donors must obtain their receipts no later than the due date, plus any extension, of their federal income tax return or the date the return was filed, whichever date is earlier. If a donor obtains the acknowledgment after this date, the gift does not qualify for a contribution deduction even on an amended return.

Sample Charitable Gift Acknowledgment

Acknowledgment #1

Received from: Howard K. Auburn

Cash received as an absolute gift:

Date Cash Received	Amount Received
1/2/16	$250.00
1/16/16	50.00
3/13/16	300.00
3/27/16	100.00
6/12/16	500.00
7/10/16	150.00
8/21/16	200.00
10/16/16	400.00
11/20/16	350.00
	$2,300.00

Any goods or services you may have received in connection with this gift were solely intangible religious benefits.

(*Note:* It is very important for a religious organization to use wording of this nature when no goods or services were given in exchange for the gift.)

This document is necessary for any available federal income tax deduction for your contribution. Please retain it for your records.

Acknowledgment issued on: January 10, 2017

Acknowledgment issued by: Harold Morrison, Treasurer
Castleview Church
1008 High Drive
Dover, DE 19901

1. This sample acknowledgment is based on the following assumptions:
    A. No goods or services were provided in exchange for the gifts other than intangible religious benefits.
    B. The acknowledgment is issued on a periodic or annual basis for all gifts whether over or under $250.
2. All acknowledgments should be numbered consecutively for control and accounting purposes.

Sample Letter to Noncash Donors

**Charitable Gift Acknowledgment for Noncash Gifts
(other than for autos, boats, or airplanes)**

Noncash Acknowledgment #1
(All acknowledgments should be
numbered consecutively for control
and accounting purposes.)

RETAIN FOR INCOME TAX PURPOSES

Donor's name and address

Date Acknowledgment Issued

Thank you for your noncash gift as follows:
    Date of gift:
    Description of gift:
    (Note: No value is shown for the gift. Valuation is the responsibility of the donor.)

To substantiate your gift for IRS purposes, the tax law requires that this acknowledgment state whether you have received any goods or services in exchange for the gift. You have received no such goods or services. (***Note:*** If goods or services were provided to the donor, replace the previous sentence with: In return for your contribution, you have received the following goods or services ___ (description) , which we value at _(good-faith estimate)_. The value of the goods and services you received must be deducted from the value of your contribution to determine your charitable deduction.)

If your noncash gifts for the year total more than $500, you must include Form 8283 (a copy of Form 8283 and its instructions are enclosed for your convenience) with your income tax return. Section A is used to report gifts valued at $5,000 or under. You can complete Section A on your own. When the value of the gift is more than $5,000, you will need to have the property appraised. The appraiser's findings are reported in Section B of Form 8283. The rules also apply if you give "similar items of property" with a total value above $5,000—even if you gave the items to different charities. Section B of Form 8283 must be signed by the appraiser. It is essential to attach the form to your tax return.

You might want an appraisal (even if your gift does not require one) in case you have to convince the IRS of the property's worth. You never need an appraisal or an appraisal summary for gifts of publicly traded securities, even if their total value exceeds $5,000. You must report those gifts (when the value is more than $500) by completing Section A of Form 8283 and attaching it to your return.

For gifts of closely held stock, an appraisal is not required if the value of the stock is under $10,000, but part of the appraisal summary form must be completed if the value is over $5,000. If the gift is valued over $10,000, then both an appraisal and an appraisal summary form are required.

If we receive a gift of property subject to the appraisal summary rules, we must report to both the IRS and you if we dispose of the gift within three years.

Again, we are grateful for your generous contribution. Please let us know if we can give you and your advisors more information about the IRS's reporting requirements.

Your Nonprofit Organization

If a charity issues acknowledgments on an annual basis, it is helpful to provide them to donors at least by January 31 each year, and earlier in January if possible. This will assist your donors in gathering the necessary data for tax return preparation.

Form 1098-C must be provided within 30 days after the date that a donated auto, boat, or airplane is sold by the ministry or within 30 days of the donation date if the charity keeps the property.

➤ **Frequency of issuing acknowledgments.** The receipts or acknowledgments can be issued gift-by-gift, monthly, quarterly, annually, or any other frequency. For ease of administration and clear communication with donors, many charities provide an acknowledgment for all gifts, whether more or less than $250.

➤ **Form of acknowledgments.** No specific design of a charitable gift receipt is required, except for Form 1098-C, used for gifts of autos, boats, or airplanes. The IRS has not issued any pro forma acknowledgments.

An acknowledgment may be in hard-copy or electronic form. An acknowledgment can be issued as a letter, e-mail, or as an attachment to an e-mail. Additionally, a gift acknowledgment may be downloaded from the ministry's website. There is no requirement for the acknowledgment to be signed. There is also no requirement to include the donor's social security number. Although the IRS has not issued any guidance requiring the ministry's Employer Identification Number (EIN) to be included on gift acknowledgments, there are reported instances for the IRS requiring EINs.

➤ **Separate gifts of less than $250.** If a donor makes separate gifts by check during a calendar year of less than $250, there is no acknowledgment requirement since each gift is a separate contribution below the $250 threshold. The donor's canceled check will provide sufficient substantiation. However, many charities provide a year-end gift summary, including all gifts regardless if each gift is under or over $250.

➤ **Donations payable to another charity.** A church member may place a check in the offering plate of $250 or more payable to a missions organization, unrelated to the church, intended to support the work of a particular missionary serving with the mission. No acknowledgment is required by the church. Since the check was payable to the missions agency, that entity will need to issue the acknowledgment to the donor for claiming the gift as a charitable contribution.

➤ **Donor's out-of-pocket expenses.** Volunteers may incur out-of-pocket expenses on behalf of your church or nonprofit. Substantiation from your organization is required if a volunteer claims a deduction for unreimbursed expenses of $250 or more. However, the IRS acknowledges that the church or nonprofit may be unaware of the details of the expenses or the dates on which they were incurred. Therefore, the organization must substantiate only the types of services performed by the volunteer which relate to out-of-pocket expenses.

➤ **Individuals.** Gifts made by a taxpayer to poor or needy individuals or to employees of a ministry, instead of to or for a ministry, generally do not qualify as charitable contributions and are not the basis for a gift acknowledgment.

➤ **Foreign organizations.** It may be inappropriate to accept gifts restricted for a foreign charity even if the charitable purposes of the foreign charity are consistent with the purposes of the U.S. charity.

> **Example 1:** An individual offers to make a $5,000 donation to a charity restricted for the Sri Lanka Relief Outreach for its relief and development purposes, a foreign charity. While the ministry provides funding for various foreign missionary endeavors, it has no connection with the Sri Lanka Relief Outreach and has no practical way to provide due diligence in relation to a gift to this entity. Based on these facts, the gift has the characteristics of a pass-through gift. The funds should generally not be accepted by the charity.

> **Example 2:** Same fact pattern as in Example 1, except the charity regularly sponsors short-term mission trips to Sri Lanka and provides funds to the Sri Lanka Relief Outreach, based on the due diligence performed by the charity's staff and volunteers on mission trips with respect to this particular foreign entity. Based on these facts, the charity is generally in a sound position to make a gift of $5,000 to the Sri Lanka-based charity as requested by the donor and provide a charitable receipt for the gift.

Since gifts by U.S. taxpayers to a foreign charity do not produce a charitable deduction, donors may try to convince a charity to accept a gift restricted for a certain foreign charity and pass it through to the entity. When a domestic charity is no more than an agent of, or trustee for, a particular foreign organization, or has purposes so narrow that its funds can go only to a particular foreign organization, or solicits funds on behalf of a particular foreign organization, the deductibility of gifts may be questioned by the IRS.

There are some acceptable situations where a U.S. charity may receive gifts for which a deduction is allowed with the money used abroad:

☐ The money may be used by the U.S. charity directly for projects that it selects to carry out its own exempt purposes. In this instance, the domestic organization would generally have operations in one or more foreign countries functioning directly under the U.S. entity. The responsibility of the donee organization ends when the purpose of the gift is fulfilled. A system of narrative and financial reports is necessary to document what was accomplished by the gift.

☐ It may create a subsidiary organization in a foreign country to facilitate its exempt operations there, with certain of its funds transmitted directly to the subsidiary. In this instance, the foreign organization is merely an administrative arm of the U.S. organization, with the U.S. organization considered the real recipient of the contributions. The responsibility of the U.S. organization ends when the purpose of the gift is fulfilled by the foreign subsidiary.

☐ It may make grants to charities in a foreign country in furtherance of its exempt purposes, following review and approval of the uses to which the funds are to be put. The responsibility of the U.S. organization ends when the purpose of the gift is fulfilled by the foreign organization. A narrative and financial report from the foreign organization will usually be necessary to document the fulfillment of the gift.

☐ It may transfer monies to another domestic entity with the second organization fulfilling the purpose of the gift. The responsibility of the first entity usually ends when the funds are transferred to the second organization.

The tax law is clear that money given to an intermediary charity but earmarked for an ultimate recipient is considered as if it has been given directly to the ultimate recipient. It is earmarked if there is an understanding, written or oral, whereby the donor binds the intermediary charity to transfer the funds to the ultimate recipient. The tax law does not allow donors to accomplish indirectly through a conduit (an intermediary charity) what the donor cannot accomplish directly.

➤ **Contingencies.** If a contribution will not be effective until the occurrence of a certain event, an income tax charitable deduction generally is not allowable until the occurrence of the event. Thus, a charitable gift acknowledgment should not be issued until the event has occurred.

> **Example:** A donor makes a gift to a college to fund a new education program that the college does not presently offer and is not contemplating. The donation would not be deductible until the college agrees to the conditions of the gift.

➤ **Charitable remainders in personal residences and farms.** The charitable gift regulations are silent on the substantiation rules for remainder interests in personal residences and farms (a life estate). It should be assumed that the $250 substantiation rules apply to those gifts unless the IRS provides other guidance.

➤ **Charitable trusts.** The $250 substantiation rules do not apply to charitable remainder trusts and charitable lead trusts.

➤ **Gift annuities.** When the gift portion of a gift annuity or a deferred payment gift annuity is $250 or more, a donor must have an acknowledgment from the church or nonprofit stating whether any goods or services—in addition to the annuity—were provided to the donor. If no goods or services were provided, the acknowledgment must so state. The acknowledgment need not include a good-faith estimate of the annuity's value.

➤ **Pooled income funds.** The substantiation rules apply to pooled income funds. To deduct a gift of a remainder interest of $250 or more, a donor must have an acknowledgment from the charity.

In addition to gifts of autos, boats, and airplanes (see pages 168–70), certain gifts require IRS reporting, or execution of a form that the donor files with the IRS:

➤ **Noncash gifts in excess of $500.** Noncash gifts in excess of $500 require the completion of certain information on page 1 of Form 8283. For gifts between $500 and $5,000, there is no requirement of an appraisal or signature of the charity.

➤ **Noncash gifts in excess of $5,000.** Additional substantiation requirements apply to contributions of property (other than money and publicly traded securities) if the total claimed or reported value of the property is more than $5,000. For these gifts, the donor must obtain a qualified appraisal and attach an appraisal summary to the return on which the deduction is claimed. There is an exception for nonpublicly traded stock. If the claimed value of the stock does not exceed $10,000, the donor does not have to obtain an appraisal by a qualified appraiser.

The appraisal summary must be on Form 8283, signed and dated by the charity and the appraiser, and attached to the donor's return. The signature by the charity does not represent concurrence in the appraised value of the noncash gifts.

If Form 8283 is required, it is the donor's responsibility to file it. The charity is under no responsibility to see that donors file this form or that it is properly completed. However, advising donors of their obligations and providing them with the form can produce donor goodwill.

➤ **Charity reporting for contributed property.** If a noncash gift requiring an appraisal summary on Form 8283 is sold, exchanged, or otherwise disposed of by the charity within three years after the date of the contribution, the charity must file Form 8282 with the IRS within 125 days of the disposition of the asset.

This form provides detailed information on the gift and the disposal of the property. A copy of the form must be provided to the donor and retained by the charity. A charity that receives a charitable contribution valued at more than $5,000 from a corporation generally does not have to complete Form 8283.

> ### Caution
>
> The IRS places certain reporting requirements on donors and charities with respect to many property gifts. They are looking for property valued at one amount on the date of the gift and sold by the charity for much less. Charities should never place a value on a gift of property. This is the responsibility of the donor.

A letter or other written communication from a charity acknowledging receipt of the property and showing the name of the donor, the date and location of the contribution, and a detailed description of the property is an acceptable contribution receipt for a gift of property.

There is no requirement to include the value of contributed property on the receipt. A tension often surrounds a significant gift of property because the donor may request the charity to include an excessively high value on the charitable receipt. It is wise for the charity to remain impartial in the matter and simply acknowledge the property by description and condition while excluding a dollar amount.

Left panel — Form 8282 (Page 1)

Form 8282
(Rev. April 2009)
Department of the Treasury
Internal Revenue Service

Donee Information Return
(Sale, Exchange, or Other Disposition of Donated Property)

▶ See instructions.

OMB No. 1545-0908

Give a Copy to Donor

Parts To Complete
• If the organization is an *original donee*, complete *Identifying Information*, Part I (lines 1a–1d and, if applicable, lines 2a–2d), and Part III.
• If the organization is a *successor donee*, complete *Identifying Information*, Part I, Part II, and Part III.

Identifying Information

Print or Type

Name of charitable organization (donee)
Oneonta First Church

Employer identification number
35 : 4829942

Address (number, street, and room or suite no.) (or P.O. box no. if mail is not delivered to the street address)
292 River Street

City or town, state, and ZIP code
Oneonta, NY 13820

Part I Information on ORIGINAL DONOR and SUCCESSOR DONEE Receiving the Property

1a Name of original donor of the property
Keith E. Chapman

1b Identifying number(s)
512-40-8076

1c Address (number, street, and room or suite no.) (P.O. box no. if mail is not delivered to the street address)
504 Church Street

1d City or town, state, and ZIP code
Solvay, NY 13209

Note. Complete lines 2a–2d only if the organization gave this property to another charitable organization (successor donee).

2a Name of charitable organization

2b Employer identification number

2c Address (number, street, and room or suite no.) (or P.O. box no. if mail is not delivered to the street address)

2d City or town, state, and ZIP code

Part II Information on PREVIOUS DONEES. Complete this part only if the organization was not the first donee to receive the property. See the instructions before completing lines 3a through 4d.

3a Name of original donee

3b Employer identification number

3c Address (number, street, and room or suite no.) (or P.O. box no. if mail is not delivered to the street address)

3d City or town, state, and ZIP code

4a Name of preceding donee

4b Employer identification number

4c Address (number, street, and room or suite no.) (or P.O. box no. if mail is not delivered to the street address)

4d City or town, state, and ZIP code

For Paperwork Reduction Act Notice, see page 4.   Cat. No. 62307Y   Form **8282** (Rev. 4-200)

Right panel — Form 8282 (Page 2)

Form 8282 (Rev. 4-2009)   Page **2**

Part III Information on DONATED PROPERTY

	1. Description of the donated property sold, exchanged, or otherwise disposed of and how the organization used the property. (If you need more space, attach a separate statement)	2. Did the disposition involve the organization's entire interest in the property?		3. Was the use related to the organization's exempt purpose or function?		4. Information on use of property. • If you answered "Yes" to question 3 and the property was tangible personal property, describe how the organization's use of the property furthered its exempt purpose or function. Also complete Part IV below. • If you answered "No" to question 3 and the property was tangible personal property, describe the organization's intended use (if any) at the time of the contribution. Also complete Part IV below, if the intended use at the time of the contribution was related to the organization's exempt purpose or function and it became impossible or infeasible to implement.
		Yes	No	Yes	No	
A	Real estate/Vacant lot, 82 White St. Oneonta, NY	X			X	
B						
C						
D						

Donated Property

		A	B	C	D
5	Date the organization received the donated property (MM/DD/YY)	9 / 1 / 16	/ /	/ /	/ /
6	Date the original donee received the property (MM/DD/YY)	/ /	/ /	/ /	/ /
7	Date the property was sold, exchanged, or otherwise disposed of (MM/DD/YY)	11 / 10 / 16	/ /	/ /	/ /
8	Amount received upon disposition	$ 3,780	$	$	$

Part IV Certification

You must sign the certification below if any property described in Part III above is tangible personal property and:
• You answered "Yes" to question 3 above, or
• You answered "No" to question 3 above and the intended use of the property became impossible or infeasible to implement.

Under penalties of perjury and the penalty under section 6720B, I certify that either: (1) the use of the property that meets the above requirements, and is described above in Part III, was substantial and related to the donee organization's exempt purpose or function; or (2) the donee organization intended to use the property for its exempt purpose or function, but the intended use has become impossible or infeasible to implement.

▶ _(signature)_ ___ Treasurer ___ 12/1/16
Signature of officer   Title   Date

Under penalties of perjury, I declare that I have examined this return, including accompanying schedules and statements, and to the best of my knowledge and belief, it is true, correct, and complete.

Sign Here

▶ _____ _____ _____
Signature of officer   Title   Date

Type or print name

Form **8282** (Rev. 4-2009)

Bottom caption

This form must generally be filed by a charity if it disposes of charitable deduction property within three years of the date the original donee received it and the items are valued at $500 or more.

Form **8283**	**Noncash Charitable Contributions**	OMB No. 1545-0908
(Rev. December 2014) Department of the Treasury Internal Revenue Service	▶ Attach to your tax return if you claimed a total deduction of over $500 for all contributed property. ▶ Information about Form 8283 and its separate instructions is at *www.irs.gov/form8283*.	Attachment Sequence No. **155**

Name(s) shown on your income tax return	Identifying number
Mark A. and Joan E. Murphy	392-83-1982

Note. Figure the amount of your contribution deduction before completing this form. See your tax return instructions.

Section A. Donated Property of $5,000 or Less and Publicly Traded Securities—List in this section **only** items (or groups of similar items) for which you claimed a deduction of $5,000 or less. Also list publicly traded securities even if the deduction is more than $5,000 (see instructions).

Part I **Information on Donated Property**—If you need more space, attach a statement.

1	(a) Name and address of the donee organization	(b) If donated property is a vehicle (see instructions), check the box. Also enter the vehicle identification number (unless Form 1098-C is attached).	(c) Description of donated property (For a vehicle, enter the year, make, model, and mileage. For securities, enter the company name and the number of shares.)
A	Endless Mountain Church 561 Maple, Rochester, NY 14623	☐	Used bedroom furniture
B		☐	
C		☐	
D		☐	
E		☐	

Note. If the amount you claimed as a deduction for an item is $500 or less, you do not have to complete columns (e), (f), and (g).

	(d) Date of the contribution	(e) Date acquired by donor (mo., yr.)	(f) How acquired by donor	(g) Donor's cost or adjusted basis	(h) Fair market value (see instructions)	(i) Method used to determine the fair market value
A	10/1/16	4/00	Purchased	3,400	750	Sales of comparable used furniture
B						
C						
D						
E						

Part II **Partial Interests and Restricted Use Property**—Complete lines 2a through 2e if you gave less than an entire interest in a property listed in Part I. Complete lines 3a through 3c if conditions were placed on a contribution listed in Part I; also attach the required statement (see instructions).

2a Enter the letter from Part I that identifies the property for which you gave less than an entire interest ▶ _____
If Part II applies to more than one property, attach a separate statement.

b Total amount claimed as a deduction for the property listed in Part I: **(1)** For this tax year ▶ _____
(2) For any prior tax years ▶ _____

c Name and address of each organization to which any such contribution was made in a prior year (complete only if different from the donee organization above):
Name of charitable organization (donee)

Address (number, street, and room or suite no.)

City or town, state, and ZIP code

d For tangible property, enter the place where the property is located or kept ▶ _____
e Name of any person, other than the donee organization, having actual possession of the property ▶ _____

		Yes	No
3a	Is there a restriction, either temporary or permanent, on the donee's right to use or dispose of the donated property?		
b	Did you give to anyone (other than the donee organization or another organization participating with the donee organization in cooperative fundraising) the right to the income from the donated property or to the possession of the property, including the right to vote donated securities, to acquire the property by purchase or otherwise, or to designate the person having such income, possession, or right to acquire?		
c	Is there a restriction limiting the donated property for a particular use?		

For Paperwork Reduction Act Notice, see separate instructions.   Cat. No. 62299J   Form **8283** (Rev. 12-2014)

This form must be completed and filed with the donor's income tax return for gifts of property valued at $500 or more. There is no requirement of an appraisal or signature of the donee organization for gifts valued between $500 and $5,000.

Form 8283 (Rev. 12-2014)   Page **2**

Name(s) shown on your income tax return	Identifying number
Mark A. and Joan E. Murphy	392-83-1982

Section B. Donated Property Over $5,000 (Except Publicly Traded Securities)—Complete this section for one item (or one group of similar items) for which you claimed a deduction of more than $5,000 per item or group (except contributions of publicly traded securities reported in Section A). Provide a separate form for each property donated unless it is part of a group of similar items. An appraisal is generally required for property listed in Section B. See instructions.

Part I   **Information on Donated Property**—To be completed by the taxpayer and/or the appraiser.

4   Check the box that describes the type of property donated:

- **a** ☐ Art* (contribution of $20,000 or more)
- **b** ☐ Qualified Conservation Contribution
- **c** ☐ Equipment
- **d** ☐ Art* (contribution of less than $20,000)
- **e** ☒ Other Real Estate
- **f** ☐ Securities
- **g** ☐ Collectibles**
- **h** ☐ Intellectual Property
- **i** ☐ Vehicles
- **j** ☐ Other

*Art includes paintings, sculptures, watercolors, prints, drawings, ceramics, antiques, decorative arts, textiles, carpets, silver, rare manuscripts, historical memorabilia, and other similar objects.

**Collectibles include coins, stamps, books, gems, jewelry, sports memorabilia, dolls, etc., but not art as defined above.

Note. In certain cases, you must attach a qualified appraisal of the property. See instructions.

5	(a) Description of donated property (if you need more space, attach a separate statement)	(b) If tangible property was donated, give a brief summary of the overall physical condition of the property at the time of the gift	(c) Appraised fair market value
A	Residence and two lots:	Good Repair	242,500
B	2080 Long Pond Road		
C	Syracuse, NY		
D			

	(d) Date acquired by donor (mo., yr.)	(e) How acquired by donor	(f) Donor's cost or adjusted basis	(g) For bargain sales, enter amount received	(h) Amount claimed as a deduction	(i) Date of contribution
					See instructions	
A	7/20/09	Purchased	236,900		242,500	
B						
C						
D						

Part II   **Taxpayer (Donor) Statement**—List each item included in Part I above that the appraisal identifies as having a value of $500 or less. See instructions.

I declare that the following item(s) included in Part I above has to the best of my knowledge and belief an appraised value of not more than $500 (per item). Enter identifying letter from Part I and describe the specific item. See instructions. ▶ _____

Signature of taxpayer (donor) ▶ *Mark A. Murphy*   Date ▶ **11/28/16**

Part III   **Declaration of Appraiser**

I declare that I am not the donor, the donee, a party to the transaction in which the donor acquired the property, employed by, or related to any of the foregoing persons, or married to any person who is related to any of the foregoing persons. And, if regularly used by the donor, donee, or party to the transaction, I performed the majority of my appraisals during my tax year for other persons.

Also, I declare that I perform appraisals on a regular basis; and that because of my qualifications as described in the appraisal, I am qualified to make appraisals of the type of property being valued. I certify that the appraisal fees were not based on a percentage of the appraised property value. Furthermore, I understand that a false or fraudulent overstatement of the property value as described in the qualified appraisal or this Form 8283 may subject me to the penalty under section 6701(a) (aiding and abetting the understatement of tax liability). In addition, I understand that I may be subject to a penalty under section 6695A if I know, or reasonably should know, that my appraisal is to be used in connection with a return or claim for refund and a substantial or gross valuation misstatement results from my appraisal. I affirm that I have not been barred from presenting evidence or testimony by the Office of Professional Responsibility.

Sign Here   Signature ▶ *Andrew J. Noble*   Title ▶ President   Date ▶ 11/20/16

Business address (including room or suite no.)	Identifying number
1100 North Adams Street	541-90-9796

City or town, state, and ZIP code
Elmira, NY 14904

Part IV   **Donee Acknowledgment**—To be completed by the charitable organization.

This charitable organization acknowledges that it is a qualified organization under section 170(c) and that it received the donated property as described in Section B, Part I, above on the following date ▶   8/31/15

Furthermore, this organization affirms that in the event it sells, exchanges, or otherwise disposes of the property described in Section B, Part I (or any portion thereof) within 3 years after the date of receipt, it will file **Form 8282**, Donee Information Return, with the IRS and give the donor a copy of that form. This acknowledgment does not represent agreement with the claimed fair market value.

Does the organization intend to use the property for an unrelated use?   . . . . ▶ ☐ Yes   ☒ No

Name of charitable organization (donee)	Employer identification number
Fairlawn Heights Church	35-4029876

Address (number, street, and room or suite no.)	City or town, state, and ZIP code
PO Box 829	Oswego, NY 13126

Authorized signature	Title	Date
James A. Black	Executive Pastor	12/15/16

Form **8283** (Rev. 12-2014)

Section B must be completed for gifts of items (or groups of similar items) for which a deduction was claimed of more than $5,000 per item or group.

Example: A charity receives a gift of real estate. The receipt should include the legal description of the real property and a description of the improvements with no indication of the dollar value.

➤ **Acknowledging and reporting gifts of autos, boats, and airplanes.** Charities are required to provide contemporaneous written acknowledgments containing specific information to donors of autos, boats, and airplanes (IRS Publication 4302). Taxpayers are required to include a copy of the written acknowledgment (Form 1098-C may be used as the acknowledgment) with their tax returns in order to receive a deduction. The donee organization is also required to provide the information contained in the acknowledgment to the IRS. The information included in such acknowledgments as well as the meaning of "contemporaneous" depends on what the charity does with the donated vehicle.

Auto, boat, or airplane sold before use or improvement. If the donated auto, boat, or airplane is sold before significant intervening use or material improvement of the auto, boat, or airplane by the organization, the gross proceeds received by the donee organization from the sale of the vehicle will be included on the written acknowledgment. Therefore, for donated property sold before use or improvement, the deductible amount is the gross proceeds received from the sale. A written acknowledgment is considered contemporaneous if the donee organization provides it within 30 days of the sale of the vehicle. The written acknowledgment provided by the charity should include the following information:

- the name and taxpayer identification number of the donor,

- the vehicle, boat, or airplane identification number or similar number,

- certification that the property was sold in an arm's length transaction between unrelated parties,

- the gross proceeds from the sale, and

- a statement that the deductible amount may not exceed the amount of the gross proceeds.

Auto, boat, or airplane not sold before use or improvement. Charities may plan to significantly use or materially improve a donated auto, boat, or airplane before or instead of selling the property. In such circumstances, the charity would not include a dollar amount in the written acknowledgment. Instead, the written acknowledgment (prepared within 30 days of the contribution of the vehicle to be considered contemporaneous) should include the following information:

- the name and taxpayer identification number of the donor,

- the vehicle, boat, or airplane identification number or similar number,

- certification of the intended use or material improvement of the property and the intended duration of such use, and

7878 ☐ VOID ☐ CORRECTED			

DONEE'S name, street address, city or town, state or province, country, ZIP or foreign postal code, and telephone no.

Lamont Community Church
101 East Main Street
Lamont, KS 66855

1 Date of contribution
1/15/15

2a Odometer mileage
81,980

OMB No. 1545-1959

20**16**

Form **1098-C**

Contributions of Motor Vehicles, Boats, and Airplanes

2b Year	**2c** Make	**2d** Model
2006	Chevy	S10 Pickup

DONEE'S federal identification number	DONOR'S identification number
35-0189211	514-41-8007

3 Vehicle or other identification number

1FAP58923V159753

DONOR'S name
Fred Wilbur

4a ☒ Donee certifies that vehicle was sold in arm's length transaction to unrelated party

Street address (including apt. no.)
512 North Main

4b Date of sale
1/25/16

City or town, state or province, country, and ZIP or foreign postal code
Lamont, KS 66855

4c Gross proceeds from sale (see instructions)
$ 3,000

Copy A

For Internal Revenue Service Center

File with Form 1096.

5a ☐ Donee certifies that vehicle will not be transferred for money, other property, or services before completion of material improvements or significant intervening use

5b ☐ Donee certifies that vehicle is to be transferred to a needy individual for significantly below fair market value in furtherance of donee's charitable purpose

5c Donee certifies the following detailed description of material improvements or significant intervening use and duration of use

For Privacy Act and Paperwork Reduction Act Notice, see the **2016 General Instructions for Certain Information Returns.**

6a Did you provide goods or services in exchange for the vehicle? . . . . ▶ Yes ☐ No ☐

6b Value of goods and services provided in exchange for the vehicle
$

6c Describe the goods and services, if any, that were provided. If this box is checked, donee certifies that the goods and services consisted solely of intangible religious benefits . . . . ▶ ☐

7 Under the law, the donor may not claim a deduction of more than $500 for this vehicle if this box is checked . . . . . ▶ ☐

Form **1098-C**   Cat. No. 39732R   www.irs.gov/form1098c   Department of the Treasury - Internal Revenue Service

---

- certification that the property will not be transferred in exchange for money, other property, or services before completion of such use or improvement.

The deductible amount for contributed autos, boats, or airplanes that will be used or improved by the charity is the fair market value of the property, as determined by the donor, taking into consideration accessories, mileage, and other indicators of the property's general condition.

In certain instances, an auto, boat, or airplane may be sold at a price significantly below fair market value (or gratuitously transferred) to needy individuals in direct furtherance of the donee organization's charitable purpose.

For property that meets this definition, the gift acknowledgment must also contain a certification that the donee organization will sell the property to a needy individual at a price significantly below fair market value (or, if applicable, that the donee organization gratuitously will transfer the property to a needy individual). Additionally, the ministry must certify that the sale or transfer will be in the direct furtherance of the donee organization's charitable purpose of relieving the poor and distressed or the underprivileged who are in need of a means of transportation.

> **Example:** On March 1, 2016, a donor contributes a qualified vehicle to a qualified charity. The organization's charitable purposes include helping needy individuals who are unemployed develop new job skills, finding job placements for these individuals, and providing transportation for these individuals who need a means of transportation to jobs in areas not served by public transportation. The charity determines that, in direct further-ance of its charitable purpose, the charity will sell the qualified vehicle at a price significantly below fair market value to a trainee who needs a means of transportation to a new workplace. On or before March 31, 2016, the charity provides Form 1098-C to the donor containing the donor's name and taxpayer identification number, the vehicle identification number, a statement that the date of the contribution was March 1, 2016, a certifi-cation that the charity will sell the qualified vehicle to a needy individual at a price significantly below fair market value, and a certification that the sale is in direct furtherance of the organization's charitable purpose.

Generally, no deduction is allowed unless donors receive Form 1098-C within 30 days after the date that the vehicle is sold or within 30 days of the donation date if the charity keeps the car. If the vehicle is sold, donors must be informed of the gross selling price.

If the charity keeps the car, the private-party sale price must be used by donors to figure the charitable tax deduction for donations, not the higher dealer retail price.

Quid Pro Quo Disclosure Requirements

When a donor receives goods or services of value approximate to the amount transferred to a ministry, there is no gift. This is because the person received a "quid pro quo" of an equivalent amount in exchange for the transfer. If the payment to a ministry exceeds the approximate amount of goods or services provided by the ministry to the donor, the difference qualifies as a charitable gift.

The charity is required to provide an acknowledgment for all transactions where the donor makes a payment of more than $75 to the charity and receives goods or services (other than intangible religious benefits or items of token value).

Form of the acknowledgment

The charitable gift acknowledgment, in quid pro quo situations, must

➤ inform the donor that the amount of the contribution that is deductible for federal income tax purposes is limited to the difference of the amount of money and the value of any property contributed by the donor over the value of the goods or services provided by the organization, and

➤ provide the donor with a good-faith estimate of the value of goods or services that the charity is providing in exchange for the contribution.

Only single payments of more than $75 are subject to the quid pro quo rules. Payments are not cumulative. It is not a difference of $75 between the amount given by the donor and the value of the object received by the donor that triggers the disclosure requirements, but the amount actually paid by the donor.

Calculating the gift portion

It is not a requirement for the donee organization to actually complete the subtraction of the benefit from a cash payment, showing the net charitable deduction. However, providing the net amount available for a charitable deduction is a good approach for clear communication with donors.

When to make the required disclosures

The disclosure of the value of goods or services provided to a donor may be made in the donor solicitation as well as in the subsequent acknowledgment. However, sufficient information will generally not be available to make proper disclosure upon solicitation (for example, the value of a dinner may not be known at the time the solicitation is made).

Warning

An organization must furnish a disclosure statement in connection with either the solicitation or the receipt of a quid pro quo contribution of over $75. The statement must be in writing and must be made in a manner that is likely to come to the attention of the donor. For example, a disclosure in small print within a larger document might not meet this requirement.

Goods provided to donors

To determine the net charitable contribution, a gift must generally be reduced by the fair market value of any premium, incentive, or other benefit received by the donor in exchange for the gift. Common examples of premiums are books, CDs, DVDs, Bibles, and other resources.

For gifts of more than $75, organizations must advise the donor of the fair market value of the premium or incentive and explain that the value of the premium is not deductible for income tax purposes.

Donors must reduce their charitable deduction by the fair market value of goods or services they receive, even when the goods or services were donated to the charity for use as premiums or gifts or when they were bought wholesale by the charity. Therefore, charities cannot pass along to donors the savings realized by receiving products at no cost or buying products at a discount.

In certain circumstances, if donors receive unsolicited free, low-cost articles (free to the donor and low-cost to the distributing ministry) as part of the ministry's stewardship efforts, they are allowed a full tax deduction for the donation:

> ➤ **Low-cost items.** If an item that has a cost (not retail value) of less than $10.60 (2016 inflation-adjusted amount) and bears the name or logo of your ministry is given in return for a donation of more than $53.00 (2016 inflation-adjusted amount), the donor may claim a charitable deduction for the full amount of the donation. Examples of low-cost items are coffee mugs, key chains, bookmarks, and calendars.

> ➤ ***De minimis* benefits.** A donor can take a full deduction if the fair market value of the benefits received in connection with a gift does not exceed 2% of the donation or $106 (2016 inflation-adjusted amount), whichever is less.

Examples of the quid pro quo rules

Here are various examples of how the quid pro quo rules may apply:

> ➤ **Admission to events.** Many organizations sponsor banquets, concerts, or other events to which donors and prospective donors are invited in exchange for a contribution or other payment. Typically, the donor receives a benefit equivalent to the payment and no charitable deduction is available.
>
> But if the amount paid is more than the value received, the amount in excess of the fair market value is deductible if the donor intended to make a contribution.

> ➤ **Auctions.** The IRS generally takes the position that the fair market value of an item purchased at a charity auction is set by the bidders. The winning bidder, therefore, cannot pay more than the item is worth. That means there is no charitable contribution in the IRS's eyes, no deduction, and no need for the charity to provide any charitable gift substantiation document to the bidder.

Remember

Many charities offer products and suggest a donation amount with respect to the products. For example, a charity may offer a book with a suggested donation amount of $30. If the fair market value of the book is $30 and the individual sends $30 to the charity, no charitable donation has been made. However, if the charity receives $50, a $20 charitable deduction is available.

However, many tax professionals take the position that when the payment (the purchase price) exceeds the fair market value of the items, the amount that exceeds the fair market value is deductible as a charitable contribution. This position also creates a reporting requirement under the quid pro quo rules.

> **Example:** Your church youth group auctions goods to raise funds for a missions trip. An individual bought a quilt for $1,000. The church takes the position that the quilt had a fair market value of $50 even though the bidder paid $1,000. Since the payment of $1,000 exceeded the $75 limit, the church is required to provide a written statement indicating that only $950 of the $1,000 payment is eligible for a charitable contribution.

➤ **Bazaars.** Payments for items sold at bazaars and bake sales are not tax-deductible to donors since the purchase price generally equals the fair market value of the item.

➤ **Banquets.** Whether an organization incurs reporting requirements in connection with banquets where funds are raised depends on the specifics of each event.

> **Example 1:** A church sponsors a banquet for missions charging $50 per person. The fair market value of the meal provided is $15 per person. There is no disclosure requirement since the amount charged was less than $75. However, the amount deductible by each donor is only $35.

> **Example 2:** A church invites individuals to attend a missions banquet without charge. Attendees are invited to make contributions or pledges at the end of the banquet. These payments probably do not require disclosure even if the amount given is $75 or more because there is only an indirect relationship between the meal and the gift.

➤ **Deduction timing.** The same quid pro quo rule applies to goods and services received in a different year. Thus, a donor's deduction for the year of the payment is limited to

Charitable Contribution Substantiation Requirements

	Not more than $75	Over $75 and under $250	At least $250 and under $500	At least $500 and under $5,000	$5,000 and over
Canceled check acceptable for donor's deduction?	Yes	Yes	No	No	No
Contribution receipt required for deduction?	No*	No*	Yes	Yes	Yes
Charity's statement on donor's receipt of goods or services required?	No	Yes **	Yes**	Yes**	Yes**

*Generally, no if paid by check, credit card, or wire transfer. Yes, if paid by cash.

**May be avoided if the charity meets the low-cost items or *de minimis* benefits exceptions described on page 172.

Sample Charitable Gift Acknowledgment

Acknowledgment #2 [2]

Received from: Charles K. Vandell

Cash received:

Date Cash Received	Gross Amount Received	Value of Goods or Services	Net Charitable Contribution
1/23/16	$80.00	$25.00 [1]	$ 55.00
3/20/16	300.00		300.00
4/24/16	60.00		60.00
6/19/16	500.00	100.00	400.00
9/04/16	275.00		275.00
10/30/16	200.00		200.00
12/18/16	1,000.00		1,000.00
		Total	$2,290.00

Property received described as follows:

Received on October 22, 2016, 12 brown Samsonite folding chairs.

In return for certain gifts listed above, we only provided you with the following goods or services (our estimate of the fair market value is indicated):

(1) Christian music CDs $25.00
(2) Limited edition art print $100.00

You may have also received intangible religious benefits, but these benefits do not need to be valued for tax purposes.

The deductible portion of your contribution for federal income tax purposes is limited to the excess of your contribution over the value of goods and services we provided to you.

This document is necessary for any available federal income tax deduction for your contribution. Please retain it for your records.

Receipt issued on: January 15, 2017

Receipt issued by: Harold Morrison, Treasurer
Castleview Church
1008 High Drive
Dover, DE 19901

---

1. This sample receipt is based on the following assumptions:
    A. Goods or services were provided in exchange for the gifts.
    B. The receipt is issued on a periodic or annual basis for all gifts whether over or under $250.

2. All receipts should be numbered consecutively for control and accounting purposes.

the amount, if any, by which the payment exceeds the value of the goods and services received in a previous or subsequent year.

➤ **Good-faith estimates.** A donor is not required to use the estimate provided by a donee organization in calculating the deductible amount. When a taxpayer knows or has reason to know that an estimate is inaccurate, the taxpayer may ignore the organization's estimate in determining the fair market value of the goods or services received.

➤ **Rights of refusal.** A donor can claim a full deduction if he or she refuses a benefit from the charity. However, this must be done affirmatively. Simply not taking advantage of a benefit is not enough. For example, a donor who chooses not to make use of tickets made available by your organization must deduct the value of the tickets from his or her contribution before claiming a deduction. However, a donor who rejects the right to a benefit at the time the contribution is made (for example, by checking off a refusal box on a form supplied by your charity) can take a full deduction.

➤ **Sale of products or a service at fair market value.** When an individual purchases products or receives services approximate to the amount paid, no part of the payment is a gift.

> **Example 1:** An individual purchases recordings of a series of Sunday morning worship services for $80. The sale price represents fair market value. Even though the amount paid exceeds the $75 threshold, the church is not required to provide a disclosure statement to the purchaser because the value of the products is approximate to the amount paid to the church.

> **Example 2:** The Brown family uses the fellowship hall of the church for a family reunion. The normal rental fee is $300. The Browns give a check to the church for $300 marked "Contribution." No acknowledgment should be given because no charitable contribution was made. The Browns received a benefit approximate to the amount of their payment.

> **Example 3:** The Smith family uses the church sanctuary and fellowship hall for a wedding and the reception. The church does not have a stated use fee but asks for a donation from those who use the facility. The comparable fee to rent similar facilities is $250. The Smiths give a check to the church for $250 marked "Contribution." No acknowledgment should be given because no charitable contribution was made. The Smiths received a benefit approximate to the amount of their payment. *Note:* It is inappropriate for the church to try to mask a fee by calling it a donation.

> **Example 4:** A church operates a Christian school. The parent of a student at the school writes a check payable to the church for his child's tuition. No acknowledgment should be given because a payment of tuition does not qualify as a charitable contribution.

Donor-Restricted Gifts

The two fundamental concepts relating to donor-restricted gifts are charity discretion and control and donor preferences:

➤ **Charity discretion and control over donor-restricted gifts.** A common misconception is that the control a charity board must exercise over any donor-restricted gift is in conflict with, or contradictory to, stipulations by donors. *This is not true.*

Some believe that organizations should not follow donor restrictions, from time to time, to demonstrate their control. *This is inappropriate.*

Board control and donor restrictions are really a "hand in glove" concept. It is not *either/or* but *both/and*! Restricted gifts must be used for a specific exempt purpose, whereas unrestricted gifts may be used for any exempt purpose.

The board must control all contributions to an exempt organization, unrestricted and restricted, to be used exclusively for its exempt purposes. In addition, the board must provide reasonable measures to assure that donor-restricted gifts are used for the intended exempt purpose(s).

Notifying the donor on the gift response vehicle that the charity will exercise discretion and control over the gift does not remove the donor's restriction placed on a gift. Charities must exercise discretion and control over all charitable gifts, whether unrestricted (may be used for any exempt purpose) or restricted (must be used for a specific purpose).

Donor restrictions arise when a charity accepts contributions that are solicited for or restricted by a donor for a specific area of ministry, such as a program, project, or a type of missionary work (vs. missionary work anywhere in the world); e.g., missionary work in Sri Lanka preferenced for a particular missionary. Unrestricted contributions have no implicit or explicit donor restrictions and are available to be used in any exempt operations of the charity.

Donors often like to retain some control over their gifts. However, if too much control is retained, the donor's income tax deduction may be endangered.

➤ **Donor preferences vs. restrictions.** In charitable giving, there is a distinction between a donor's restriction and a donor's preference. This distinction can make a difference between the donor's eligibility for a charitable tax deduction and no tax deduction.

The preferencing of a gift does not determine whether the gift is unrestricted or restricted for accounting purposes. When a gift is preferenced to support a particular worker, the preferencing may qualify the gift for a charitable tax deduction, but other factors must be reviewed to determine whether the gift is unrestricted or restricted for accounting purposes.

Example 1: Accompanying a gift, a donor communicates: "My preference is that the gift be used for scholarships. However, I give the charity permission to use the gift for any exempt purpose consistent with the charity's mission statement." This gift is an unrestricted gift because the charity has full discretion as to the use of the gift.

Example 2: A prayer letter or appeal letter from a charity that conducts work in several countries describes the need for religious workers in India. The request is for funds preferenced to enable a particular worker employed by the charity to carry out certain work in India. A gift in response to this appeal is temporarily restricted for the ministry's program in India (a geographical restriction), and the gift is preferenced to support a particular worker.

A donor's *restriction* on a gift limits the charity's use of the funds to the purposes specified by the donor; e.g., "This gift is made on the condition that," or "This gift is restricted for XYZ project." This type of gift is generally tax-deductible as a charitable contribution.

It may be inappropriate for a charity to accept a gift if the restrictions accompanying a gift

☐ Prevent the charity from using the donation in the furtherance of its charitable purposes. For example, if a donor restricts a gift for the benefit of a specific individual and the charity is prevented from exercising discretion and control over the gift (such as a gift restricted for a particular benevolent recipient, an employee of the charity, etc.), the gift is generally not deductible as a charitable contribution.

☐ Are incompatible with the mission of the charity. Even though a restricted gift is exclusively charitable, it is generally inappropriate for a charity to accept a gift requiring the expenditure of funds outside the mission of the charity. For example, if a ministry whose sole purpose is international child sponsorship is offered a gift restricted for inner-city evangelism in the U.S., the gift should generally not be accepted by the charity because it is inconsistent with the mission of the charity (the overall mission of the charity is generally described in the organization's governing documents).

☐ Are at odds with the best interests of the charity. A restricted gift could be exclusively charitable and compatible with the mission of the charity and still not be in the best interests of the charity. A charity might not have the capacity to comply with gift restrictions. For example, the amount of funds raised for a particular disaster may exceed the charity's capacity to effectively spend the funds in a reasonable period of time.

Alternatively, the administrative requirements of a restricted gift could consume an inordinate amount of the charity's resources. For example, the gift of a time share property could be offered to a ministry. However, the charity may decide the time share is not in the best interest of the charity because (1) time shares are often unmarketable properties laden with annual costs, and (2) even when sales are made, the low resale market prices can minimize or erase profits.

A donor's *preference* communicates a desire or suggestion which is advisory in nature. A desire or suggestion does not restrict the use of the gift and allows the charity full discretion to use the gift in relation to the desire or suggestion or use the funds for any other purpose. Factors that imply a charity has received a donor preferenced gift and not a restricted gift include:

☐ **Donor intention.** The donor intends to only express a desire or make a suggestion with respect to a gift.

☐ **Charity communication.** Both the solicitation letter and response form (and perhaps the gift acknowledgment) from the charity clearly communicate to the donor that preferenced gifts are sought. Materials include statements such as "We appreciate your desire or suggestion as to the use of the funds. While we will endeavor to use the funds as you desire or suggest, we may use the gift for another purpose." This is very different from the statement "Gifts made to our charity are under the discretion and control of the charity." All gifts must be under the discretion and control of the charity, so making that statement does not turn an otherwise donor-restricted gift into an unrestricted gift.

☐ **Donor communication.** The donor communicated in writing or verbally a desire or suggestion as to the use of the funds, but the donor did not restrict the funds for a certain purpose.

If the donor preferences a gift, even when the preference is for the funds to go to a particular individual, the gift may qualify for a charitable tax deduction if the charity exercises adequate due diligence with respect to the gift. For example, a gift restricted for missions and preferenced for the missionary endeavors involving a certain identified individual or a gift for benevolence preferenced for a particular benevolent recipient may qualify for a charitable tax deduction if the charity exercises adequate due diligence related to the gift.

Some charities request that donors not place the name of a preferenced worker on the memo line of the donor's check. This request may send an inappropriate message to donors—i.e., implying that hiding information from the IRS is an acceptable and/or desirable practice. If a donor wants to use the memo line on the check to indicate a preference to support the work of a particular individual ("preferenced for the ministry of Jill Smith"), this should be no more problematic for IRS purposes than checking a box on the response form which contains preferenced wording.

Contributions to Support Missionaries and Other Workers

Donations may be received, payable to your church or nonprofit organization, for the support of a particular missionary (often called deputized fundraising). These gifts generally qualify as a charitable contribution if the charity exercises sufficient discretion and control over the gift. If so, the charity should include the amounts in gift acknowledgments issued to donors.

The IRS has acknowledged that deputized support-raising is a widespread and legitimate practice, and the contributions properly raised by this method are tax-deductible.

In its 1999 Technical Instruction Program materials, the IRS outlined two general tests to determine whether a tax-deductible contribution is made to or for the use of a ministry, or whether a gift is a non-deductible pass-through gift to a particular individual who ultimately benefits from the contribution. These two tests, the intended benefit test and discretion and control test, are explained below.

Key Issue

There is an extremely fine line between a personal nondeductible gift to a missionary (or other religious worker) and a tax-deductible gift to a charity to provide funding for the ministry of a particular missionary. The key is the intention of the donor to benefit the charity and the charity's discretion and control over the gift.

➤ **Intended benefit test.** The donor's intention must be to benefit the charity. While the donor's intention is often only in the donor's mind, communication provided by the charity when the gift is solicited and the gift receipt is provided may help clarify donor intent:

☐ **Solicitation.** The best time for the donor to understand that a charity will have complete discretion and control over a gift is at the point of solicitation—before the gift is ever made—underscoring the principle of truthfulness in fundraising. And using the suggested wording at the point of solicitation is the best way to communicate the pertinent facts to the prospective donor before the donation is made.

The IRS formally indicated that the following language in solicitations for contributions, with no conflicting language in the solicitations and no conflicting understandings between the parties, will help show that the qualified donee has exercised the necessary control over contributions, that the donor has reason to know that the qualified donee has the necessary discretion and control over contributions, and that the donor intends that the qualified donee is the actual recipient of the contributions:

"Contributions are solicited with the understanding that [insert name of donee organization] has complete discretion and control over the use of all donated funds."

☐ **Gift receipt.** The IRS has provided the following suggested language for use in gift acknowledgment to help clarify the record of the true intentions of a donor at the time of the contribution:

> "This contribution is made with the understanding that [insert name of donee organization] has complete control and administration over the use of the donated funds."

Thus, use of this language should provide strong evidence of both donor intent and organizational control in the deputized fundraising context.

➤ **Discretion and control test.** The IRS uses the phrase "discretion and control" with respect to a charity's obligation over deputized funds. Informally, the IRS has stated that discretion and control may be evidenced by such factors as adequate selection and supervision of the self-supported worker (a worker who raises part or all of his or her support) and formalizing a budget that establishes the compensation limit and expenses of each deputized individual. Establishing compensation limits and expense reimbursements with reference to considerations other than an amount of money a deputized fundraiser collects is very important. For a complete list of the factors indicating adequate discretion and control, see the box on page 181.

Example 1: When worker A leaves the employment of charity B, the worker may mistakenly believe that the balance in his or her account should be transferred to charity C (worker A's new employer), where the worker will be employed. While a transfer to charity C may be made if it furthers the charitable purpose of charity B, it is not required.

Example 2: When worker D leaves the employment of charity E after completing a two-year missionary term, there is a substantial excess of funds raised for the charity by worker D above what was spent for the ministry of this worker. The worker may mistakenly believe the excess in his or her account should be paid to the worker. While a modest severance payment might be made to the worker in conformity with the charity's policies, the excess is an asset of the charity and subject to the charity's discretion and control.

But how does a charity know if the "intended benefit" and "control" tests have been met? Unfortunately, the IRS provides little guidance for these tests. Charities, with advice from their CPAs and attorneys, must design their action plan based on applicable law and informal IRS guidelines. (*Note:* In 1999, Dan Busby and five attorneys participated in the last significant meeting conducted with the IRS National Office on the deputized fundraising topic.) The following is a review of issues that should be considered by ministries using the deputized fundraising approach:

> **Caution**
>
> Prayer or support letters should clearly communicate that gifts are being solicited for the charity. It is permissible to request that the gift be designated for the ministry of John Doe, who is a missionary employed by the charity. But letters should not request gifts "for a certain missionary" because of the implication that it is a nondeductible conduit transaction.

Factors Demonstrating Discretion and Control Over the Deputized Fundraising Process

According to the IRS, charities that receive revenues through deputized fundraising—through individual missionaries, staff members, or volunteers conducting grassroots fundraising to support the organization—can demonstrate discretion and control by the following factors:

➤ Control by the governing body of donated funds through a budgetary process;

➤ Consistent exercise by the organization's governing body of responsibility for establishing, reviewing, and monitoring the programs and policies of the organization;

➤ Staff salaries set by the organization according to a salary schedule approved by the governing body. Salaries must be set by reference to considerations other than an amount of money a deputized fundraiser collects. There can be no commitments that contributions will be paid as salary or expenses to a particular person;

➤ Amounts paid as salary, to the extent required by the Internal Revenue Code, reported as compensation on Form W-2 or Form 1099-MISC;

➤ Reimbursements of legitimate ministry expenses approved by the organization, pursuant to guidelines approved by the governing body. Reimbursements must be set by considerations other than the amount of money a deputized fundraiser collects;

➤ Thorough screening of potential workers pursuant to qualifications established by the organization that are related to its exempt purposes and not principally related to the amount of funds that may be raised by the workers;

➤ Meaningful training, development, and supervision of workers;

➤ Workers assigned to programs and project locations by the organization based upon its assessment of each worker's skills and training, and the specific needs of the organization;

➤ Regular communication to donors of the organization's full discretion and control over all its programs and funds through such means as newsletters, solicitation literature, and donor receipts; and

➤ The financial policies and practices of the organization annually reviewed by an audit committee, a majority of whose members are not employees of the organization.

➤ Determine how to put donors on notice that you will exercise discretion and control over the donations. Using the IRS-recommended language in solicitations—written or verbal—*and* on receipts is prudent.

➤ Be sure your organization consistently communicates with your donors. Eliminating written conflicts between solicitation letters (including prayer letters), donor response forms, deputized worker training materials, receipts, and other related documents can be accomplished by a careful review of your current documents. It is also important to establish procedures to ensure that the reviews are ongoing. The more daunting task is the proper training and continuing reinforcement to self-supported workers of the need to clearly and consistently communicate the discretion and control concept to donors.

➤ Use appropriate terminology when communicating with donors. Since the charity should not infer that contributions will be paid as salary, fringe benefits, and expense reimbursements to a particular person, communication to donors from the charity or self-supported workers should consistently underscore the charity's discretion and control over donations. A donor may indicate a preference that a gift to a charity be used to support the ministry of a certain individual, and the charity may track the dollars based on the preference. But the charity and the deputized worker should refrain from any inference that the contributions will be paid as salary or expense reimbursements to the worker. This is a fine line but one that should be observed.

Clear communication with donors about the discretion and control issue not only places donors on notice but also serves to reinforce this concept in the mind of deputized workers. Too often, self-supported workers assume they have an element of personal ownership of funds that they raise for the charity. For example, when the worker leaves the employment of charity A, he or she may mistakenly believe that the balance in his account will be transferred to charity B, where he or she will be employed. While a transfer to charity B may be appropriate, it is not required.

For more information on this topic, see the *The Guide to Charitable Giving for Churches and Ministries* by Dan Busby, Michael Martin, and John Van Drunen, published by ECFAPress (ECFA.org).

Contributions to Support Short-Term Mission Trips

Many churches and other nonprofit organizations sponsor individuals and/or teams of individuals that serve on short-term mission trips, domestically and internationally. The proper handling of funds raised and expended for short-term mission trips often presents challenging tax, finance, and legal issues for trip participants and sending organizations alike.

The definition of "short-term" varies from one sponsoring organization to another. For church-sponsored trips, a short-term mission trip often means a trip of a week or two in duration. However, for a missions organization, a short-term trip may last as long as two years. Short-term mission trips sometimes only involve adults. Other times, participants are minors supervised by adults, or some combination of adults and minors.

Funding options for short-term mission trips. Short-term mission trips may be funded in a variety of ways. For example, the sponsoring organization may pay part or all of the expenses of the trip from the organization's general budget. Or a donor may give funds restricted for short-term mission trips without any preference for particular mission trip participants—the donor simply wishes to support the program of sending short-term missionaries. However, most organizations sponsoring short-term mission trips seek gifts that are preferenced for particular trip participants.

➤ **Funding from the sponsoring organization's general budget.** Expenses relating to short-term mission trips may be funded in full by the sponsoring organization. This use of funds from the sponsoring organization's general budget is appropriate if short-term mission trips are consistent with its tax-exempt purposes.

➤ **Funds directly expended by the trip participant with no financial involvement of the sponsoring organization.** A participant in a short-term mission trip may partially or totally fund trip expenses by making direct payments for airfare, lodging, meals, and other expenses. If a trip is sponsored by a charity, the trip is consistent with the tax-exempt purposes of the charity, and there is no significant element of personal pleasure, recreation, or vacation, expenses related to the trip are generally deductible as charitable contributions on the taxpayer's Schedule A, Itemized Deductions. The deduction will not be denied simply because the taxpayer enjoys providing services to the charitable organization. Personal expenses relating to "side-trips" or vacation days unrelated to the mission trip included in the trip are generally not deductible.

➤ **Funding based on donor-restricted gifts for the trip but with no preference in relation to any trip participant.** Donors may make gifts restricted for a short-term mission trip project. Gifts for the project could be solicited by the charity, or the donor might make an unsolicited gift. These gifts generally qualify as charitable contributions, and it is appropriate for the sponsoring charity to provide a charitable gift acknowledgment.

If a charity accepts gifts that are donor-restricted for a short-term mission trip project, the charity is obligated to spend the funds for the intended purpose.

A donor could change the gift restriction by redirecting the gift to another project. This scenario presumes the donated funds have not already been expended or obligated for the mission trip.

Additionally, an organization could establish, and disclose with gift solicitation information, a board policy regarding the possible redirection of donor-restricted gifts if a mission trip event is canceled or oversubscribed (more funds are received than needed).

➤ **Funding based on gifts preferenced for particular trip participants.** Generally, mission trip participants are responsible for soliciting gifts to cover part or all of the expenses necessary for the particular trip (see pages 186–87 for a sample letter from a potential short-term mission trip participant to a potential donor).

When mission trip participants raise part or all of the funds required for a trip, the sponsoring organization generally identifies the amounts preferenced for particular participants to monitor whether sufficient funds have been raised to cover the expenses for each individual's trip.

There is generally no basis for refunding gifts if the preferenced individual does not go on the trip. Refunding gifts demonstrates that the sponsoring charity does not have adequate discretion and control over the gifts and may raise a question of the tax-deductibility of the gifts given in relation to the particular trip.

When a worker or a volunteer (a short-term mission trip participant typically qualifies as a "volunteer") raises some of his or her own support, the IRS has proposed the following two general tests to determine whether a tax-deductible contribution was made to or for the use of a charitable organization, or whether the gift was a nondeductible, pass-through gift to a particular individual who ultimately benefited from the contribution.

1. **The intended benefit test.** The purpose of this test is to determine whether the contributor's intent in making the donation was to benefit the organization or the individual.

   > **Caution**
   >
   > Gifts preferenced for particular trip participants should generally not be refunded to donors if the preferenced individual does not go on the trip.

   The IRS has formally indicated that organizations should avoid the use of conflicting language in their solicitations for contributions and conflicts in understandings between the parties. This is to demonstrate that

   a. the organization has exercised the necessary control over contributions;

   b. the donor has reason to know that the organization will have the necessary discretion and control over contributions; and

   c. the donor intends for the organization to be the actual recipient of the contributions.

   The authors recommend the following statement be used in solicitations for contributions:

   > *Contributions are solicited with the understanding that [insert name of sponsoring organization] has complete discretion and control over the use of all donated funds.*

2. **The discretion and control test.** The IRS uses the phrase "discretion and control" to indicate a charity's obligation regarding charitable gifts. The IRS has stated that charities receiving funds for the support of mission endeavors can demonstrate discretion and control with the following factors:

   a. Reimbursement of legitimate ministry expenses are approved by the organization, consistent with the governing body's guidelines. Reimbursement should be set by considerations other than the amount of money collected by the individuals who raise funds.

b. Potential trip members are screened according to qualifications established by the organization.

c. Trip members are given meaningful training, development, and supervision.

d. The organization assigns trip members to programs and project locations based upon its assessment of each individual's skills and training, and the specific needs of the organization.

e. Donor acknowledgments communicate the organization's full discretion and control over its programs and funds.

f. Since the organization should not commit to restricting the use of contributions to a particular person, potential trip participants should not imply the opposite, verbally or in writing. A donor may indicate a preference that the charity use a gift to support the trip of a certain individual, and the charity may track the dollars based on that preference. However, the organization and the potential trip participant should refrain from any inference that the contributions will be paid as expenses to or for a particular worker.

Even if the intended benefit and discretion and control tests are met, there may be charitable tax-deductibility issues based on age of trip participants (see Example 2 below), charity authorization, and the pursuit of pleasure or personal gain. Two potentially tax-deductible scenarios follow.

> ### Remember
>
> Apply both the intended benefit test and the discretion and control test when soliciting and administering funds related to short-term mission trips.

Example 1: **Trip participants are adults.** The following two examples illustrate different funding patterns when trip participants are adults:

a. **Participants contribute to the charity to cover part or all of the trip expenses.** The payments by the participants to the charity are deductible as charitable contributions if the trip involves no significant element of personal pleasure, recreation, or vacation. These trip contributions may be acknowledged by the charity as charitable contributions.

b. **All trip expenses are paid by the charity, and non-participants make contributions to cover trip expenses.** If the charity has preauthorized the mission trip, the trip furthers the exempt purposes of the charity, and if the trip involves no significant element of personal pleasure, recreation, or vacation, gifts to cover the trip expenses are generally tax-deductible, even if the donors indicate a

185

Sample Short-Term Mission Trip Fundraising Letter

This short-term mission trip fundraising letter demonstrates elements consistent with IRS guidance. The notes in the letter relate to accounting for the gift and qualifying it for a tax deduction.

1232 Main Street
Yakima, WA 98904
509/248-6739

Date

Dear Mr. and Mrs. Donor,

| This paragraph confirms it is a church-sponsored mission trip. |

This summer, I have an exciting opportunity to serve the Lord on a mission trip sponsored by our church, Yakima Fellowship, to East Africa. Fifteen members of my church youth group plan to participate in a 10-day trip. We will fly into Nairobi, Kenya on July 21.

Our ministry during this trip is in Nairobi at an orphanage where most of the children have AIDS. Our team will lead a Vacation Bible School, distribute clothes we will take with us, and be available to work with and support the children in the orphanage. Sponsors from our church will accompany our team and provide ministry oversight.

| This paragraph confirms that ministry will be performed on the trip. |

One of the ways you can help me is to pray for the trip, the ministry we will perform, and for me personally. Only with prayer support will I be able to bless the children in the orphanage.

| This paragraph confirms that gifts are preferenced for Jodi's trip expenses. (For accounting purposes, gifts are temporarily restricted for the mission trip.) |

Yes, there are financial needs. The cost of the trip is $2,100, which each team member is responsible to raise in gifts for our church. Please pray with me that the funds to cover my trip expenses will be provided.

Gifts to the church, with an expression of a preference for my trip expenses, are tax-deductible to the extent allowed by law.

If you will commit to pray, please check the appropriate box on the enclosed card. If you are able to make a gift to the church to assist with my expenses, please check the appropriate box, indicating your interest in helping fund my portion of the trip expenses, and make your check payable to the sponsoring church, Yakima Fellowship. If I am unable to participate in the trip, your gifts will be used to support the short-term missions program of the church.

> This paragraph confirms the church will exercise discretion and control over the funds, implied in: "There are no refunds to donors if I don't go."

May God bless you richly as you consider your involvement in this mission trip!

Sincerely,

Jodi Hunter

Sample Short-Term Mission Trip
Response Form (Trip Expenses Paid by the Charity)

We want to support the missions outreach of Yakima Fellowship and are sending our gift of $_____.

Our preference is that this gift be used to support the short-term mission trip of Jodi Hunter. We understand that the use of the gift is subject to the discretion and control of Yakima Fellowship.

> These paragraphs make it clear that the donor's intent is to benefit the charity. Their financial support of Jodi Hunter is simply a desire.

Donor(s):

Bill and Karen Smith
2315 Main
Wenatchee, WA 98801

Sample Short-Term Mission Trip
Gift Acknowledgment (Trip Expenses Paid by the Charity)

Gift Acknowledgment • Please keep this acknowledgment for your tax records

	Preferenced for the mission trip of:	Total Amount	Gift Amount	Other Amount
Acknowledgment #2675 Gift Date: 01/02/XX Acknowledgment Date: 01/15/XX Bill and Karen Smith 2315 Main Wenatchee, WA 98801	Jodi Hunter	**$100.00**	**$100.00**	0

Thank you for your contribution which is tax-deductible to the extent allowed by law. While every effort will be made to apply your gift according to an indicated preference, if any, **Yakima Fellowship** has complete discretion and control over the use of the donated funds. We thank God for you and appreciate your support.

Yakima Fellowship
PO Box 4256
Yakima, WA 98904
509/248-5555

No goods or services were provided in exchange for this contribution.

Sample Short-Term Mission Trip
Gift Check (Trip Expenses Paid by the Charity)

Bill and Karen Smith
2315 Main
Wenatchee, WA 98801

DATE: December 1, 2016

PAY TO
THE ORDER OF: Yakima Fellowship $ 200.00

Two Hundred and no/100---------------------------------- DOLLARS

FOR   Missions Work   *Bill Smith*

Note: If a donor wishes to identify the preferenced participant on the check, the "preferential" or "to support the trip of" terminology should be used to avoid communicating the gift is earmarked for a particular participant. It is generally preferable for the donor to check an appropriately worded box on the response form indicating a preference to support the ministry of a particular trip participant.

Sample Short-Term Mission Trip
Gift Acknowledgment (Trip Expenses Paid by the Participant)

Gift Acknowledgment • Please keep this acknowledgment for your tax records

Acknowledgment #4575 Gift Date: 01/02/XX Acknowledgment Date: 01/15/XX Bill and Karen Smith 2315 Main Wenatchee, WA 98801	Description of Services Provided	Built church building in Nairobi, Kenya, on July 21-28, 2016

Thank you for your contribution which is tax-deductible to the extent allowed by law. While every effort will be made to apply your gift according to an indicated preference, if any, **Yakima Fellowship** has complete discretion and control over the use of the donated funds. We thank God for you and appreciate your support.

Yakima Fellowship
PO Box 4256
Yakima, WA 98904
509/248-5555

No goods or services were provided
in exchange for this contribution..

ECFA
ACCREDITED

preference that gifts be applied to the trip expenses of a particular participant.

Example 2: **Trip participants are minors.**

If a trip participant is a minor, the minor must actually provide services to carry out the tax-exempt purposes of the trip. The age of the minor and the minor's development may be important factors in determining the minor's capability of providing services to the charity.

If parents, relatives, and/or friends contribute to the charity with a preference for a child's trip expenses and the charity pays the trip expenses, these contributions are generally tax-deductible, assuming the minor significantly contributes to the trip purposes.

➤ **Funding based on gifts _restricted_ for particular trip participants.** A donor may express a _preference_ for a particular trip recipient, but if a donor expresses a _restriction_ for a certain trip recipient, the gift is generally an earmarked gift. Therefore, the gift may

Caution

Earmarked gifts (for personal benefit of missionaries) should generally not be accepted by an organization sponsoring a mission trip.

Sample Short-Term Mission Trip and Mission Field Assessment Visit Policy

ABC Church occasionally sponsors short-term mission trips. While these trips may provide essential ministry services and encouragement on the field, the visits are primarily intended to introduce trip participants to missions.

Additionally, it is occasionally desirable for church staff and/or volunteers to visit a supported missionary (national or expatriate) in the field, assess a potential field of service for potential future missionary support, or assess a potential field of service for a future short-term mission trip. Visits to missionaries currently supported by the church are to (1) demonstrate the church's commitment to their ministry, (2) provide face-to-face encouragement, and (3) assess the effectiveness of the ministry.

The church desires that God will be honored in every aspect of these trips. Therefore, this policy has been developed and adopted by the church Governing Board to provide general guidance for these trips.

Trip approval. All short-term mission trips and field assessment visits are recommended by the Missions Committee and approved by the church Governing Board to be considered under these policies. (*Note:* The trip approval process will vary based on the governance structure of a particular church. In some instances, the Governing Board may delegate trip approval responsibility to the Executive Pastor, for example.)

Approval, training, supervision, and assignment of trip participants. Potential non-staff trip members will be screened according to qualifications established by the church, and trip participants are given meaningful training and adequately supervised.

Non-staff trip participants are assigned to programs and project locations based on the assessment of church leaders of each individual's skills and training.

Funding trips. Based on the funding method approved by the church Governing Board for a particular trip, the following funding approaches may be used:

A. Trip expenses may be fully or partially funded by the church. Funds from the missions or other budget line-items may be identified for this purpose.

B. Trip expenses may be fully or partially funded through resources raised by the trip participants. Funding may be raised to cover direct and indirect trip costs, based on the approval by the Church Board of the funding plan. While the church will accept gifts preferenced for the trip of a particular participant, the church will not accept gifts restricted or designated for a particular trip participant. (Reason: Gifts restricted or designated for a particular gift participant do not qualify to receive a charitable gift acknowledgment, and such gifts are not consistent with the tax-exempt status of the church.)

If trip expenses are fully or partially funded by resources raised by the trip participants, all communication to donors—sample text for letters, websites, and blog posting and talking points for the verbal communication about the trip—will be approved by the church.

If resources are raised beyond the goal for a particular trip participant, the excess may be used to provide resources for a trip participant who is under-funded.

If the resources raised by a potential trip participant are less than the financial goal established by the church, the church will determine whether to assign funds sufficient to allow the individual to participate in the trip. The additional funds could come from the church's mission or general funds. Or the additional funds could come from resources raised beyond the goal to fund other potential trip participants.

Issuing charitable gift acknowledgments. At the discretion of the church, charitable gift acknowledgments will be prepared by the church and provided for all gifts that conform with this policy, including gifts from family members and trip participants. However, gifts will not be acknowledged if the trip participant is unable to, or for any reason does not plan to, significantly perform services to carry out the purposes of the trip (for example, a child of age three).

The church will determine the appropriateness of issuing charitable gift acknowledgments when trip participants pay their own expenses for a church-sponsored trip. No charitable gift acknowledgments will be issued for short-term mission trips that have not been approved by the church.

Charitable gift acknowledgments issued by the church will include the following wording:

- An indication that the church has discretion and control over the gifts.
- A statement indicating "no goods or services were provided in exchange for the gifts," if this is true.

In determining whether a gift is preferenced or restricted for a potential trip participant, the church will use the following principles for guidance:

- A preferenced gift merely comes with a preference or a desire that the gift be used to support the trip expenses of a particular trip participant.
- Preferenced gifts generally may be accepted with a gift acknowledgment provided.
- An earmarked gift is a transfer that is intended to benefit an individual, not the church. It is a transfer over which the church does not have sufficient discretion and control. For example, if accepted, the church would not have the freedom to use the funds for a trip participant who fell short of the financial goal for the trip.

  Earmarked gifts generally should not be accepted; therefore, a gift acknowledgment is a moot issue.

Refunding of gifts related to trips. Gifts preferenced for particular gift recipients will not be refunded to donors except in unusual circumstances, such as the cancellation of a trip. Funds preferenced for the trip of a particular participant could be carried forward for a future trip at the discretion of the church.

Discretion and control over gifts. All gifts given to support trips are the property of the church and will be expended under the discretion and control of the church.

Accounting records. The church will separately record revenue and expenses related to each short-term mission trip.

Determining accountable expenses related to trips. Expenses will be reimbursed under the church's accountable expense reimbursement plan. Allowable volunteer expenses include transportation expenses and reasonable expenses for meals and lodging necessarily incurred while away from home. Expenses will not be reimbursed for individuals who only have nominal duties relating to the performance of services for the church or who for significant portions of the trip are not required to render services.

While "a significant element of personal pleasure" is not defined by the tax code or regulations, the current edition of IRS publication 526 provides the following guidance:

> Generally, you can claim a charitable contribution deduction for travel expenses necessarily incurred while you are away from home performing services for a charitable organization only if there is no significant element of personal pleasure, recreation, or vacation in the travel. This applies whether you pay for the expenses directly or indirectly. You are paying the expenses indirectly if you make a payment to the charitable organization and the organization pays for your travel expenses.

> The deduction for travel expenses will not be denied simply because you enjoy providing services to the charitable organization. Even if you enjoy the trip, you can take a charitable contribution deduction for your travel expenses if you are on duty in a genuine and substantial sense throughout the trip. However, if you have only nominal duties, or if for significant parts of the trip you do not have any duties, you cannot deduct your travel expenses.

To prove the extent and duration of services, each trip participant will keep an hour-by-hour itinerary of the entire trip. The itinerary should separate those times when the trip participant is on duty for the church from those times when the participant is free to choose his or her own activities.

Church staff participation in trips. Church staff are encouraged to participate in mission trips by providing them with one week of paid time for one trip per year subject to the approval and staff member's supervisor. (*Note:* Your church may determine it is appropriate for staff to have more paid time for trips; for example, two weeks of paid time for up to two trips per year.)

Staff members are responsible to raise the same financial support as other trip participants. (*Note:* Your church may determine it is appropriate for a staff member who is leading a team to raise support for the team as a whole, whereby the funding for the leader is paid from the overall trip budget.)

If a staff participant is a non-exempt employee for purposes of the Fair Labor Standards Act and the mission trip responsibilities are not clearly outside the scope of their position description, the church will define the hours on and off duty during the trip to clearly determine any overtime hours. (*Note:* Your church may determine staff members participating outside the scope of their position description must use leave time instead of receiving their regular pay.)

not qualify for a charitable deduction and should generally not be accepted (or not acknowledged as a charitable gift if accepted).

Sponsors of short-term mission trips generally should not accept gifts earmarked for individuals because the gifts are not consistent with the charity's tax-exempt purposes. An earmarked gift is a transfer that is intended to benefit an individual, not the charity ("for Joe Smith's trip costs"). It is a transfer over which the charity does not have sufficient discretion and control. For example, in the short-term mission trip context, if the charity accepted a gift restricted for a particular trip participant, the charity would not have the freedom to use the funds given for another trip participant who fell short of the financial goal for the trip.

Accounting issues. Gifts to a ministry preferenced to support particular short-term trip participants are generally considered to be temporarily restricted contribution revenue under Generally Accepted Accounting Principles (GAAP), because the purpose of the gift is more narrow than the general purposes of the charity while still meeting the IRS requirements for charitable contributions.

A ministry should have sufficient discretion and control over gifts to permit the charity to redirect the gifts for other short-term trip participants (for example, redirection of funds often occurs when a trip participant raises more or less funds than required for a trip). This redirection does not negate or negatively impact the charitable nature of the gifts. Rather, it is a clear demonstration of a charity properly exercising discretion and control over gifts.

Ministries may wish to utilize separate accounts for each trip participant. This treatment should not jeopardize the donor's charitable tax deduction as long as the ministry maintains discretion and control over the funds.

Other Special Charitable Contribution Issues

Gifts of inventory

Donors may contribute some of their business inventory to a charity and ask for a charitable contribution acknowledgment for the retail value of the merchandise. This is inappropriate because inventory contributions are generally deductible at cost and not at retail value. Acknowledgments issued by a church or other nonprofit organization for inventory contributions should not state the value of the gift—only the date of the gift and a description of the items donated.

Caution

What is the bottom line of inventory contributions? An inventory item can only be deducted once—there is no contribution deduction and also a deduction as a part of cost of goods sold. The tax benefit to the donor is generally equal to the donor's cost of the items, not their retail value.

> **Example:** Bill owns a lumberyard. The charity is constructing a building, and Bill donates some lumber for the project. Bill's company purchased the lumber during his current business year for $10,000. The retail price of the lumber is $17,000, and it would have generated a $7,000 profit if Bill's company had sold it. What is the tax impact for Bill's company? Since Bill's company acquired the item in the same business year that the lumber was donated, there is no charitable contribution for his company. The cost of the lumber, $10,000, is deducted as part of the cost of goods sold.

Payments to private schools

Tuition payments to private schools are generally nondeductible since they correspond to value received. The IRS has ruled that payments to private schools are not deductible as charitable contributions if

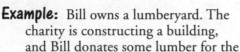

Remember

Tuition payments are personal expenses. However, taxpayers often attempt to construe tuition payments as charitable deductions. The IRS is particularly alert to arrangements that require a certain amount of contributions from a parent in addition to some tuition payments or where education is provided tuition-free.

➤ a contract exists under which a parent agrees to make a "contribution" and that contains provisions ensuring the admission of the child;

➤ there is a plan allowing a parent either to pay tuition or to make "contributions" in exchange for schooling;

➤ there is the earmarking of a contribution for the direct benefit of a particular individual (student); or

➤ there is the otherwise unexplained denial of admission or readmission to a school for children of individuals who are financially able to, but do not contribute.

Some churches operate related private schools on a "tuition-free" basis. These churches typically request that families with children in the school increase their contributions by the amount that they would otherwise have paid as tuition. In reviewing "tuition-free" situations, the IRS often questions the deductibility of gifts to the church if

➤ contributions of several families increased or decreased markedly as the number of their children enrolled in the school changed;

➤ the contributions of parents of students dropped off significantly in the summer months when the school was not in session; and

➤ the parents were not required to pay tuition.

Generally, contributions to a church by parents are not deductible as charitable contributions to the extent that the church pays the parents' tuition liabilities for their children.

Gifts to staff

Churches and nonprofits often make gifts to employees to show appreciation for their dedicated service. These payments may take several forms and have important implications to the organization, to staff members, and to donors:

➤ **Gifts made by an individual directly to a staff member with no church involvement.** When the payer of the funds makes the payment directly to a staff member of the church or nonprofit, this is a gift which is not tax-deductible to the giver and is generally not taxable to the recipient. A gift of this nature does not raise any tax issues for the church or nonprofit.

➤ **Gifts made by an individual to the church but earmarked by the donor for a particular staff member and not intended for use by the church or nonprofit.** If contributions are earmarked by the donor and treated as being gifts to the designated individual, they are not tax-deductible as charitable gifts. The earmarking of gifts by donors prevents a church or nonprofit from using the funds to carry out its functions and purposes at its discretion. The use of terminology such as a "love gift for an individual" or a "desire to bless an individual" does not impact the nondeductibility of the gift.

➤ **Gifts to staff members from church or nonprofit funds.** Often gifts are made from organizational funds which are not required by contract or a typical employment plan. The gifts may be given in appreciation near a holiday, a birthday, or an employee anniversary. The gifts may be given in relation to personal medical or financial crises.

Gifts to staff members from church or nonprofit funds are taxable and subject to payroll tax treatment and reporting unless they meet one of the following exceptions:

1. *De minimis* **gifts.** These gifts are impracticable of specific valuation and are generally less than $25 in value. IRS rulings have emphasized that the difficulty in valuing a *de minimis* gift is just as important as the small value. Cash, gift cards, or other cash equivalents are not *de minimis* gifts, regardless of how small the value.

195

2. **Employee achievement awards.** To avoid taxation, achievement awards must meet specific tax law requirements. The law generally requires a written, non-discriminatory achievement award program, which provides awards either upon attaining longevity goals or safety standards and meets other requirements for type of gift and limits on amounts.

3. **Staff member is a church attender.** If the staff member is also a church attender, it is possible for the staff member to receive benevolence assistance in the capacity of a church attender without the assistance being taxable. The benevolence need must be handled and paid through the normal benevolence process. While dual status of being both church attender and employee does not require taxation of assistance provided to the person as church attender, it does require careful documentation to ensure the employee is treated just like nonemployees. Due to the challenge of documenting that the staff member would have received a benevolence payment, and in the same amount if the individual had not been a staff member, many churches adopt policies prohibiting the payment of benevolence funds to employees.

➤ **Gifts to "bless" a particular staff member by raising a "love offering."** In the typical love offering scenario, the funds are received by the church or nonprofit (payments directly to an individual are discussed above). When the donor knows that a gift will go to a specific person, tax law generally treats the gifts as if they were made to the specific person and the gifts are not deductible as charitable contributions. The payment of the love offering is taxable and subject to payroll tax treatment and reporting unless one of the three exceptions is met as noted above.

➤ **Gifts to "bless" multiple staff members by raising a "love offering."** When an occasional love offering is raised for more than one staff person (e.g., when an offering is received for a Christmas gift or for a Pastor's Appreciation gift and the funds will be distributed to more than one staff member), if the church or nonprofit leadership determines the recipients and the allocation of the offering between staff members, then donations to the love offering are generally tax-deductible. The payment of the love offering is taxable as compensation and subject to payroll tax treatment and reporting unless one of the three exceptions is met as noted above.

➤ **Gifts to an educational institution to pay tuition for a staff member's dependent.** There is no charitable tax deduction for a gift to a church or other nonprofit which is designated for the educational expenses of a staff member's dependent. If the organization uses the funds to pay the tuition of a staff member's dependent, even if the funds are paid directly to the educational institution, the amount is taxable and subject to payroll tax treatment and reporting with respect to the staff member.

Contributions that benefit specific individuals other than staff members and other than the needy

Occasionally individuals give money to a ministry but request that it be sent to a particular recipient who is not on the staff of the ministry, is not a missionary related to the ministry, and does not qualify as a "needy" individual. When told that this "conduit" role is improper, the donor usually responds, "But I can't get a tax deduction otherwise!" The donor is absolutely correct.

In a conduit transaction, the donor is making a gift to the ultimate beneficiary. The IRS will look to the ultimate beneficiary to decide whether the gift qualifies for a charitable contribution deduction.

There are certain limited circumstances in which a ministry may appropriately serve as an intermediary with respect to a gift that will be transferred to another ministry or to a specific individual. In such circumstances, it is essential that the ministry that first receives the monies has the right to control the ultimate destination of the funds.

Donor intent is also a key factor. If the donor intends for a gift to benefit a specific individual instead of supporting the mission of the ministry, the gift is generally not deductible.

> **Example:** Frank Lee makes a gift of $5,000 to Shady Lane Church. Mr. Lee
> stipulates that the gift must go to a particular music group of which his son is
> a member. The money will be used to purchase sound equipment. The group
> will go on tour to present religious music in churches. The group is not an
> approved ministry of Shady Lane Church. This gift would generally be termed
> personal gift to the music group and would not be deductible as a charitable
> contribution. It is best if the church returns the gift to Mr. Lee. If the church
> accepts the gift and passes the money on to the music group, the church
> should advise Mr. Lee that the gift is not deductible and should not provide a
> charitable acknowledgment.

Contributions to needy individuals and benevolence funds

Gifts made directly by a donor to needy individuals are not deductible. To qualify for a charitable deduction, contributions must be made to a qualified charitable organization. Contributions to benevolence funds may be claimed as charitable deductions if they are not earmarked for particular recipients.

A gift to a charitable organization involved in helping needy people marked "to aid the unemployed" is generally deductible. Yet if the gift is designated or restricted for the "Brown family" and the organization passes the money on to the Browns, the gift is generally not tax-deductible.

If a donor makes a suggestion about the beneficiary of a benevolent contribution, it may be deductible if the recipient organization exercises proper control over the benevolence fund. The donor's suggestion

Warning

An area of frequent abuse involves a monetary donation that the donor specifies must go to a particular individual (or family) to assist their financial needs. Before accepting such a gift, a charity must determine if it can exercise due diligence to ensure the transaction does not actually constitute earmarking of the funds by a donor, which is not deductible as a charitable contribution.

Sample Benevolence Fund Policy

Whereas, New Haven Church has a ministry to needy individuals; and

Whereas, The church desires to establish a Benevolence Fund through which funds for the support of needy individuals may be administered; and

Whereas, The church desires to operate the Benevolence Fund according to the highest standards of integrity;

Resolved, That New Haven Church establish a Benevolence Fund to help individuals in financial need and will develop written procedures to document the need, establish reasonable limitations of support per person during a specified time period, and obtain external verification of the need; and

Resolved, That the church will accept only contributions to the Benevolence Fund that are "to or for the use" of the church, and their use must be subject to the control and discretion of the church board. Donors may make suggestions but not designations or restrictions concerning the identity of the needy individuals; and

Resolved, That the church will provide a charitable contribution receipt for gifts that meet the test outlined in the previous resolution. The church reserves the right to return any gifts that do not meet the test.

---

must be only advisory in nature, and the charity may accept or reject the suggestion. However, if every "suggestion" is honored by the organization, the earmarking could be challenged by the IRS.

A church or nonprofit organization may want to help a particular individual or family that has unusually high medical bills or other valid personal financial needs. To announce that funds will be received for the individual or family and acknowledge the monies through the church or nonprofit organization makes the gifts personal and not deductible as charitable contributions. One option is for the organization to set up a trust fund at a local bank. Contributions to the trust fund are not deductible for tax purposes, but payments from the trust fund do not represent taxable income to a needy individual or family. This method of helping the needy person or family represents personal gifts from one individual to another.

Granting of scholarships

When scholarship assistance is provided by a church or nonprofit, it requires careful compliance with tax laws and regulations. Three distinct areas of the tax law must be addressed:

> ➤ **Protecting the contributor's tax deduction.** The contribution deduction requires the gift be "to or for the use of" a charitable entity, not an individual. To qualify,

the gift must be to a church or other qualified nonprofit organization, knowing it will be used for scholarships, but without knowing who will receive the scholarship. A gift designated for a specific individual will not qualify.

Five guidelines for protecting the contribution deduction are as follows:

1. The charity determines all scholarship recipients through the use of a scholarship committee.

2. The charity has a well-published policy stating that it determines the recipients according to its own policies and that it expressly rejects any effort to honor a donor's recommendation(s).

3. All scholarship policies contain the following statement: "Scholarships are awarded without regard to sex, race, nationality, or national origin."

4. Recipients of scholarships and the amount they are to receive will be based on funds already received.

5. The criteria for scholarship qualification are in writing.

> **Protecting the status of the payments to the scholarship recipient.** Only a candidate for a degree can exclude amounts received as a scholarship. A qualified scholarship is any payment to or for the student if it is for "tuition and fees" or for enrollment or "fees, books, supplies, and equipment" required for specific courses. It is not necessary for an organization granting a scholarship to confirm that it will be used only for qualified uses. The person receiving the scholarship must report excess amounts as taxable income.

> **Employee dependent scholarship programs.** Generally, scholarships for an employee's dependents will be considered taxable compensation to the employee unless they meet the following precise guidelines. A few of the requirements include the following:

1. The existence of the program must not be presented as a benefit of employment by the organization.

2. Selection of beneficiaries must be made by an independent committee.

3. Selection must be based solely upon substantial objective standards that are completely unrelated to the employment of the recipients or their parents and to the employer's line of business.

4. Generally, not more than 25% of eligible dependents may be recipients of scholarships.

Key Issue

Too often, well-meaning people want to help a relative or a friend pay their school bills; plus they want a tax deduction for the assistance. So instead of making a personal nondeductible gift to the intended beneficiary, they make a "gift" to a charity with a request to provide a scholarship for a designated individual. This transfer of funds is not a charitable contribution, and the funds should not be accepted by the charity.

Donated travel and out-of-pocket expenses

Unreimbursed out-of-pocket expenses of a volunteer performing services for a church or nonprofit are generally deductible. (Volunteer reimbursements using the per diem method triggers taxable income to the volunteers for the reimbursements in excess of actual expenses.) The expenses must be directly connected with and solely attributable to the providing of the volunteer services.

The type of expenses that are deductible include transportation; travel (mileage at 14 cents per mile for 2016), meals, and lodging while away from home if there is no significant element of personal pleasure, recreation, or vacation associated with the travel; postage; phone calls; printing and photocopying; expenses in entertaining prospective donors; and required uniforms without general utility.

It is generally inappropriate to provide a volunteer with a standard charitable receipt, because the charity is usually unable to confirm the actual amount of a volunteer's expenses. But a letter of appreciation may be sent to the volunteer thanking the individual for the specific services provided. The burden is on the volunteer to prove the amount of the expenses.

Volunteers who incur $250 or more in out-of-pocket expenses in connection with a charitable activity are subject to the acknowledgment rules. The acknowledgment should identify the type of services or expenses provided by the volunteer and state that no goods or services were provided by the charity to the donor in consideration of the volunteer efforts (see page 201 for a sample letter to volunteers).

When a donor requests a refund or transfer of gift funds

Occasionally, donors request a refund of a charitable gift they have made. Since contributions must be irrevocable to qualify for a charitable deduction, there generally is no basis to return a charitable gift to a donor. In the rare instances where a refund is justified, legal and tax advice should be sought (at least for refunds of significant amounts).

In some instances, after a donor makes a restricted gift to a charity, the donor requests that the funds be transferred to a second charity. This sometimes occurs when a deputized worker moves from one charity to a second charity, and a donor who has given funds to charity A asks that the money be transferred to charity B. It is within the discretion of charity A to determine whether the funds are retained by charity A or a gift/grant is made to charity B. A gift/grant by charity A to charity B is appropriate only if charity B is qualified to carry out the donor's restrictions and is consistent with charity A's exempt purposes.

A few preventive steps may be helpful in this area:

> **Adopt a proactive policy.** Start from a position of generally providing no refunds of charitable gifts. Include guidance relating to how the charity will communicate

Sample Letter to Volunteers

Date _____

Dear Volunteer:

We appreciate the time, energy, and out-of-pocket costs you devote to our cause as follows:

<u>Description of Services/Expenses Provided/Date Provided</u>

_____

_____

_____

No goods or services were provided to you by our church, except intangible religious benefits, in consideration of your volunteer efforts.

You may deduct unreimbursed expenses that you incur incidental to your volunteer work. Transportation costs (travel from home to our church or other places where you render services), phone calls, postage stamps, stationery, and similar out-of-pocket costs are deductible.

You can deduct the IRS approved charitable mileage rate (14 cents per mile for 2016) in computing the costs of operating your car while doing volunteer work as well as unreimbursed parking and toll costs. Instead of using the cents-per-mile method, you can deduct your actual auto expenses, provided you keep proper records. However, insurance and depreciation on your car are not deductible.

If you travel as a volunteer and must be away from home overnight, reasonable payments for meals and lodging as well as your travel costs are deductible. Your out-of-pocket costs at a convention connected with your volunteer work are deductible if you were duly chosen as a representative of our church.

You cannot deduct travel expenses as charitable gifts if there is a significant element of personal pleasure, recreation, or vacation in the travel.

You cannot deduct the value of your services themselves. If you devote 100 hours during the year to typing for us and the prevailing rate for these services is $8.00 per hour, you can't deduct the $800 value of your services. Although deductions are allowed for property gifts, the IRS doesn't consider your services "property." Nor is the use of your home for meetings a "property contribution."

Finally, you may be required to substantiate your deduction to the IRS. Be prepared to prove your costs with canceled checks, receipted bills, and diary entries. If your expenses total $250 or more for the calendar year, you must have this acknowledgment in hand before you file your income tax return.

Again, thank you for furthering our cause with that most precious commodity: your time.

Castleview Church

with donors relating to situations where a restricted project may be overfunded, underfunded, or cancelled. Provide guidance on how the charity will communicate with donors concerning gift preferences.

➤ **Clearly communicate with donors.**
Particularly when accepting gifts with donor preferences (see pages 176–93), clearly communicate that the charity has discretion and control over the gift. This does not suggest that donor preferences will be ignored. It simply means that the charity has the right to expend the funds for similar purposes if the preferences are not honored.

> **Warning**
>
> Charities should have policies and procedures in place to address requests for the return of charitable donations. Significant gifts should be returned only after consulting with legal and tax counsel and after approval by the governing board.

When raising or accepting gifts with donor restrictions, it is often wise to communicate to donors that if gift restrictions cannot be met by the charity, the charity will use the funds for another project or make a grant to another charity that is able to fulfill the donor's restrictions.

Avoid duplicity in communicating with donors. *Example:* A church offering envelope providing an opportunity to check a box for a gift for the building fund, the missions fund, or to use where needed most. The following sentence is added: "The church may use this money for any purpose at the discretion of the board." Wording of this nature is very confusing to givers. It suggests to them that a gift they may wish to restrict for missions might be used to pay the pastor's salary.

➤ **Make wise administrative decisions.** When gifts with donor restrictions cannot be spent for the intended purpose, make a decision within a reasonable period regarding how the funds will be expended. While there are no hard and fast rules on how quickly restricted gifts must be used, the longer the time it takes the charity to expend the funds, the greater the risk of creating a public relations issue with donors.

Receipting a taxpayer other than the donor

Donors or prospective donors often present challenging requests to churches and non-profits. Some requests relate to the receipting of a gift or potential gift. If a donor asks a charity to issue a gift receipt to a taxpayer other than the one making the gift, what should the organization do?

➤ Should the charity automatically issue the receipt as requested by the donor?

➤ Should the charity ask for an explanation?

➤ If the donor provides an explanation that evidences an attempt to understate income or social security taxes, what should the charity do?

➤ If the charity provides a receipt to a taxpayer other than the donor, is the charity aiding tax evasion?

➤ Even if the law does not cover these issues, is there a position of "high ground" for the charity?

Policy on Issuing Receipts to Someone Other Than the Remitter of the Funds

When the charity receives requests for receipts to be issued to a taxpayer other than the remitter of the funds, receipts will be issued only to the taxpayer making the gift.

➤ For a cash gift, the person or entity named on the check (or the individual delivering the cash) is the one to whom the receipt is addressed.

➤ The person or entity transferring ownership of noncash assets to a charity is the donor.

The following exceptions to this policy may be permitted:

➤ If the donor documents the appropriateness of issuing a receipt to a taxpayer other than the donor, an exception may be made to the policy.

➤ To facilitate the processing of modest gifts, an exception may be made for small gifts where the risk of significant fraud is diminished.

Donor privacy

While donor information is treated with the utmost confidentiality by most churches and nonprofit organizations, there is no federal law that mandates donor privacy.

Is it acceptable for a church pastor, charity executive, or fundraising consultant to be given a list of donors, identified either within dollar ranges or with actual contribution amounts? This practice is not prohibited or considered unethical if this information is used within a limited context on a "need to know" basis for a specific function. However, circulating this information outside the charity would be considered unethical.

It is wise and prudent for a ministry to maintain a donor privacy policy to help assure its donors of their privacy in contributing to the organization. Charities should consider including several components in developing donor privacy policies:

Sample Donor Privacy Policy

Our charity is committed to respecting the privacy of our donors. We have developed this privacy policy to assure our donors that donor information will not be shared with any third party.

Awareness. This policy is shared to make you aware of our privacy policy and to inform you of the way your information is used. We also provide you with the opportunity to remove your name from our mailing list, if you desire to do so.

Information collected. Here are the types of donor information that we collect and maintain:

- contact information: name, organization/church, complete address, phone number, email address;

- payment information: credit card number and expiration date, and billing information;

- shipping information: name, organization/church, complete address;

- information concerning how you heard about our charity;

- information you wish to share: questions, comments, suggestions; and

- your request to receive periodic updates: e.g., to individuals who request them, we will send periodic mailings related to specific fundraising appeals, prayer concerns, and newsletters.

How information is used. Our charity uses your information to understand your needs and provide you with better service. Specifically, we use your information to help you complete a transaction, communicate back to you, and update you on ministry happenings. Credit card numbers are used only for donation or payment processing and are not retained for other purposes. We use the comments you offer to provide you with information requested, and we take seriously each recommendation as to how we might improve communication.

No sharing of personal information. Our charity will not sell, rent, or lease your personal information to other organizations. We assure you that the identity of all of our donors will be kept confidential. Use of donor information will be limited to the internal purposes of our charity and only to further our ministry activities and purposes.

Removing your name from our mailing list. It is our desire to not send unwanted mail to our donors. Please contact us if you wish to be removed from our mailing list.

Contacting us. If you have comments or questions about our donor privacy policy, please send us an email at info@XYZCharity.org or call us at (800) 555-5555.

➤ **How the donor information is used.** The donor privacy policy should explain how donor information will be used. Common uses are to process contributions, communicate with donors, and update them about charity events or programs.

➤ **Who the donor information is shared with.** The privacy policy should specify whether the charity will share donor information with other organizations. Most ministries have a policy not to share any form of donor information. If, however, a nonprofit does share donor information with other organizations, it is important that it disclose that fact in the donor privacy policy. Doing so allows donors to be aware that any personal information given may be passed on to another organization.

➤ **Removal from the mailing list.** A good donor privacy policy will also include instructions that persons may follow to remove their name from the mailing list.

Charities may communicate their donor privacy policy in several different places. The policy may be included in fundraising appeals, response vehicles, contribution receipts, annual reports, and on the ministry's website. Charities can publish their entire donor privacy policy or create a simplified donor privacy statement to be used on documents and websites.

Charitable solicitation registration

Approximately forty states and the District of Columbia currently have laws regulating the solicitation of funds for charitable purposes. These statutes generally require organizations to register with a state agency before soliciting the state's residents for contributions, providing exemptions from registration for certain categories of organizations. In addition, organizations may be required to file periodic financial reports. State laws may impose additional requirements on fundraising activity involving paid solicitors and fundraising counsel. Before soliciting contributions, charitable organizations may wish to contact the appropriate state agency to learn more about the requirements that may apply in their state. In some states, municipal or other local governments may also require organizations soliciting charitable contributions to register and report.

To determine in what state(s) you may be required to register to solicit charitable contributions or hold assets subject to a charitable trust, see the website of the National Association of State Charity Officials: www.nasconet.org/agencies/document.

Child adoption gifts

It is not surprising that charities and donors often seek ways to provide financial support to couples involved in the adoption process. The cost to adopt a child often exceeds the financial resources of the adopting couple.

While there are a few ways charities can legitimately assist adoptive parents, these options are very limited. A charity should carefully scrutinize any gifts that are designated for a particular adoptive family. The IRS may consider such gifts as conduit or pass-through transactions which do not qualify for a charitable receipt by a charity or a charitable deduction by a donor and could endanger the tax status of a charity.

The following are some considerations for providing support for adoptive parents:

➤ **Personal gifts to the adoptive parents.** An individual may make a personal gift to adoptive parents to assist with adoption expenses. Personal gifts are not deductible as charitable gifts but are not taxable to the adoptive parents.

➤ **Gifts for adoptive parents by a charity whose purpose and nature are not consistent with such gifts.** If gifts by a charity to adoptive families are not consistent with the broad limits imposed by the charity's purpose and nature, the gifts are generally not a proper use of tax-exempt funds.

➤ **Gifts for adoptive parents from the operating fund of a charity.** If adoption assistance is consistent with the charity's purpose and nature, a charity generally has a sound basis to provide assistance for adoptive parents from the charity's general funds (budgeted or unbudgeted); e.g., the charity has available funds that were not designated by a donor for a particular adoptive family. Payments for adoptive families are often made on the basis of financial need and paid directly to the adoption agency to assure that the funds are properly used. These payments are tax-free to the adopted parents.

➤ **Gifts to a charity's adoption fund not preferred for a particular adoptive family and gifts for an adoptive family from the fund.** If adoption assistance is consistent with the charity's purpose and nature, a charity generally has a sound basis to establish a restricted fund (either temporarily restricted or permanently restricted) to accept gifts that are not designated by a donor for a particular adoptive family. Gifts to such a fund will generally qualify as charitable gifts. Payments for adoptive families are often made on the basis of financial need. Payments should typically be made directly to the adoption agency or reimbursed to the adoptive parents based on adequate documentation to assure that the funds are properly used.

➤ **Gifts to a charity preferred for a particular adoptive family and gifts for the adoptive family from the fund.** Even if adoption assistance is consistent with the charity's governing documents, gifts that are preferred by a donor for a particular adoptive family may raise conduit or pass-through transaction issues. To be deductible, the charity must generally have discretion and control over the contribution without any obligation to benefit a preferred individual, obtain adequate information about the potential recipient of the funds (including financial resources), avoid refunding gifts to donors if a particular adoption is not completed, and avoid conflicts of interest between those approving and receiving a loan or a grant. Before considering accepting gifts of this nature and making related gifts to adoptive parents, a charity should seek qualified legal counsel.

Providing Assistance to or for Adoptive Parents Implications for Charitable Deduction Purposes	
Type of Gift	**Qualifies as a Charitable Deduction**
Gift from a charity to/for an adoptive family based on need [1] [2]—not based on gifts designated by the donor(s), e.g., from the charity's general fund.	Yes
Gift from a charity to/for an adoptive family based on gifts restricted for the charity's adoption fund but not restricted or preferenced for a particular adoptive family.	Yes
Personal gifts from one individual to/for another individual to assist in an adoption.	No
Gift from a charity to/for an adoptive family based on gifts preferenced for a particular adoptive family and the donor's intent is to benefit the adoptive family, not the charity.	No
Gift from a charity to/for an adoptive family based on gifts restricted for a particular adoptive family. *The charity is unable to provide adequate discretion and control over the payment because of the donor(s) restriction.*	No
Gift from a charity to/for an adoptive family based on gifts restricted for a particular adoptive family—the adoptive family and the donor are the same taxpayer.	Generally, no (may be tax fraud because of the circular nature of the transaction)
Gift from a charity to/for an adoptive family based on gifts preferenced for a particular adoptive family. *The charity exercises adequate discretion and control over the gift.*	Based on facts and circumstances

[1] As a best practice, the payments should either be made directly to the adoption agency or reimbursed to the adoptive parents based on adequate documentation to assure that the funds are properly used.

[2] Personal gifts from an individual to another individual may have estate tax implications if the gifts to an individual exceed the annual gift tax limitation.

INTEGRITY*Points*

- **Crossing the line from a restricted to an earmarked gift.** Donors may restrict gifts either as to purpose or to time. When the restriction only relates to a project (such as a capital campaign, the mission budget of a church, or the benevolence fund), the issue of earmarked gifts does not arise. When gifts are preferenced for the support of a particular missionary or a benevolent recipient and the preferencing is only an expression of a desire, not a restriction, the gift is restricted for accounting purposes and the earmarking line generally has not been crossed.

  However, when the gift is not preferenced, but restricted for an individual, the earmarked issue arises. Charitable gift deductions are generally not available for earmarked gifts. Integrity requires carefully monitoring the restricted, preferenced, and earmarked issues.

- **Raising money for a mission trip.** The deputized fundraising concept applies to raising money for career and short-term missionaries. When an organization accepts gifts under this concept, it assumes the responsibility for the discretion and control of the gifts. Additionally, the charity must be precise in its proper communication with the supported missionary and the donors. It is very easy to cross the line from a gift restricted for missions, perhaps even in a particular region of the world or a specific country, to a gift earmarked for a particular missionary.

  Sponsors of short-term mission trips most often cross the restricted to earmarked line when refunds are provided in relation to individuals who planned to go on a mission trip but were unable to make the trip. These refunds should be avoided.

- **Transactions which are part gift/part purchase.** These transactions trigger the "quid pro quo" rules and require churches and other nonprofits to demonstrate integrity. Unless the charity fulfills its responsibility to report to the donor the fair market value of the goods or services provided, the donor lacks the necessary information to claim the correct charitable contribution amount.

Citations

Chapter 1, Financial Accountability

- **Expenses of spouses of board members**

  INFO 2000-0236

- **Per diem expense payments to board members**

  Rev. Rul. 67-30

Chapter 2, Tax Exemption

- **Criteria for qualifying as a church**

  Spiritual Outreach Society v. Commissioner, T.C.M. 41 (1990)

  Joseph Edward Hardy v. Commissioner, T.C.M. 557 (1990)

- **Exemption from filing Form 990 for certain missions organizations**

  Treas. Reg. 1.6033-2(g)(1)(iv)

- **General**

  501(c)(3) organization established for religious purposes
  Treas. Reg. 1.511-2(a)(3)(ii)

- **Local sales taxes**

  Thayer v. South Carolina Tax Commission, 413 S.E. 2d 810 (S.C. 1992)

  Quill Corp. v. North Dakota, S. Ct. No. 91-194

  Jimmy Swaggart Ministries v. Board of Equalization of California, 110 S. Ct. 688 (1990)

- **Private benefit/private inurement**

  Treas. Reg. 1.501(a)-1(c)

  G.C.M. 37789

- **Property taxes**

  Trinity Episcopal Church v. County of Sherburne, 1991 WL 95745 (Minn. Tax 1991)

- **Public Disclosure of Information Returns**

  P.L. 100-203

- **Tax-exempt status revoked for excessive UBI**

  United Missionary Aviation, Inc. v. Commissioner, T.C.M. 566 (1990)

  Frazee v. Illinois Department of Employment, 57 U.S.L.W. 4397, 108 S. Ct. 1514 (1989)

  Hernandez v. Commissioner, 819 F.2d 1212, 109 S. Ct. 2136 (1989)

- **Unrelated business income: general**

  Code Sec. 511-13

- **Unrelated business income: affinity credit card programs**

  T.C.M. 34 (1996)

  T.C.M. 63 (1996)

- **Unrelated business income: jeopardy to exempt status**

  Ltr. Rul. 7849003

- **Unrelated business income: organization's tour programs**

  Ltr. Rul. 9027003

- **Unrelated business income: affinity card programs**

  Ltr. Rul. 9029047

  G.C.M. 39827, July 27, 1990

- **Unrelated business income: mailing list profits**

  Disabled American Veterans v. U.S., 94 TC No. 6 (1990)

  American Bar Endowment v. U.S., 477 U.S. 105 (1986)

- **Unrelated business income: rental income**

  Ltr. Rul. 200222030

- **Unrelated business income: other**

  Hope School v. U.S., 612 F.2d 298 (7th Cir. 1980)

  Rev. Rul. 64-182

Chapter 3, Compensating Employees

- **Accountable expense reimbursement plans**

  Treas. Reg. 1.62-2

  Treas. Reg. 1.274-5(e)

  Ltr. Rul. 9317003

- **Deferred compensation**

  Code Sec. 409A

  IRS Notice 2005-1

- **Documenting employee expenses**

  T.A.M. 200435018-22

- **Fair Labor Standards Act**

  DeArment v. Harvey, No. 90-2346 (8th Cir. 1991)

  U.S. Department of Labor v. Shenandoah Baptist Church, 899 F.2d 1389 (4th Cir.) cert. denied, 111 S. Ct. 131 (1990)

  Shaliehsabou v. Hebrew Home of Greater Washington, 363 F.3d 299 (4th Cir. 2004)

- **Flexible spending accounts**

  Rev. Rul. 2003-102

  Code Sec. 125

- **Health reimbursement arrangements**

  Code Sec. 105

  Rev. Rul. 2002-41

  Notice 2002-45

  IRP 80,600

- **Health Savings Accounts**

  Code Sec. 233

  IRS Notice 2004-2

  Rev. Proc. 2004-22

  IRS Notice 2004-23

  Rev. Rul. 2004-38

  Rev. Rul. 2004-45

  IRS Notice 2004-50

- **Health care flexible spending accounts**

  Code Sec. 105(b), (e)

  IRS Notice 2004-42

- **Ministerial exception**

  Hosanna Tabor v. EEOC, 132 S. Ct. 694 (2012)

- **Tax-sheltered annuities**

  Code Sec. 403(b)

  Code Sec. 1402(a)

  Code Sec. 3121(a)(5)(D)

  Rev. Rul. 78-6

  Rev. Rul. 68-395

  Azad v. Commissioner, 388 F. 2d74(8th Cir.1968)

  Rev. Rul. 66-274

Chapter 5, Employer Reporting

- **Classification of workers**

  Rev. Proc. 85-18

  Sec. 530 of the Revenue Act of 1978

- **Employee v. self-employed for income tax purposes**

  Rev. Rul. 87-41

- **Moving expenses**

  Code Sec. 82

  Code Sec. 3401(a)(15)

- **Noncash remuneration**

  Code Sec. 3401(a)

- **Payment of payroll taxes**

  Triplett 115 B.R. 955 (N.D. Ill. 1990)

  Carter v. U.S., 717 F. Supp. 188 (S.D. N.Y. 1989)

- **Per diem allowances**

  IRS Publication 1542

  T.D. 9064

- **Personal use of employer-provided auto**

  Temp. Reg. Sec. 1.61-2T

  IRS Notice 91-41

- **Rabbi trusts**

  Rev. Proc. 92-64

- **Reasonable compensation**

  Truth Tabernacle, Inc. v. Commissioner of Internal Revenue, T.C.M. 451 (1989)

  Heritage Village Church and Missionary Fellowship, Inc., 92 B.R. 1000 (D.S.C. 1988)

- **Taxability of benefits paid under cafeteria plans**

  Ltr. Rul. 8839072

  Ltr. Rul. 8839085

- **Temporary travel**

  Rev. Rul. 93-86

  Comprehensive National Energy Policy Act of 1992

- **Unemployment taxes**

  Code Sec. 3309(b)

  St. Martin Evangelical Lutheran Church v. South Dakota, 451 U.S. 772 (1981)

  Employment Division v. Rogue Valley Youth for Christ, 770 F.2d 588 (Ore. 1989)

- **Voluntary withholding for ministers**

  Rev. Rul. 68-507

Chapter 6, Information Reporting

- **Backup withholding**

  Code Sec. 3406

- **Cash reporting rules for charities**

  T.D. 8373

  G.C.M. 39840

- **Issuing Forms 1099-MISC**

  Rev. Rul. 84-151

  Rev. Rul. 81-232

- **Moving expense reporting**

  IRS Announcement 94-2

- **Nonresident alien payments**

  Code Sec. 1441

  Code Sec. 7701(b)

- **Volunteer fringe benefits**

  Prop. Reg. 1.132-5(r)

- **Withholding of tax on nonresident aliens**

  Pub. 515

Chapter 8, Charitable Gifts

- **Charitable remainder unitrusts**

  IRS Notice 94-78

- **Church school gifts**

  Rev. Rul. 83-104

- **Contribution denied/indirectly related school**

  Ltr. Rul. 9004030

- **Contribution designated for specific missionaries**

  Hubert v. Commissioner, T.C.M. 482 (1993)

- **Contribution earmarked for a specific individual**

  Ltr. Rul. 9405003

  IRS Announcement 92-128

  Ltr. Rul. 8752031

Rev. Rul. 79-81

- **Contribution of autos**

  IRS Publication 4302

  American Jobs Creation Act of 2004

- **Contribution of church bonds**

  Rev. Rul. 58-262

- **Contribution of promissory note**

  Allen v. Commissioner, U.S. Court of Appeals, 89-70252 (9th Cir. 1991)

- **Contribution of services**

  Rev. Rul. 67-236

  Grant v. Commissioner, 84 T.C.M. 809 (1986)

- **Contribution of unreimbursed travel expenses**

  Tafralian v. Commissioner, T.C.M. 33 (1991)

  Rev. Rul. 84-61

  Rev. Rul. 76-89

- **Contribution sent to children who are missionaries**

  Davis v. U.S., 110 S. Ct. 2014 (1990)

- **Contribution that refers to donor's name**

  IR-92-4

- **Contribution to needy individuals**

  Stjernholm v. Commissioner, T.C.M. 563 (1989)

  Ltr. Rul. 8752031

  Rev. Rul. 62-113

- **Criteria used to determine deductibility of payments to private schools**

  Rev. Rul. 83-104

  Rev. Rul. 79-99

- **Deductibility of gifts to domestic organizations for foreign use**

  Ltr. Rul. 9211002

  Ltr. Rul. 9131052

  Ltr. Rul. 9129040

  Rev. Rul. 75-65

  Rev. Rul. 63-252

- **Deductibility of membership fees as contributions**

  Rev. Rul. 70-47

  Rev. Rul. 68-432

- **Deductibility of payments relating to fundraising events**

  Pub. 1391

  Rev. Rul. 74-348

- **Deduction of out-of-pocket transportation expenses**

  Treas. Reg. 1.170A-1(g)

  Rev. Rul. 76-89

- **Determining the value of donated property**

  IRS Pub. 561

  Rochin v. Commissioner, T.C.M. 262 (1992)

- **Gift of inventory**

  Code Sec. 170(e)

  Reg. 1.161-1

  Reg. 1.170A-1(c)(2), (3), (4)

  Reg. 1.170A-4A(c)(3)

  Rev. Rul. 85-8

- **Gift of life insurance**

  Ltr. Rul. 9147040

  Ltr. Rul. 9110016

- **Incentives and premiums**

  IRS. Pub. 1391

  Rev. Proc. 96-59

  Rev. Proc. 92-102

Rev. Proc. 92-49

Rev. Proc. 90-12

- **IRA rollovers**

  Pension Protection Act of 2006

- **Payments in connection with use of ministry services**

  Rev. Rul. 76-232

- **Payments to a retirement home**

  T.A.M. 9423001

  U.S. v. American Bar Endowment, 477 U.S.105 (S. Ct. 1986)

- **Scholarship gifts**

  Ltr. Rul. 9338014

  Rev. Rul. 83-104

  Rev. Rul. 62-113

- **Substantiation rules**

  Omnibus Budget Reconciliation Act of 1993

  T.D. 8690

- **Travel tours**

  Ltr. Rul. 9027003

Federal Tax Regulation (Reg.)

Treasury Decision (T.D.)

Private Letter Ruling (Ltr. Rul.)

Field Service Advice (F.S.A.)

Revenue Ruling (Rev. Rul.)

Revenue Procedure (Rev. Proc.)

Tax Court Memorandum (T.C.M.)

Technical Advice Memorandum (T.A.M.)

Index

10 *B*iggest *T*ax and *F*inancial *M*istakes *M*ade by *C*hurches and *N*onprofits

1. Not setting up and adequately monitoring an accountable expense reimbursement plan for employees. Chapter 3.

2. Failure to comply with the Fair Labor Standards Act for churches and other nonprofits. Chapter 3.

3. Not reporting taxable fringe benefits and social security reimbursements as additional compensation to employees. Chapter 3.

4. Deducting FICA tax from the salary of qualified ministers, whether employed by a church or other nonprofit. Chapter 5.

5. Failing to file Form 1099-MISC for independent contractors. Chapter 6.

6. Weak controls over revenue, including failing to have offerings and other cash and checks controlled by two individuals until the funds are counted. Chapter 7.

7. Inadequate controls over disbursements, leaving the ministry at risk for embezzlement. Chapter 7.

8. Failure to issue a proper receipt (including the fair market value of the goods or services provided) when a donor makes a payment of more than $75 and receives goods or services. Chapter 8.

9. Providing receipts for the donation of services and the rent-free use of property. Receipting contributions designated for individuals without proper discretion and control exercised by the donee organization. Placing values on noncash gifts. Chapter 8.

10. Accepting earmarked gifts with the charity exercising inadequate control when the gift is disbursed to another charity or benevolent recipient. Chapter 8.

10 *Tax and Finance Questions Most Frequently Asked by Churches and Nonprofits*

1. **Tax exempt status.** Should our church or nonprofit file for tax exemption with the Internal Revenue Service? Are we required to annually file Form 990? Chapter 2.

2. **Unrelated business income exposure.** Do we have any filing requirements for unrelated business income? If we have some unrelated business income, will we lose our tax-exempt status? Chapter 2.

3. **Public disclosure.** Is our organization required to disclose any documents to the public based on appropriate requests for them? If so, which documents? Chapter 2.

4. **Political activities.** Are the activities of our organization consistent with the political activity law? Chapter 2.

5. **Housing allowance.** How do we determine whether a minister qualifies for a housing allowance designation? Are the rules for qualifying for the housing allowance identical for churches and other nonprofits? Chapter 3.

6. **Reporting compensation.** Which payments to employees are taxable and must be reported on the annual Form W-2? Chapter 5.

7. **Handling gifts.** What steps can we take to ensure the highest integrity in processing gifts, especially cash offerings, and providing acknowledgments to donors? Chapter 7.

8. **Internal and external auditing.** Should we have an audit, review, or compilation by an independent CPA? If not, how can we perform a valid internal audit of our financially related processes? Chapter 7.

9. **Noncash gifts.** How do we handle noncash gifts? What type of receipt should we provide? Should we ever place a value on a noncash gift, including gifts of services? Chapter 8.

10. **Donor-restricted gifts.** When a donor restricts a gift, how do we determine whether we should accept the gift and whether it qualifies as a charitable contribution? Chapter 8.